D1272360

The
Transformation
of Psychology

The Transformation of Psychology

Influences of 19th-Century Philosophy, Technology, and Natural Science

Edited by
Christopher D. Green, Marlene Shore,
and Thomas Teo

American Psychological Association
Washington, DC

Published by
American Psychological Association
750 First Street, NE
Washington, DC 20002
www.apa.org

To order
APA Order Department
P.O. Box 92984
Washington, DC 20090-2984

Tel: (800) 374-2721, Direct: (202) 336-5510
Fax: (202) 336-5502, TDD/TTY: (202) 336-6123
Online: www.apa.org/books
Email: order@apa.org

In the U.K., Europe, Africa, and the Middle East, copies may be ordered from
American Psychological Association
3 Henrietta Street
Covent Garden, London
WC2E 8LU England

Typeset in Goudy by EPS Group Inc., Easton, MD
Printer: Sheridan Books, Ann Arbor, MI
Dust jacket designer: NiDesign, Baltimore, MD
Technical/Production Editor: Amy J. Clarke

The opinions and statements published are the responsibility of the authors, and such opinions and statements do not necessarily represent the policies of the American Psychological Association.

Library of Congress Cataloging-in-Publication Data
The transformation of psychology : influences of 19th-century philosophy, technology, and natural science / edited by Christopher D. Green, Marlene Shore, and Thomas Theo.—1st ed.
    p.   cm.
Includes bibliographical references and index.
ISBN 1-55798-776-9 (cb : acid-free paper)
1. Psychology—History—19th century—Congresses.   I. Green, Christopher D.
II. Shore, Marlene Gay, 1953-   .   III. Teo, Thomas, 1963-   .
BF103.T73 2001
150'.9'034—dc21   00-068985

British Library Cataloguing-in-Publication Data
A CIP record is available from the British Library.

Printed in the United States of America
First Edition

CONTENTS

CONTRIBUTORS

Katharine Anderson, PhD, Department of Science & Technology Studies, York University, Toronto, Ontario, Canada

John G. Benjafield, PhD, Department of Psychology, Brock University, St. Catherines, Ontario, Canada

Kurt Danziger, DPhil, professor emeritus, York University, Toronto, Ontario, Canada.

Raymond E. Fancher, PhD, Department of Psychology, York University, Toronto, Ontario, Canada

Christopher D. Green, PhD, Department of Psychology, York University, Toronto, Ontario, Canada

Marlene Shore, PhD, Department of History, York University, Toronto, Ontario, Canada

Michael M. Sokal, PhD, Department of Humanities and Arts, Worcester Polytechnic Institute, Worcester, MA

Thomas Teo, PhD, Department of Psychology, York University, Toronto, Ontario, Canada

Charles W. Tolman, PhD, Centre for Studies in Religion and Society, University of Victoria, Victoria, British Columbia, Canada

Fredric Weizmann, PhD, Department of Psychology, York University, Toronto, Ontario, Canada

Andrew S. Winston, PhD, Department of Psychology, University of Guelph, Guelph, Ontario, Canada

ACKNOWLEDGMENTS

The chapters of this collection first took shape in the meetings of a seminar series held at York University in Toronto over the course of the 1998–1999 school year. The seminar's topic was the 19th-century transformation that psychology underwent—from being a largely philosophical discipline to being a largely scientific one. We sought from the beginning to produce an intellectual atmosphere that was both interdisciplinary and inter-institutional. As a consequence, we included in the group psychologists and historians, Americans and Canadians, men and women. We have all benefited from being exposed to these diverse points of view and from considering how they might be integrated with each other.

The seminar was supported by a grant from the Gerstein Foundation, administered by York University, and we thank them both for their generous assistance. We would also like to thank APA Acquisitions Editor Susan Reynolds, APA Development Editor Kristine Enderle, APA Production Editor Amy Clarke, and York Research Assistant Daniel Denis for their valuable contributions to this project.

INTRODUCTION

CHRISTOPHER D. GREEN, MARLENE SHORE, AND THOMAS TEO

Near the end of the 18th century, Immanuel Kant declared in the *Metaphysical Foundations of Natural Science* (1786/1970) that psychology would never become a true natural science. It did not operate within the kind of a priori framework that Kant considered necessary for a proper natural science, similar to the one he was in the process of erecting for Newtonian physics. Without that sort of framework, Kant believed, any discipline purporting to be a natural science would fall prey to Hume's corrosive skepticism—the philosophy that he famously claimed had roused him from his "dogmatic slumber" in the *Prologema to Any Future Metaphysics* (1783/1950, p. 8). Moreover, psychology faced further obstacles in becoming a science because, according to Kant, "mathematics is inapplicable to the phenomena of the internal senses and their laws" (p. 8).

By the outbreak of World War I, however, the intellectual and institutional obstacles that had seemed to stand in the way of the development of a scientific psychology had virtually disappeared. Psychological laboratories proliferated in universities throughout Europe and the United States and were producing doctorates and experimental studies at a tremendous rate. Professional societies and journals dedicated to the pursuit of experimental psychology were multiplying rapidly as well. Scientific psychology was gaining acceptance in some governmental departments, and even the general public was showing an interest in the ideas and results generated by psychologists. Sometimes public audiences mistook psychology for the study of paranormal phenomena, equating it with the spiritism and telepathy that had also caught hold of the popular imagination, but psychological knowledge was being applied in educational and legal systems as well as in clinical contexts. Psychology was put to use in the war effort, especially in the United States, where psychologists led in developing mental tests to ascertain which individuals were intellectually suited for the rigors of army life (and, of course, which were not).

American psychologists also became adept at selling various approaches to psychology as a kind of general social ideology. On the one hand, there was the apparently optimistic vision of John B. Watson, whose extreme environmentalism held that ultimately most human ills would be eliminated simply by conditioning people correctly. On the other hand was the vision of the hereditarians and eugenicists, who pushed for the exclusion from America of all potential immigrants who were unable to pass tests of presumably innate intelligence and for the segregation of the so-called "feeble-minded" (all too often members of the racial and economic underclasses) who happened to be born in America.

The question addressed in this book is the path—or paths—that psychology took between the two "bookends" of Kant and Word War I. How could such a profound transformation in the nature of psychological study come about in a period of just over a century? How was it possible that in this relatively short space of time, the qualms expressed by the leading intellectuals of the age, who had ruled out the very possibility of a scientific psychology, were cast aside, and scientific psychology became commonplace, with the few remaining voices of dissent decidedly in retreat? What intellectual, social, technological, and institutional currents occurred in the 19th century such that the philosophical approach to mind was abandoned by so many in favor of an apparently more scientific approach? Were the uncertainties expressed by Kant and others overcome, neglected, or simply forgotten?

The standard historical reply to these questions, most famously articulated by E. G. Boring (1929) and evident even today in most history of psychology textbooks, presents a relatively simple account of the development of scientific psychology. Kant's dictum was ignored for the most part, whereas E. H. Weber's and G. T. Fechner's successes in psychophysics, combined with advances in psychophysiology by Johannes Müller, Hermann von Helmholtz, and others, ultimately led to the establishment of the first experimental psychology laboratory by Wilhelm Wundt in Leipzig, Germany, in 1879. Wundt's many students went on to populate the chairs of universities not only in Germany but in America as well, where the new experimental approach was merged with the ideas of pragmatists and evolutionists, establishing the foundations of modern scientific psychology. When combined with Francis Galton's advances in the measurement of mental abilities and applied statistics, what was once the bare possibility of a new scientific discipline dedicated to the study of perception, cognition, and action rapidly became a thriving reality. With the help of a number of active promoters such as G. Stanley Hall, Hugo Münsterberg, and Robert M. Yerkes, the "new" psychology demonstrated its usefulness in educational institutions, in the workplace, in hospitals, in the army, and in the court of law.

This is the standard account, but surely such an explanation for psychology's transformation from a primarily philosophical discipline to a scientific one is too linear and simplistic for the historian to accept with equanimity. Although such "founding myths" contain some truth, they have generated a "triumphalist" narrative of the discipline that tends to obscure as much as it reveals. As we hope to demonstrate in this book, the establishment of a "scientific" psychology was not a project that was simply passed from Müller to Helmholtz to Wundt and then to Hall and Cattell. Indeed, there were a wide variety of efforts to create a psychological discipline that might be described as "scientific." Some of these were ultimately incorporated into the version that was to dominate North America, but others were not. Some of these alternatives died away; others gave rise to approaches that continue to flourish in Europe to the present day. They should all attract the interest of the historian of psychology because they can all tell us something about why it was considered so important in the 19th century that psychology be "scientized." They also reveal how science itself was regarded in that era—not only was scientific psychology expected by many to bestow great benefits on society at large, but succeeding in the project itself would speak very highly of the overall quality of the civilization that finally managed to achieve it.

Embedded in so general a question are a number of important "externalist" questions, often glossed over in the standard accounts. What role did social, political, and economic developments play in the rapid growth of scientific psychology in the second half of the 19th century? What was psychology's relationship to philosophy, and how did it change? To what extent was psychology's development driven by the invention of new instruments, new institutions, and new spaces, which enabled it to develop and thrive?

The concept of *science* itself is shaped by historical change. Kant, who discriminated between a body of knowledge (which he regarded as systematically organized facts about natural objects) and science (which he saw as organized according to principles), was no longer considered authoritative among many 19th-century scientists, especially those outside of Germany. In particular, his distinction between *apodictic* certainty (proper science) and *empirical* certainty (improper science) was rapidly losing ground to fallibilism—the belief that scientific knowledge is forever tentative, subject to being overturned by new discoveries—especially in America. Moreover, 19th-century German academics, in the main, had little problem accepting religion and art as "sciences" (*Wissenschaften*), as long as these subject matters were investigated, described, and presented systematically. The problem for them was whether the *human* sciences were significantly different from the *natural* sciences, whether they required the same or different methodologies, and whether one type of science could account for all knowledge produced.

The contributors to this volume attempt to address these questions within an integrated collection of chapters, each discussing a different aspect of psychology's transition from philosophy to science during the 19th century. No sophisticated historical explanation can any longer claim to present a complete picture, and we do not pretend that we have done so here. Rather, we have made a concerted effort to tell some of psychology's "other" histories, including attempts that "failed" outright or movements that "succeeded" to some degree but did not gain acceptance in the dominant Anglo American psychological tradition. We also explore some of the uncomfortable aspects of apparently "successful" attempts that have been half-forgotten or half-suppressed because they did not sit well with the primary thrust of the standard narrative. What emerges is a picture that is in some ways much clearer, but in others far more complex, of the ways in which the philosophical, economic, and political uncertainties of the 19th century buffeted psychology's development over the "long 19th century" (1789–1914).

ORGANIZATION OF THIS BOOK

We have attempted to organize the chapters in this book such that subjects that are likely to be more familiar to the reader are covered in the earlier chapters, thereby setting a context for the subjects of the later chapters, which are not often found in the standard accounts of the development of psychology.

In chapter 1, Raymond E. Fancher explores the influence of the 1859 publication of the theory of natural selection on the course of psychology, paying particular attention to the impact that Charles Darwin's theory had on the religious faith of members of the English scientific community. The main focus is on Francis Galton's eugenics, which Fancher argues played for Galton the role of a "secular religion," replacing the conventional faith, which had been shattered by his conversion to evolutionism.

In chapter 2, Michael M. Sokal explores the value of the work of the antebellum practicing phrenologists in the United States. He argues that these phrenologists, far from being mere quacks and charlatans, often provided a real, if apparently scientifically misguided, service to their clients. He suggests in this regard that phrenology should be seen alongside of Medieval alchemy and Renaissance astrology as another serious effort "to make rational the course of events and to fit humankind into the scheme of the universe."

Chapter 3 presents Kurt Danziger's investigation of the conflicting conceptions of memory that were used in the scientific work of Wundt and Hermann Ebbinghaus during the last quarter of the 19th century. Whereas Wundt saw the term *memory* as an imprecise popular term that had little to offer a scientific psychology, Ebbinghaus molded it to his purposes, stripping it down to the recollection of nonsense syllables, thereby enabling the development of an experimental technique that could easily be adapted by what Danziger identifies as the "potential consumers of psychological knowledge"—the most prominent example being educators. By contrast, Wundt's more abstruse academic approach held little appeal for professionals interested in the products of the new psychology, in no small part because he failed to make the needed concessions to what he regarded as "vulgar psychology."

In chapter 4, Marlene Shore explores this thread further, examining one of the most significant events in the popularization of scientific psychology in North America during the 19th century: the psychological exhibit at the World's Columbian Exposition held in Chicago in 1893. She sets her discussion in the context of the rise to pre-eminence of both academic and popular concerns with history and memory at the end of the 19th century, seeing these developments, which profoundly influenced psychology, as part and parcel of the rising culture of modernism and the very technological innovation celebrated by the Columbian Exposition itself.

In chapter 5, John G. Benjafield explores J. F. Herbart's efforts to develop a mathematical psychology and the impact that this work had on the development of Fechner's psychological experimentalism. Benjafield's main interest here, however, is not with Fechner's well-known psychophysical work but with his less well recognized attempt to establish an experimental aesthetics during the 1870s. The focus of Fechner's investigations in this area was the then-popular phenomenon of the Golden Section, an irrational mathematical proportion widely believed to be the basis of visual beauty. Benjafield shows that this work was not a sideline of Fechner's research but was central to his efforts to create a discipline that blended romantic ideals with scientific rigor.

Then Andrew S. Winston, in chapter 6, discusses the implications of a revolutionary philosophical view that would become dominant by the end of the 19th century—Ernst Mach's attempt to purge scientific discourse of all metaphysical vocabulary. In particular, he is concerned with Mach's effort to replace the age-old notion of *causation* with the seemingly metaphysically neutral concept of *function*. Winston first examines the scientific impact of this move and then shows how it became intertwined with the social progressivism of Mach's close colleague and friend, Josef Popper-Lynkeus.

In chapter 7, Christopher D. Green examines the intentions that lay behind Charles Babbage's invention of the Analytical Engine during the 1830s and 1840s. Contrary to commonly made current claims, Green shows, Babbage did not believe his machine to stimulate activity of the mind and indeed took pains to distance himself from the controversial thesis of psychological materialism that such a belief might imply.

In chapter 8, Katharine Anderson describes and analyzes the significance of a curious device displayed at the Great Exhibition of 1851 in London. Called the Tempest Prognosticator, a device intended to predict the weather by using the presumed instincts of leeches. Anderson's treatment of this unlikely contraption opens a window on to a number of issues salient to 19th-century investigations of the mind, illuminating the conceptual boundaries between the mechanical and the rational; between human being and animal; and among sensation, intellect, and will.

Chapter 9 presents Charles W. Tolman's examination of Kant's and Georg Wilhelm Friedrich Hegel's views of the "proper" position of psychology in relation to other academic disciplines, arguing that psychology may have taken the wrong path when it turned away from an analysis of the *reasons* for behavior in favor of the attempt to uncover merely its determining stimuli. Tolman suggests that the so-called scientific psychology that developed in the 19th century and came to dominate in the 20th century was largely that which Kant described as empirical psychology and pragmatic anthropology. Moreover, Tolman argues that there is still a case to be made for the conclusion that in the past 150 years what qualifies as psychology has not been science, and what qualifies as science has not been psychology. As an alternative, he presents Hegel's psychology as conceptualized in his encyclopedia of the sciences.

This is followed by Thomas Teo's related investigation in chapter 10 of the rise of the view that mind should be understood as a socio–historical rather than a purely individual phenomenon—a *cogitamus*—an alternative that grew from the ground of Hegel's idealism. He looks closely at two approaches to this idea, the first advanced in the middle part of the century by Karl Marx, whose position on mind and consciousness was deeply socio–historical, and the second, developed later in the century, by Wilhelm Dilthey, whose hermeneutic approach was put forward, Teo argues, as an explicit challenge to attempts to reduce psychological phenomena and the mind to the results of natural-scientific experimentation. In addition, Teo contrasts the methodologies of Marx and Dilthey as alternatives to scientific methodologies in 19th-century German academia.

In chapter 11, Fredric Weizmann explores the contributions made in the late 19th and early 20th centuries by the developing fields of genetics and embryology to early developmental psychology. He critically surveys the vociferous debate over the impact of the prenatal environment on the developing fetus and shows how the terms of that debate—particularly the hypothesis of the "critical period"—were transferred to and adapted by those attempting to forge a scientific study of psychological development.

What we hope to show in these pages is not just that the standard narrative of the rise of scientific psychology is incomplete. We aim primarily to elucidate the various cross-currents of thought—in philosophy, science, technology, and institution-building practices—that led a wide array of people to render psychology scientific by putting the various available facets together in myriad ways. In addition, as several of the chapters in this collection also demonstrate, many psychologists were attuned to popular interests and concerns. As studies in the history of science and the sociology of knowledge have shown in recent decades with respect to many other disciplines, scientific psychology grew out of particular historical, socioeconomic, and technological contexts that would have a profound impact on the condition in which the discipline found itself at the opening of the 20th century.

REFERENCES

Boring, E. G. (1929). *A history of experimental psychology*. New York: Appleton-Century.

Kant, I. (1950). *Prologema to any future metaphysics* (L. W. Beck, Trans.). Indianapolis, IN: Bobbs-Merrill. (Original work published 1783)

Kant, I. (1970). *Metaphysical foundations of natural science* (J. Ellington, Trans.). Indianapolis, IN: Bobbs-Merrill. (Original work published 1786)

The
Transformation
of Psychology

1

EUGENICS AND OTHER VICTORIAN "SECULAR RELIGIONS"

RAYMOND E. FANCHER

Francis Galton (1822–1911) is widely recognized as one of modern psychology's most important—and controversial—founders. His "anthropometric laboratories" of the 1880s established the prototype for later "mental testing" and eventually intelligence testing (cf. Shore, chap. 4, this volume). His pioneering statistical studies directly inspired mathematician Karl Pearson and others to develop the modern techniques of correlation and regression analysis (cf. Winston, chap. 6, this volume). His studies of similarities between twins and biological relatives of lesser degree laid the foundations of modern behavior genetics and the ongoing debate over *nature versus nurture* (a phrase that Galton himself introduced and popularized). For more details about his psychological contributions, see Fancher (1996, chap. 7).

Galton conceived of nearly all of these contributions in the service of his visionary plan to improve the hereditary status of the human species, which he named *eugenics* and to which he passionately devoted the second half of his long life. Indeed, although he may never have used the exact phrase *secular religion*, it is clear that he thought about his eugenics program in precisely those terms. The concluding paragraph of *Inquiries Into Human*

Faculty and Its Development—the work in which Galton first introduced eugenics—declared that "the chief result of these Inquiries has been to elicit the religious significance of the doctrine of evolution" (1883/1907, p. 220). In *The National Review* he wrote, "The direction of the emotions and desires towards the furtherance of human evolution, recognized as rightly paramount over all objects of selfish desire, justly merits the name of a religion" (1894, p. 758). Furthermore, his autobiography asserted that eugenic principles "ought to become one of the dominant motives in a civilised nation, much as if they were one of its religious tenets" (1907, p. 322).

Galton's conception of eugenics as a secular religion developed over the course of a tumultuous decade in the middle of his life and entailed a profound transformation in his professional and scientific identity as well as in his religious outlook. Consider this brief "before-and-after" sketch. In 1860, before the transformation, Galton's reputation and expertise were confined to the fields of geography and travel. He had come to prominence as an African explorer in the early 1850s and subsequently won a place on the council of the Royal Geographical Society (see Fancher, 1983, for details). Throughout the 1850s his writings focused almost exclusively on geography and travel, with the best known being *The Art of Travel* (Galton, 1855). At this time he was neither expert nor even interested in the fields of biology and natural history. Although he was on friendly terms with his older cousin Charles Darwin, he was not among Darwin's scientific intimates and was just as surprised as the rest of the world when the *Origin of Species* burst on the scene in late 1859. Galton was impressed when he read it, but it made no immediate impact on his own life and work. His major research in the early 1860s continued to focus on subjects unrelated to biology, namely meteorology and weather maps. When Darwin in 1860 compiled a list of the naturalists who had responded favorably to his theory, Galton's name was not on it (F. Darwin, 1887, Vol. 2, p. 87). Indeed, Darwin then had no reason to think of Galton as a naturalist—or even as someone whose opinion might be important.

At this point in his life Galton was also a conventional and sincere Anglican believer. His African exploration had been partly inspired by the missionary journeys of David Livingstone, and Galton consulted with the London Missionary Society before and after his exploration; as late as 1861 he was writing in the society's journal about missionary prospects in Zanzibar. He had married into an eminent clerical family—his father-in-law was Dean of Peterborough Cathedral, and three of his brothers-in-law also took holy orders. In 1860, the 3rd edition of *The Art of Travel* contained passages speculating about how Adam, Eve, and Cain might have learned how to make fire—demonstrating Galton's acceptance at that time of the literal interpretation of the Book of Genesis (Pearson, 1924, p. 4).

By the end of the 1860s this picture had changed radically. Galton's book *Hereditary Genius* (1869/1962) was received respectfully by most Darwinians and seen as a valuable contribution to the new evolutionary discourse. In this work Galton coincidentally adopted a negative and not always consistent attitude toward traditional religion. On the one hand, he railed against enforced clerical celibacy as a virtual eugenic crime, on the grounds that it disproportionately removed men of a contemplative nature from the breeding pool. But on the other hand, he attributed unusual amounts of instability and waywardness to the offspring of clergy who did marry and remarked on "how large a part of religious biographies is commonly given up to occurrences of the sick-room" (1869/1962, p. 327). But even as he denigrated orthodox religion, Galton attributed "religious" significance to the general Darwinian worldview. He argued that evolutionary connectedness "points to the conclusion that all life is single in its essence. . . . Men and all other animals are active workers and sharers in a vastly more extended system of cosmic action than any of us can possibly comprehend" (p. 428). The anthropomorphic deities of the past should be replaced by a pantheistic over-soul, comprising the entire organic universe and expressing itself through the evolution of ever-higher forms of life. What better way to express devotion to this over-soul than first to study and understand and then deliberately to abet the workings of natural selection by enacting a program of the still unnamed but fully conceptualized eugenics?

Galton emphasized Darwin's personal role in his transformation when he wrote his cousin in 1869, "your book drove away the constraint of my old superstition as if it had been a nightmare" (quoted in Pearson, 1914, Plate I). Galton's autobiography states that the effect of the *Origin of Species* "was to demolish a multitude of dogmatic barriers by a single stroke, and to arouse a spirit of rebellion against all ancient authorities whose positive and unauthenticated statements were contradicted by modern science" (1907, p. 287). But whereas Darwin's influence was undoubtedly great, these statements obscure an important fact: namely, that Galton's transformation did not occur quickly or easily and certainly not at "a single stroke." In fact it took nearly a decade for the transition to become complete.

In the remainder of this chapter I consider another set of influences on Galton that I believe acted gradually and as a complement to Darwin during the crucial early years of the 1860s. Galton does not explicitly acknowledge these, so the evidence is circumstantial. But it seems highly significant that throughout this period Galton had increasing personal and professional contact in London with several of the figures who were prime creators of the broad movement the historian of science Frank Turner (1974) called "Victorian scientific naturalism." Although varying on their individual points and emphases, these men all agreed that all supernatural modes of explanation must be vehemently rejected in favor of interpretations according to the emerging findings and theories of empirical science. Among the most important of these were biologist T. H. Huxley (1825–1895), philosopher Herbert Spencer (1820–1903), journalist George Henry Lewes (1817–1878), physicist John Tyndall (1820–1893), and archeologist John Lubbock (1834–1913).

Of this group only Lubbock came from the same wealthy and privileged class with whom Galton customarily associated. The others represented the emerging group of middle-class, *professional* intellectuals who had to earn a living from their labors. But in 1861 the highly sociable Lubbock moved to London and began holding weekend parties whose guest lists included not only wealthy amateurs like himself and Galton but also rising young professional intellectuals including Huxley, Lewes, Spencer, and Tyndall. Galton also shared a passion for mountain climbing and membership in the Alpine Club with several of these men, and a certain social intimacy developed that gradually led to collaborations of a more professional nature. In 1863, for example, Lubbock, Huxley, and Galton all became officers of the Ethnological Society of London. A year later, Spencer convinced Galton to join himself, Tyndall, Lubbock, Darwin, and a few others in buying *The Reader,* a weekly journal intended to cover all major intellectual developments of the day. Huxley was also involved in this project as a nonshareholder, along with Lewes and several other luminaries including John Stuart Mill. Each major participant was to take responsibility for his particular specialty: for example, Huxley covered biology, Spencer philosophy and psychology, Tyndall physics, Lewes fiction and poetry, and Galton travel and geography.

Not only were Galton's new colleagues at the cutting edge of new scientific and intellectual developments in Victorian Britain, but they also had for the most part rejected orthodox Christianity earlier in their lives and were strongly committed to the view that naturalistic modes of explanation would have to supplant the supernaturalism characteristic of orthodox church doctrines. At the same time, however, these men considered themselves to be profoundly "religious" in a broad sense of the term. Further, they propounded their iconoclastic views particularly clearly during the early 1860s as Galton was getting to know them. It seems almost inevitable that some of this message must have rubbed off on him at the same time that he was absorbing the implications of Darwin's theory.

HUXLEY AND AGNOSTICISM

The most outspoken of Galton's new associates was T. H. Huxley, who in 1860 established his public reputation as "Darwin's bulldog." In June of that year he openly embraced the issue of human evolution—which the timid Darwin had largely evaded in the *Origin*—in his celebrated British Association debate with Samuel Wilberforce, the Bishop of Oxford. Asked sarcastically by the bishop whether he claimed descent from a monkey through his grandmother or his grandfather, Huxley responded that it was far preferable to have an ape for a grandfather than a man who used his high position to introduce unwarranted and ignorant ridicule into a grave scientific discussion. This public rebuke of a bishop scandalized the orthodoxy but electrified those of more liberal opinion (for an account of the debate, see L. Huxley, 1900, pp. 179–189). In private Huxley was sarcastic about Wilberforce, and when he learned in 1873 that his old antagonist had died after hitting his head on a rock, Huxley wrote to Tyndall, "For once, reality and his brains came into contact, and the result was fatal" (quoted in Clark, 1984, p. 146).

Soon after the Oxford debate Huxley reinforced the case for humanity's apelike ancestry in his popular 1863 book, *Evidence of Man's Place in Nature*, which summarized the available scientific information about the apes while emphasizing their humanlike physical and behavioral characteristics. The book had a provocative frontispiece depicting a procession of walking skeletons led by "man" and followed by the gorilla, chimpanzee, orangutan, and gibbon. Darwin was thrilled by this bold statement and wrote Huxley, "I declare I never in my life read anything grander" (quoted in Desmond, 1997, p. 313).

As he defended Darwin in the 1860s, Huxley was also privately and publicly staking out a distinctive position on religion. Despite his disdain for formal religion, Huxley considered himself to be a deeply religious person, and despite his public bombast, in private he was deeply reflective. He once described himself as having "a profound religious tendency capable of fanaticism, but tempered by no less profound theological scepticism" (quoted in Pearson, 1924, p. 178). As a child he had dressed like a priest and delivered mock sermons to his family, but gradually his theological skepticism developed. As a teenager he was impressed by William Hamilton's (1788–1856) *Philosophy of the Unconditioned*, a work that helped introduce Kantian philosophy to Great Britain while arguing that ultimate reality, like Kant's noumenal things-in-themselves, lay beyond the grasp of human awareness. During a long voyage as a ship's surgeon in the 1840s Huxley gradually drifted into a state of complete theological unbelief, and by the time he returned in 1850, "the fundamental principles of what is now understood as Agnosticism were clearly fixed in my mind" (quoted in Lightman, 1987, p. 96).

Huxley had to put those principles to a difficult personal test almost immediately after his debate with Wilberforce in 1860, when his young son died suddenly of scarlet fever. Among his condolences was a letter from Charles Kingsley (1819–1875), the novelist and liberal Anglican priest. Unlike Wilberforce, Kingsley was open to at least part of Darwin's message and wrote, "I dare say I am descended from some animal from whom also the chimpanzee has sprung." He added, however, that a human being's *moral* nature was "nearer to a God than to a Chimpanzee" and further that the moral self was immortal in the mind of God. Therefore he assured Huxley that his son survived in the Lord's sight and would one day be reunited with his parents (quoted in Desmond, 1997, p. 288). A deeply touched Huxley (L. Huxley, 1900) penned a long reply that constituted a cogent statement of his still unnamed agnosticism:

> I neither deny nor affirm the immortality of man. I see no reason for believing in it, but, on the other hand, I have no means of disproving it. Pray understand that I have no *a priori* objections to the doctrine. . . . It is not half so wonderful as the conservation of force, or the indestructibility of matter. (p. 217, emphasis added)

He added,

> I have champed up all the chaff about the ego and the non-ego, about noumena and phenomena, and all the rest of it, too often not to know that in attempting even to think of these questions, the human intellect flounders at once out of its depth. (p. 218)

Huxley continued to correspond with Kingsley, and in an 1863 letter (L. Huxley, 1900, Vol. 1, pp. 242–244), he extended his agnosticism into the realm of metaphysics:

> I am quite as ready to admit your doctrine that souls secrete bodies as I am the opposite one that bodies secrete souls—simply because I deny the possibility of obtaining any evidence as to the truth and falsehood of either hypothesis. My fundamental axiom of speculative philosophy is that *materialism and spiritualism are opposite poles of the same absurdity* —the absurdity of imagining that we know anything about either spirit or matter. (p. 243, emphasis in original)

But still, he continued, the materialistic assumptions of the scientific method promised to reveal at least a few of the "rules of the game" of existence: "We call them 'Laws of Nature' and honour them because we find that if we obey them we win something for our pains" (p. 243). This pragmatic and strategic assumption of the validity of scientific laws, even while admitting that they fall short of explaining the "ultimate" nature of the universe, enabled Huxley to endorse materialistic modes of explanation in his later debates with the physiologist William Carpenter (see Anderson, chap. 8, this volume, for details).

Just how much Galton knew about Huxley's private philosophizing in the early 1860s cannot be determined. Undoubtedly, however, he would have read a provocative letter Huxley published in *The Reader* in December 1864. Benjamin Disraeli had just given a highly publicized speech to the Anglican bishops in which he asked the rhetorical question "Is man an ape or an angel," and then replied "I, my lord, am on the side of the angels." Enraged, Huxley's letter excoriated Disraeli as a "political intriguer" who pandered "grotesquely" to the bishops. Although acknowledging that true religion had an "unshakeable throne . . . in the deeps of man's nature," Huxley asserted that this arose from the appreciation of the grandeur of nature and its laws and had nothing to do with the "old traditions" of orthodox theology. Science provided the way to express the truest religion, and science had "no intention of signing a treaty of peace" with the old traditions, "nor of being content with anything short of absolute victory and uncontrolled domination over the whole realm of the intellect" (quoted in Desmond, 1997, pp. 330–331). Huxley's outspokenness in this letter offended even some of his friends from the liberal clergy and may well have contributed to the ultimate financial failure of *The Reader*.

Still, Huxley remained in dialogue with Kingsley and other liberal-minded clerics, and toward the end of the decade joined the Metaphysical Society—an eclectic group whose members ranged from orthodox believers to outspoken skeptics, but all dedicated to the open discussion of philosophical and theological questions. Challenged to name his personal point of view, Huxley rejected the term *freethinker* as too vague and others such as *atheist, pantheist, theist, idealist,* or *materialist* because those who adopted those names

> were quite sure they had attained a certain "gnosis,"—had, more or less successfully solved the problem of existence; while I was pretty sure I had not, and had a pretty strong conviction that the problem was insoluble. . . . [The term *agnostic*] came into my head as suggestively antithetic to the "gnostic" of Church history, who professed to know so much about the very things of which I was ignorant. (quoted in Lightman, 1987, pp. 11–12)

The broadly religious connotations of Huxley's agnosticism were far from lost on his contemporaries, who referred to him as "the great apostle of the modern gospel of science," "the John Knox of agnosticism," the "prophet of science," and even "Pope Huxley" (Lightman, 1987, p. 120). Historian Adrian Desmond invoked this same idea in the subtitle of his 1997 biography, *Huxley: From Devil's Disciple to Evolution's High Priest.*

SPENCER'S "UNKNOWABLE" AND LEWES'S PANTHEISM

Huxley's coining of "agnosticism" was welcomed by many of his friends who had independently adopted similar views. Herbert Spencer, for example, came from an evangelical Methodist family but rejected his parents' faith while in his teens. He recalled that he had disliked the oppressive atmosphere of his religious household and very early developed objections to the notions of original sin and hell; moreover, the acquisition of scientific knowledge about physical cause and effect "practically excluded the ordinary idea of the supernatural" (1904, p. 172). He experienced no violent crisis of faith, but discarded Christianity gradually. By the mid-1850s his views were much like Huxley's, as he explicitly denied a charge of atheism while declaring, "I hold, in common with most men who have studied the matter to the bottom, that the existence of a Deity can neither be proved nor disproved" (quoted in Duncan, 1908, p. 81).

Throughout the 1850s Spencer made his name and his living as an editor, journalist, and professional author. His *Social Statics* in 1851 and the *Principles of Psychology* in 1855 promoted the notion of evolution, although without positing a plausible mechanism by which it might occur. (This, of course, is what Darwin provided with natural selection in 1859.) Spencer postulated a universal tendency toward progressive development, in societies as well as in organisms, from simpler into increasingly complex and more highly organized forms. When Galton first met him, Spencer was projecting and promoting a 10-volume series to be called a "System of Synthetic Philosophy." A pamphlet advertising the series appeared in the spring of 1860, endorsed by a list of 60 charter subscribers including younger notables such as Huxley, Kingsley, Lewes, and Tyndall—as well as several eminent elder statesmen such as Darwin, John Stuart Mill, and Charles Babbage (see Green, chap. 7, this volume, for a discussion of Babbage's attitudes toward religion).

In 1860 Galton was still a marginal figure in these circles and not on the list. But he surely learned about the first volume in his new friend's series, *First Principles of a New System of Philosophy*, when it duly appeared in 1862. The first chapter of this work, "The Unknowable," attempted to reconcile science and religion. Spencer here argued that most religions agree that there are ultimate mysteries to be solved and that science's most basic ideas represent realities that can never be directly comprehended. The ultimate nature of matter is incomprehensible, for example, because one cannot conceive of it as either infinitely or finitely divisible. Thus, both science and religion at least implicitly infer the existence of some ultimately unknowable actuality lying behind appearances. Here, in somewhat more abstract language than Huxley used, was the basic idea of agnosticism. Indeed, Lightman called Spencer's chapter "the first major statement of agnosticism and most comprehensive account of its basic tenets"—even though Huxley had not yet coined the term *agnosticism*. After he did, Spencer was content to accept that designation, and Victorians came to regard *First Principles* as "the agnostic bible" (Lightman, 1987, p. 82).

Spencer's belief in an "unknowable" universal principle, like Huxley's agnosticism, derived in part from the influence of Continental idealist philosophy. As previously noted, Huxley explicitly referred to Kantian philosophy and discussed it knowledgeably when describing the origins of his own views. Spencer, by contrast, deliberately practiced what Lewes's biographer Rosemary Ashton (1991, p. 50) called "cerebral hygiene"—"keeping the mind free of the clutter produced by the reading of the works of others." Thus, Spencer recalled that "I had in 1844 got hold of a copy of Kant's *Critique* . . . and had read its first pages; rejecting the doctrine in which, I went no further" (1904, Vol. 1, p. 438). He did, however, have a *secondary* source of some Continental philosophical clutter, in the writings of his friend George Henry Lewes. Although probably best remembered today as the consort of writer George Eliot, Lewes was himself a successful writer whose works included popular expositions of Continental philosophical thought for the English lay audience. Inasmuch as Lewes was also one of Galton's new colleagues on *The Reader,* he deserves mention here.

As an impoverished and rebellious teenager Lewes chanced on the Latin version of Spinoza's *Ethics*. Finding himself impressed by this systematic argument for pantheism, Lewes published an essay on Spinoza's life and work in the 1843 *Westminster Review*—the first serious and sympathetic presentation of the previously anathematized philosopher's work to the English public. His study of Spinoza inspired Lewes to seek firsthand knowledge of other continental philosophers, so he traveled and studied extensively in Germany and France. Among those he met and came to admire (if not always completely to believe) was the "positivist" philosopher Auguste Comte. Lewes now produced a series of accessible biographical essays beginning with Plato and concluding with Comte, which in the mid-1840s were published together as a *Biographical History of Philosophy*; among his most successful works, this remained constantly in print and underwent four revisions and enlargements before Lewes's death.

For Spencer, Lewes's book provided exactly what he needed to know about the history of philosophy:

> [It] made me acquainted with the general course of philosophical thought, and with the doctrines which throughout the ages have been the subjects of dispute, [and] gave me an increased interest in psychology, and an interest, not before manifest, in philosophy at large. (1904, Vol. 1, p. 439)

Particularly important—both for Spencer and for much of the English public—were Lewes's presentations of Spinoza's pantheism, Kant's idealism, and Comte's "positive philosophy" with its associated "religion of humanity." All of these represented attempts to come to grips with broadly "religious" issues but on a nontheological basis that accommodated recent scientific attitudes, and thus they were precursors to Victorian agnosticism. Comte's postulation of three inevitable stages of human development—starting with the theological or fictitious and passing through the metaphysical to culminate in the scientific or "positive"—resonated with Spencer's hypothesis of progressive evolutionary development. And even though Huxley sarcastically described Comte's proposed religion of humanity as "Catholicism minus Christianity," it nonetheless represented one of the first of the "secular religions" that came to wide notice in Victorian times.

A second edition of Lewes's *Biographical History* appeared in 1857; whether or not Galton was aware of it is unclear. But in any case, the two would have met when working together on *The Reader*, and later in the 1870s they collaborated as skeptical investigators of spiritualistic seances (Oppenheim, 1985, p. 291). Thus it seems reasonable to suggest that Lewes was at least indirectly one of the promoters of a theologically skeptical but pantheistically "religious" worldview that Galton first seriously encountered during the first half of the 1860s.

TYNDALL AND THE EFFICACY OF PRAYER

The son of an Irish shoemaker, John Tyndall began his career as a surveyor in rural Ireland and England, where he saw much poverty and coincidentally read and was radicalized by the works of the outspoken Scottish essayist Thomas Carlyle (1795–1881). In his 20s he found himself unable to imagine that a good and merciful God could make salvation dependent on "such slender links as a conformity with what some are pleased to call the essentials of religion" (quoted in Lightman, 1987, p. 99). Rejecting Christian dogma, he still retained a diffuse but strong sense of religious awe, inspired by the newly discovered laws of science and by the majesty of the natural world. The mountains provided a particular source of wonder, and he became an avid climber. His religious transformation, like Huxley's and Spencer's, occurred gradually and without an acute crisis.

Tyndall earned a PhD in chemistry at Marburg, Germany, in 1851, and on returning to England met and befriended Huxley. The two had much in common—scientifically, philosophically, religiously, and above all practically in their search for paying jobs in a country where science was still dominated by wealthy amateurs and the conservative clergy. In 1854 Tyndall finally obtained a post as professor of natural philosophy at the Royal Institution, where he worked closely with chemist and physicist Michael Faraday and began to achieve a reputation both as an original researcher and as a popularizer of recent developments in physics. His book *Heat, a Mode of Motion*, which interpreted heat as a consequence of molecular vibrations, appeared in 1863 just as Galton was getting to know him.

Among the most important scientific concepts Tyndall worked to popularize was the law of conservation of energy, which had been established in the 1840s through the combined efforts of the physicists Julius

Mayer, James Joule, and Hermann Helmholtz. For Tyndall and his fellow scientific naturalists, this law represented one of the most impressive indications of the ultimate unity and lawfulness of all of nature (recall that Huxley described it to Kingsley as more "wonderful" in its implications than the doctrine of immortality). Helmholtz had argued in 1847 that perpetual-motion machines would violate the law if they existed, and the fact that they did not exist thus substantiated the law. A decade and a half later, Tyndall modified this argument in a debate about miracles of the type commonly prayed for by the Anglican clergy. He argued that to pray for divine intervention to relieve a drought, a cattle plague, or a serious illness in the royal family was essentially to ask for a suspension of the conservation of energy. And this, he argued, was not only delusional but also harmful because it detracted attention from the real causes of events. Within the new ethos of scientific naturalism, such supplication was literally "sacrilegious."

A few of the clergy, including Kingsley, agreed with Tyndall that such prayers were inappropriate and refused requests from their parishioners to conduct them. In 1861 Tyndall praised these liberal priests in the essay "Reflections on Prayer and Natural Law": "Such men do service to public character, by encouraging a manly and intelligent conflict with the real causes of disease and scarcity instead of a delusive reliance on supernatural aid" (quoted in Turner, 1981, p. 175). These were minority attitudes in the Church, however, and in 1865 the Archbishop of Canterbury issued a special prayer for relief from a devastating cattle plague. Tyndall applauded when the liberal *Pall Mall Gazette* criticized the prayer as both selfish and offensive to those who believed the laws of nature could not be arbitrarily suspended. In a letter to the periodical, Tyndall argued,

> the antecedents [of the prayed about problem] are often very clear to one class of the community, though very dark to another and a larger class. This explains the fact, that while the latter are ready to resort to prayer, the former decline doing so. The difference between the classes is one of knowledge, not of religious feeling. (quoted in Turner, 1981, p. 176)

In a letter to a liberal cleric, Tyndall declared, "with regard to humbling ourselves in the expectation that a single beast the less will die, I would say in all frankness that I consider it a mere pagonism [sic]" (quoted in Turner, 1981, p. 177). Implicit here was the notion that the scientific attitude represented a higher form of genuine religious devotion than did traditional Christian practices and beliefs. Coincidentally, this same idea was suggested in an important 1865 book by Tyndall and Galton's friend Lubbock.

LUBBOCK AND THE EVOLUTION OF RELIGION

Although 12 years younger than Galton, John Lubbock by the early 1860s had already achieved a multifaceted and enviable public reputation. The eldest son of a knighted and wealthy banker, he had been something of a prodigy. When told by his father at age 7 that there was "a great piece of news," he was at first disappointed to discover that it was not that he was going to get a pony, but rather that Charles Darwin was to be their neighbor (Hutchinson, 1914, Vol. 1, p. 15). In due course, however, Lubbock came to appreciate what his father had said. He left school at age 14 to work at the family banking business but continued his education informally under the tutelage of his friend and neighbor. By age 20 he published four scientific papers, all about previously undescribed specimens from Darwin's crustacean collection. A skilled artist, he provided his own illustrations for the papers, as well as several for Darwin's 1854 book on barnacles. At 21 he discovered a fossilized musk ox and was elected to the Royal Geological Society; 2 years later he was named a Fellow of the Royal Society. By the early 1860s, while still working as a banker, he was elected president of the Ethnological Society and was independently pursuing research on archeology.

Lubbock's entry in the *Dictionary of National Biography* reports that "at an early period of his life, he moved away from orthodoxy and dogma, but his nature was in the highest degree reverent" (Rivière, 1978, p. xlii). This attitude, of course, would have been consistent with that of his friends Huxley, Spencer, and Tyndall. Further aspects of his belief may be inferred from *Prehistoric Times*, the book he published in 1865 describing his archeological research. This work popularized the now standard subdivision of human prehistory into the paleolithic (early stone), neolithic (late stone), bronze, and iron ages. More pertinent to the theme this essay, Lubbock also hypothesized that human beings evolved during these stages and that "modern savages" are kinds of living fossils throwing light on what European people's distant ancestry must have been like. Further, according to Lubbock's interpretation, religion numbered among the most important of evolved human institutions. He argued that the most primitive of human societies manifested no religious sensibility at all and that progressively higher stages of appreciation of the deity subsequently evolved.

Lubbock developed this idea more fully in his next book, *The Origin of Civilization and the Primitive Condition of Man* in 1870, which proposed seven distinct stages progressing from atheism through fetishism, shamanism, and idolatry before arriving at the modern state in which morality is integrated with religion. Implicit from the previous book, however, was the suggestion that religion is not a static or completed thing. Like human nature itself, it is an evolved characteristic that is still evolving. Within this context, of course, the newly emerging scientific appreciation of nature and its wonders was interpretable as the newest and highest stage of human religious development.

GALTON'S REACTION

Such, then, were some of the iconoclastic ideas the religiously conventional Galton encountered in the early 1860s. Here were bold extensions of Darwin's ideas into the realm of human evolution, along with a new interpretation of the nature of religion. It seems significant that only after his exposure to these men and their ideas did Galton himself begin to think and write about "Darwinian" subjects, at first in a very minor paper on the domestication of animals published in 1864. Then sometime in late 1864 he had the inspirational ideas he later denoted by the terms *hereditary genius* and *eugenics*. He hastily sketched these out in an 1865 article for the semipopular *Macmillan's Magazine*, "Hereditary Talent and Character." This paper contained his first statistical studies of familial eminence, the basic ideas behind both eugenics and intelligence testing, and several foundational ideas for behavior genetics. The article has been characterized by Galton's biographer Karl Pearson as "an epitome of the great bulk of Galton's work for the rest of his life" (1924, p. 86).

It is notable, however, that although this article may have served as an accurate preview of Galton's later work, it was also extremely sloppy and at times illogical. Space limitations preclude a detailed listing of its defects here, but historian Ruth Schwartz Cowan has commented, "Rarely in the history of science has such an important generalization been made on the basis of so little concrete evidence, so badly put, and so naively conceived" (1977, p. 135). Further, soon after completing the paper Galton suffered a severe and prolonged emotional breakdown marked by obsessions and anxiety that prevented him even from dining in public with friends. For three years his productivity plummeted, with his only major publication being a 4th edition of *The Art of Travel* in 1867; significantly, all biblical references were removed from this edition.

These events help resolve at least one minor mystery remarked on by earlier historians of science. In November 1864, Huxley, Lubbock, Spencer, and Tyndall joined with five other scientific friends (George Busk, Edward Frankland, Thomas Hirst, Joseph Hooker, and Galton's good friend from the Royal Geographical Society William Spottiswoode) to create the dining group that came to be called the "X Club." This small society soon became, in the words of historian James Moore, "the most powerful coterie in late-Victorian science" (quoted in Barton, 1998, p. 412). An informative account of the formation of the X Club by the historian Ruth Barton expresses surprise that Galton was not included in its original number (p. 442n). In light of what has been just discussed, however, at least two reasons why seem clear. First, Galton in late 1864 had not yet established himself as a reliable man of science; and second he was on the brink of an emotional breakdown that would curtail both his science and his social life for the next four years. Even if he had been invited, it seems unlikely he would have been able to join in.

Only in late 1868 did he begin to recover and to prepare the more detailed statistical analyses that a year later would form the heart of his book *Hereditary Genius*. In a previous paper (Fancher, 1998) I have suggested that Galton experienced a "midlife crisis" precipitated by a combination of factors, including the childlessness of his marriage, his contemplation of a new scientific worldview and, crucially, the abandonment of his orthodox religious faith. I argue that these factors conspired to make Galton's new ideas seem to him intellectually compelling but also psychologically dangerous, requiring an extended period of working through to be brought under full intellectual and emotional control.

One turning point in his recovery occurred when he began to analyze his data on eminence and intellectual ability in light of the writings of the pioneering statistician Adolphe Quetelet (1796–1874) and others on the Gaussian or "normal" distribution—works to which he had been introduced several years earlier by Spottiswoode. Here, he found not only a new tool for the statistical analysis of measures of intellectual ability but also —it seems—a "constructive" outlet for his obsessional tendencies. With better control of his ideas and better tools at his disposal for dealing with them he produced *Hereditary Genius*, which when it appeared in late 1869 presented a more cogent argument than had his clumsy paper four years earlier. The book received a respectful review in *Nature* by the eminent Darwinian Alfred Russel Wallace, and—more important to Galton—was also praised (with certain reservations) by Darwin himself.

Only now did Galton become a full member of the fraternity of scientific naturalists. His relationship with Darwin entered a new phase— one of genuine intellectual collaboration and mutual respect. Throughout 1870 and 1871 Galton conducted a series of transfusion experiments on rabbits intended to test Darwin's "pangenesis" theory of hereditary transmission. Darwin helped in the planning of these studies and took a keen interest in their progress. Even though the two cousins differed in their interpretations of the results (with Galton seeing them as a more conclusive refutation of pangenesis than did Darwin), they remained in regular and friendly discussion and debate of scientific issues for the rest of Darwin's life. When Galton proposed alternative theories of heredity in 1872 and 1875 (which anticipated the German biologist August Weismann's germ plasm theory in important ways) and also made his early discoveries of statistical regression and conducted his pioneering study of twins, Darwin remained a regular and respectful—if not always completely acquiescent —correspondent.

Galton now also joined forces with his scientific naturalist friends in their efforts to secularize religion. He collaborated with Tyndall, with whom he had also become a frequent mountain climbing companion, in the controversy over prayer. In 1871 the Prince of Wales was stricken with typhoid, and a nationwide program of prayer for his recovery was promoted by both Church and government. When he recovered, a national day of thanksgiving was declared, with a special service at St. Paul's Cathedral to celebrate the Prince's recovery through prayer. Neither thanks nor mention were given to the doctors who had tended the Prince, and only 12 invitations to the service were sent to physicians, whereas more than 1,500 members of the clergy were invited (Turner, 1981, p. 177). Tyndall was predictably outraged by this and began to campaign ever more vigorously against the control exerted by the conservative clergy over the educational system and the national consciousness in general. As part of his campaign he forwarded an anonymous letter he had received to the *Contemporary Review,* proposing an experiment in which a single ward in a large hospital would be made the subject of special national prayers by the faithful for a period of 3 to 5 years, at the end of which its mortality rates could be compared with those of other hospitals. This launched what became known as the "Prayer-Gauge Debate," a series of critiques and rebuttals in several semipopular periodicals.

Galton contributed to this debate with an 1872 article in the *Fortnightly Review,* "Statistical Inquiries Into the Efficacy of Prayer." Here he reported that the group of people whose well-being is most frequently and devoutly prayed for—namely sovereigns—had an average life span several years shorter than those of other groups such as doctors, lawyers, aristocrats, and even military officers. Here was clear evidence, he suggested, of the inefficacy of prayer to alter the laws of nature and mortality. Galton concluded the essay by admitting that, despite its lack of objective effect, prayer may still relieve the minds of the faithful and produce a sense of communion with a greater power. But a similar consolation was available to those, like himself, who were skeptical about the existence of a personal deity. Such people, he wrote,

> can dwell on the undoubted fact that there exists a solidarity between themselves and what surrounds them, through the endless reactions of physical laws, among which the hereditary influences are to be included. They know that they are descended from an endless past, that they have a brotherhood with all that is, and have each his own share of responsibility in the parentage of an endless future. . . . [Such knowledge] is quite as powerful [as prayer] in ennobling the resolves, and it is found to give serenity during the trials of life and in the shadow of approaching death. (1872, p. 135)

Clearly, Galton had now assumed a general religious stance very similar to those of the X Club members. And although the club never officially increased itself in size, he became one of its most frequently invited guests and one of only four people ever to be considered as a new member (Barton, 1990, p. 57).

It is an appropriate conclusion to this narrative to note that, following Darwin's death in 1882, Galton joined with Lubbock, Hooker, Huxley, and Spottiswoode in leading the successful campaign to have him buried in Westminster Abbey (Desmond & Moore, 1991, chap. 44). This may seem strange, given the group's hostile attitudes toward the Church and the fact that Darwin himself was an agnostic. But given the group's broader aims of biologizing religion and bringing it into accord with modern science, it made good sense. Indeed, Galton had written in *English Men of Science* about the desirability of a new "scientific priesthood" that would replace the traditional clergy in looking after the general well-being of the nation (1874/1970, p. 195). In the context of Galton's new secular religions of agnosticism and eugenics, Darwin clearly would rank among the highest of the scientific high priests. Thus it was only fitting that he should be given a reverential burial in the very seat of England's religious life.

CONCLUSION

Francis Galton was widely recognized during his lifetime as one of the most important of the new breed of English "scientists" (itself a term that came into wide use only in the latter half of the 19th century). Thus the social reformer Beatrice Potter Webb (1858–1943), who in her earlier years was Herbert Spencer's assistant and intimately acquainted with his entire circle of intellectual friends, recalled in her autobiography that out of all of these, "the one who stays in my mind as the ideal man of science is, not Huxley or Tyndall, Hooker or Lubbock, still less my guide, philosopher and friend Herbert Spencer, but Francis Galton" (1950, p. 116). Similarly, historians of "scientific" and experimental psychology have characterized Galton as one of the two or three most influential founders of that discipline. Edwin G. Boring, for example, pairs Galton with the German psychologist Wilhelm Wundt—crediting the latter as the father of a "general" experimental psychology while asserting that "Galton is founder of individual psychology—the psychology of individual differences in human capacity" (1957, p. 487). More recently, Kurt Danziger (1990) cited the "Galtonian" tradition of research—using relatively large numbers of "subjects" undergoing particular procedures, with their responses tabulated and analyzed statistically by an independent "experimenter"—as one of the three major methodological approaches adopted by early experimental psychologists.

Consistent with the theme of this volume, however, in this chapter

I have demonstrated that Galton's most influential scientific attitudes and ideas did not emerge fully formed and independently of religious and philosophical concerns. Indeed, when his most important ideas first occurred to him in their "bare" form, they severely disturbed his mental and emotional equilibrium. Only after those ideas could be securely placed within a satisfying philosophical and broadly "religious" context, suggested in part by his new circle of friends in the 1860s, was he able to develop and promote them with such consequence for modern psychology.

REFERENCES

Ashton, R. (1991). G. H. Lewes: A life. Oxford, England: Oxford University Press.

Barton, R. (1990). "An influential set of chaps": The X-Club and Royal Society politics, 1864–85. British Journal for the History of Science, 23, 53–81.

Barton, R. (1998). "Huxley, Lubbock, and half a dozen others": Professionals and gentlemen in the formation of the X-Club, 1851–1864. Isis, 89, 410–444.

Boring, E. G. (1957). A history of experimental psychology (2nd ed.). New York: Appleton-Century-Crofts.

Clark, R. W. (1984). The survival of Charles Darwin. New York: Random House.

Cowan, R. S. (1977). Nature and nurture: The interplay of biology and politics in the work of Francis Galton. In W. Coleman & C. Limoges (Eds.), Studies in history of biology (Vol. 1, pp. 133–208). Baltimore: Johns Hopkins University Press.

Danziger, K. (1990). Constructing the subject: Historical origins of psychological research. Cambridge, England: Cambridge University Press.

Darwin, F. (Ed.). (1887). The life and letters of Charles Darwin. New York: Appleton.

Desmond, A. (1997). Huxley: From devil's disciple to evolution's high priest. Reading, MA: Addison-Wesley.

Desmond, A., & Moore, J. (1991). Darwin. New York: Warner Books.

Duncan, D. (1908). The life and letters of Herbert Spencer. London: Methuen.

Fancher, R. E. (1983). Francis Galton's African ethnography and its role in the development of his psychology. British Journal for the History of Science, 16, 67–79.

Fancher, R. E. (1996). Pioneers of psychology (3rd ed.). New York: Norton.

Fancher, R. E. (1998). Biography and psychodynamic theory: Some lessons from the life of Francis Galton. History of Psychology, 1, 99–115.

Galton, F. (1855). The art of travel. London: Murray.

Galton, F. (1864). First steps towards the domestication of animals. British Association Report, pp. 93–94.

Galton, F. (1865). Hereditary talent and character. Macmillan's Magazine, 12, 157–166, 318–327.

Galton, F. (1872). Statistical inquiries into the efficacy of prayer. *Fortnightly Review, 12*, 125–135.

Galton, F. (1894). The part of religion in human evolution. *National Review, 23*, 755–763.

Galton, F. (1907). *Inquiries into human faculty and its development.* London: Dent. (Originally published 1883)

Galton, F. (1907). *Memories of my life.* London: Methuen.

Galton, F. (1962). *Hereditary genius.* Gloucester, MA: Peter Smith. (Original work published 1869)

Galton, F. (1970). *English men of science.* London: Frank Cass. (Original work published 1874)

Hutchinson, H. (1914). *The life of Sir John Lubbock, Lord Avebury* (2 vols.). London: Macmillan.

Huxley, L. (1900). *Life and letters of Thomas Henry Huxley.* London: Macmillan.

Lewes, G. (1845–1846). A biographical history of philosophy (2 vols.). London: Knight. (2nd ed. published 1857)

Lightman, B. (1987). *The origins of agnosticism: Victorian unbelief and the limits of knowledge.* Baltimore: Johns Hopkins University Press.

Lubbock, J. (1865). *Prehistoric times.* London: William & Margate.

Lubbock, J. (1870). *The origin of civilization and the primitive condition of man.* New York: Appleton.

Oppenheim, J. (1985). *The other world: Spiritualism and psychical research in England, 1850–1914.* Cambridge, England: Cambridge University Press.

Pearson, K. (1914, 1924, 1930). *The life, letters and labours of Francis Galton* (3 vols.). Cambridge, England: Cambridge University Press.

Rivière, P. (1978). Introduction. In J. Lubbock (Ed.), *The origin of civilization and the primitive condition of man.* Chicago: University of Chicago Press. (Original work published 1870)

Spencer, H. (1882). *First principles of a new system of philosophy.* New York: Appleton. (Original work published 1862)

Spencer, H. (1904). *An autobiography.* New York: Appleton.

Turner, F. (1974). *Between science and religion: The reaction to scientific naturalism in late Victorian England.* New Haven, CT: Yale University Press.

Turner, F. (1981). John Tyndall and Victorian scientific naturalism. In W. H. Brock, N. D. McMillan, & R. C. Mollan (Eds.), *John Tyndall: Essays on a natural philosopher* (pp. 169–180). Dublin, Ireland: Royal Dublin Society.

Tyndall, J. (1863). *Heat, a mode of motion.* London: Longmans, Green.

Webb, B. P. (1950). *My apprenticeship* (2nd ed.). London: Longmans, Green.

2

PRACTICAL PHRENOLOGY AS PSYCHOLOGICAL COUNSELING IN THE 19TH-CENTURY UNITED STATES

MICHAEL M. SOKAL

Most early-21st-century people in the United States who have heard of phrenology tend to think of it as quackery, on a par with fortune-telling, palm reading, and the like. After all, what can bumps on a skull tell anybody about an individual? Better informed observers tend to see phrenology as a pseudoscience, much like parapsychology, which (they argue) only those with delusions accept. Recently, however, historians of science have begun to clarify the origins of phrenology, revealing serious epistemological parallels between it and alchemy and astrology. All three emerged in their times as serious efforts to make the world intelligible. Medieval alchemists sought the elixir of life to overcome death and disease, and Renaissance astrologers tried to make rational the course of events and to fit humankind into the scheme of the universe. In the same way, 19th-century phrenologists tried to understand the relationship between human character and the human body. They sought to go beyond the folk wisdom of physiognomy to provide a scientific basis for such an analysis. More important, their claims attracted paying clients who accepted their authority and these analyses, and through the mid-19th century phrenologists in the United

States provided highly effective counseling that meant much to those who they examined.

PHRENOLOGY AND SCOTTISH COMMONSENSE REALISM

The phrenologists' analysis started from the prevalent mental philosophy of the period, Scottish commonsense realism, which emerged in 18th-century Aberdeen and Edinburgh through the work of such distinguished academic thinkers as Thomas Reid and Dugald Stewart. Their "faculty psychology" held that all humans exhibited specific mental traits, or faculties. These included, for example, the abilities to systematize, to reason, to judge, to generalize, to abstract, and to compare, as well as appetites for sex, for sleep, for air, for water, and for food. Professors at U.S. colleges taught this psychology throughout the 19th century, using such oft-reprinted textbooks as Thomas Upham's *Elements of Mental Philosophy* and Joseph Haven's *Mental Philosophy* and—perhaps most notably—*An Outline Study of Man; or, The Body and Mind in One System* by Mark Hopkins, long-time president of Williams College. His contemporaries knew Hopkins as a brilliant teacher; one described the perfect schoolroom as a log with Hopkins on one end and the student on the other. His 1873 text thus included "illustrative diagrams" and a novel "method for blackboard teaching." It closed with an "Analytical Chart" (see Figure 2.1) that detailed "the body and mind in one system" and illustrated how 19th-century U.S. academics understood their own psychic lives. Indeed, this faculty psychology was not displaced at even the most innovative U.S. colleges until the 1870s and 1880s, when men influenced by evolutionary ideas, such as William James and G. Stanley Hall, began to seek the new experimental psychology in Germany.

In their work the phrenologists took this mental philosophy and related it to human physiology by making at least four assumptions (see Sizer, 1882, pp. 372–373). The first—that the brain is the organ of the mind—aroused no controversy; indeed, many ancient Greeks (although not Aristotle) would have accepted it. Their second assumption—that specific faculties are located in specific parts of the brain—has equally ancient roots and also meshed well with slightly later studies of nervous physiology by scientists such as Charles Bell and François Magendie. The phrenologists' third and fourth assumptions—that the strength of each faculty determines the physical size and shape of the specific part of the brain in which it is localized and that the shape of the brain itself determines the shape of the skull that surrounds it—were less universally defensible even in the 18th century and, of course, no early-21st-century neurologist accepts them. But

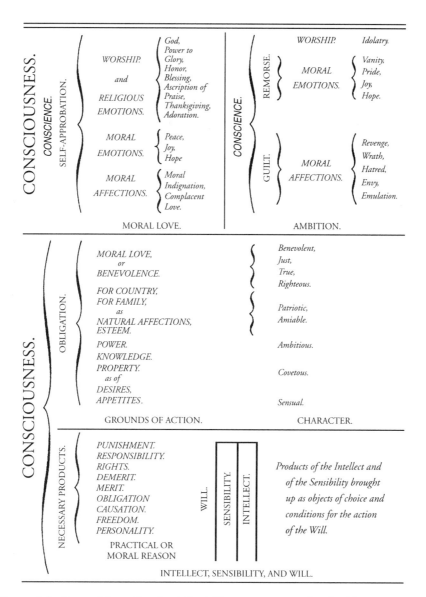

Figure 2.1. Excerpt from the Analytical Chart accompanying M. Hopkins (1873), *An Outline Study of Man; or, the Mind and Body in One System* (pp. 306–307).

these assumptions made much sense to the phrenologists and to many of their contemporaries, and they provided a foundation on which they established their science and their practice.

Other historians have analyzed phrenology as a system of the mind and have emphasized the theories of Franz Josef Gall of Germany, who first formally proposed the science. Still others have written on phrenological

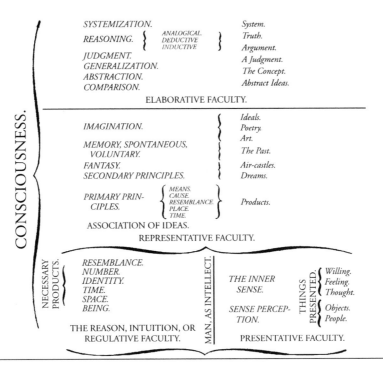

Figure 2.1. (*Continued*)

reform proposals—particularly in 19th-century Scotland—and have tried to outline the study's political implications (Cooter, 1986, 1989). This chapter, however, focuses on the work of the itinerant or "practical" phrenologists who traveled throughout the United States in the mid-19th century, offering themselves as psychological examiners, diagnosticians, prognosticians, and counselors. Historians have already written of the U.S. tour of Gall's disciple Johann Gaspar Spurzheim (Walsh, 1972), and Madeleine B. Stern's *Heads and Headlines: The Phrenological Fowlers* (Stern, 1971) effectively details the successful careers of siblings Orson, Charlotte, and Lorenzo Fowler. This chapter builds on this work and both outlines 19th-century U.S. phrenological practice and describes and analyzes the kinds of vocational guidance, marital counseling, and child-rearing advice that the phrenologists offered their clients. This chapter also seeks to go further with two ambitious goals: (a) to suggest just how these phrenological examiners arrived at the character readings they offered to those whom they examined and (b) to explain why these readings meant something to these clients. The results presented here remain tentative but go beyond previous attempts to explain the intricacies of phrenological practice, and previous audiences have found these arguments provocative.

Answers to these "how" and "why" questions depend, as noted, on a knowledge of 19th-century U.S. phrenological practice. To be sure, phrenology lingered in the United States for many years, and, for example, phrenologists operated a vocational guidance bureau in Minneapolis during the Great Depression (Risse, 1976). And Sybil Leek (1970)—until her recent death a self-identified witch—called phrenology a significant component of her craft even in the late 20th century. Phrenology began to boom, however, in the years before the U.S. Civil War. The popular journal *Annals of Phrenology* first appeared in Boston in 1834, and the Fowlers (and their heirs) sponsored the publication of the *American Phrenological Journal and Miscellany* from 1838 to 1911. During these decades the most prominent practical phrenologists, including the Fowlers, established consulting offices in major cities such as Boston, New York, and Philadelphia. But such opportunities were rare in the antebellum United States, when most people lived on farms and in smaller towns. Instead, most phrenologists during this period were itinerant, traveling from town to town, visiting during market days, setting themselves up for a short time, and offering their services for a fee. Like other itinerant lecturers, they typically hired the town hall or a large church and began their visits with free or low-cost lectures and demonstrations. At these events they sold books and charts, much as today's rock groups sell T-shirts and posters at their concerts. At larger towns the phrenologists stayed for a week or more and offered a full course of lectures at higher fees, and indeed, in such settings, phrenology retained its influence long after its authority had waned in the great cities.

From 1857, for example, Worcester, Massachusetts—long a prosperous county seat—had available the large and beautiful Mechanics Hall, at which distinguished speakers such as clergyman Henry Ward Beecher (in 1857 and after), Ralph Waldo Emerson (in 1860 and after), astronomer Ormsby McKnight Mitchel (in 1861), and Charles Dickens (in 1868) read and lectured. Through its first decades, Mechanics Hall hosted phrenological lectures and demonstrations by, among others, John Logan and Orson Fowler (see Figure 2.2). These presentations emphasized the full range of powers the phrenologists claimed for their science, particularly with respect to its abilities to advise individuals on proper patterns of behavior. Logan's lectures, for example, addressed "the training and education of children" and offered advice as to how "Phrenology . . . may be applied in Education, Business, Marriage, and Success in Life." Fowler's longer series of presentations successively treated "Health and Phrenology," "How to Rise in the World," "Love and Matrimony," "Courtship and Married Life," and "Self-Culture and Children" and concluded with two closed lectures on "Ma-

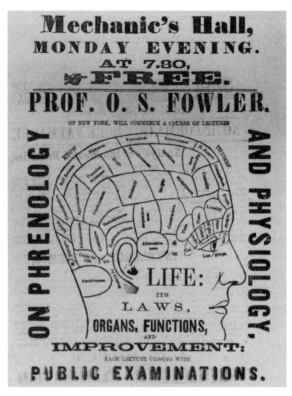

Figure 2.2. Excerpt from the broadside advertising O. S. Fowler's phrenological lectures at Mechanics Hall, Worcester, Massachusetts. Copyright 1999 American Antiquarian Society, Worcester, MA. Courtesy, American Antiquarian Society, Worcester.

ternity and Female Perfection" ("to Ladies only") and on "Sexuality and Nature's Creative Laws and Facts" ("to Men only").

Many lectures closed with one or more open examinations, at which the phrenologists set out to demonstrate publicly their ability to read an individual's character by examining his or her skull. In doing so, they rarely looked simply for individual "bumps" but instead concerned themselves with the total shape of the head and the relationship among the several "organs" they identified. The phrenologists conducted these public examinations as much for amusement—and, especially, for advertisement—as for edification and, at times, audiences tried to fool examiners by disguising subjects. These "rigged" examinations often took on a comic turn, and the phrenologists soon learned to make the best of them.

The phrenologists' primary (and most profitable) business, however, consisted of a series of private readings conducted for a fee, often at their hotels, on mornings and afternoons before each lecture. (In Worcester, e.g., Orson Fowler met his clients at the Lincoln House, the city's best hotel.)

The phrenologists based these "delineations" on careful examinations of their subjects' skulls. They identified their subjects' most prominent character traits by the development of their "organs," they usually recommended which traits should be "cultivated" and which should be "restrained," and they often even suggested how these traits might be altered. At times, the phrenologists suggested specific traits that a subject should seek in a spouse—and often advertised this aspect of their practice—or, more generally, which course of action he or she should follow. Phrenologists thus served 19th-century people in the United States in much the same way family and vocational guidance counselors do today. Indeed, in emphasizing conduct and courses of action, these practical phrenologists often proved much more directive and much less concerned with their subjects' emotional or intellectual life than are many early-21st-century psychotherapists. Some historians of science thus claim that phrenology helped prepare the United States for the emergence of behaviorism (see Bakan, 1966)—which characterized much of U.S. psychology at least through the 20th century's first half—and especially its concern for applicability, which continues in the early 21st century to dominate psychological concerns in the United States.

The phrenologists often reported their delineations by filling in blanks in large printed charts, or—if clients would pay for the service—by having stenographers record their remarks as they performed their examinations. Nelson R. Sizer, a prominent itinerant phrenologist who at times worked with the Fowlers, often urged his subjects to avail themselves of such records. More typically, however, the phrenologists simply filled in blanks in the first pages of phrenological manuals, which they then sold to their clients. Careful practitioners like the Fowlers also often annotated the texts of these manuals and provided appropriate marginalia for their subjects to consult at their leisure. Many of these reports survive—including Sizer's delineation of Clark Gillson, mayor of Worcester (available from Worcester's American Antiquarian Society)—and these provide graphic portraits of phrenological practice.

A PHRENOLOGICAL READING

One examination, detailed throughout the pages of a copy of Fowler's (1868) *The Practical Phrenologist; A Compendium of Phreno-Organic Science*, effectively illustrates this practice. The volume's printed title page notes further that it serves as the "Recorder and Delineator of the Character and Talents of _____ as marked by _____," and these blanks have been completed, in pencil, with the names of "Randolph Moetley" and "O. S. Fowler," respectively (see Figure 2.3). In the frontispiece (see

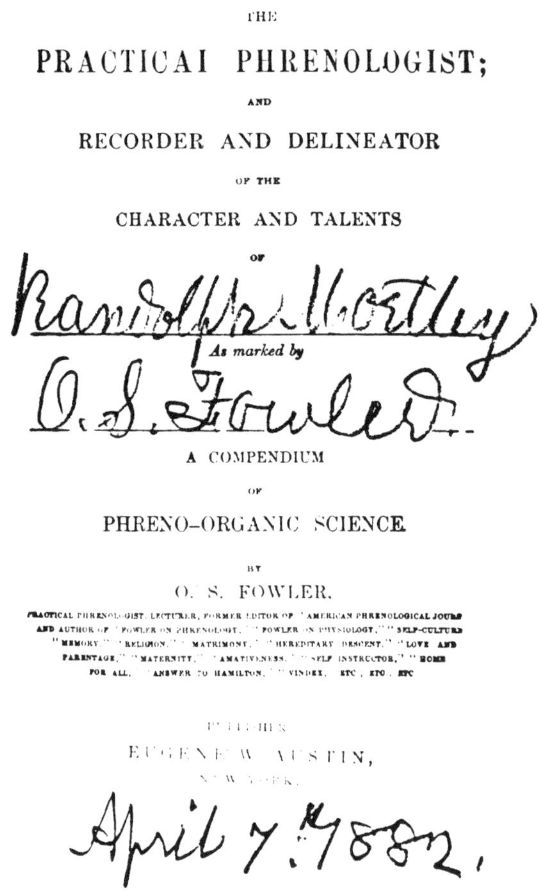

THE

PRACTICAI PHRENOLOGIST;

AND

RECORDER AND DELINEATOR

OF THE

CHARACTER AND TALENTS

OF

Randolph Moetley

As marked by

O. S. Fowler

A COMPENDIUM

OF

PHRENO–ORGANIC SCIENCE

BY

O. S. FOWLER.

PRACTICAL PHRENOLOGIST, LECTURER, FORMER EDITOR OF "AMERICAN PHRENOLOGICAL JOURNAL"
AND AUTHOR OF "FOWLER ON PHRENOLOGY," "FOWLER ON PHYSIOLOGY," "SELF-CULTURE"
"MEMORY," "RELIGION," "MATRIMONY," "HEREDITARY DESCENT," "LOVE AND
PARENTAGE," "MATERNITY," "AMATIVENESS," "SELF INSTRUCTOR," "HOME
FOR ALL," "ANSWER TO HAMILTON," "VINDEX," ETC., ETC., ETC

PUBLISHER

EUGENE W. AUSTIN,
NEW YORK.

April 7th 1882.

Figure 2.3. Title page from O. S. Fowler (1868), *The Practical Phrenologist: A Compendium of Phreno-Organic Science*, recording Fowler's delineation of the character of Randolph Moetley, April 7, 1882.

Figure 2.4), a diagram of the human skull is presented, with a detailed caption providing the "names, numbering, and definitions of the faculties." This is followed by an outline of "Business Adaptations in a Scale from 1 to 7" (see Figure 2.5), and Fowler marked several occupations—notably those of editor, elocutionist, lawyer, lecturer, politician, and reporter—with a penciled "7." A chart fills the following two pages, with each of the lines labeled with one of the previously defined phrenological faculties, and each of the first five columns headed by numbers on a scale that ranges from "7. Very Large" to "2. Small." The headings of the final three columns read "Cultivate," "Restrain," and "Marry one having," respectively. Each box of the chart (except those in the last column) contains a number referring to a particular page in the manual, and for each faculty Fowler marked in pencil his reading of Moetley's particular strengths and weaknesses. For example, Fowler found Moetley's faculties of "vital power," "ex-

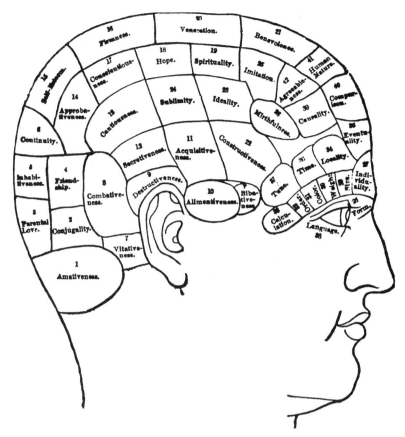

Figure 2.4. Excerpt from the frontispiece from O. S. Fowler (1868), *The Practical Phrenologist: A Compendium of Phreno-Organic Science.*

citability," "amativeness," "parental love," "cautiousness," "secretiveness," "firmness," and "benevolence" to be "very large" and "large" and, indeed, Fowler urged Moetley to "restrain" his tendencies toward excitability, amativeness, and benevolence. On the other hand, Fowler found Moetley's faculties of "friendship," "continuity," "acquisitiveness," "self-esteem," "hope," and "spirituality" to be "average," "moderate," or "small," and he urged Moetley to "cultivate" these faculties. Fowler also recommended that Moetley seek a spouse whose large and small faculties would complement his; that is (in Fowler's view) one with average excitability and amativeness, with moderate secretiveness, and with large hope. For all of these recommendations, Fowler's chart referred Moetley to specific pages in *The Practical Phrenologist*, each of which contains detailed descriptions of each faculty's characteristics. The volume noted, for example, that those with large cautiousness "are always on the lookout; take ample time to get ready; provide for prospective dangers; make everything safe; guard against losses and evils; incur no risks" and stresses that those with large benevolence

IN A SCALE FROM 1 TO 7.

Artistical.
Architect.
Designer.
Engraver.
Musician.
Music Teacher.
Painter, Orna-
mental.
do., Portra
Photographc.

Commercial.
Accountant.
Agent.
Appraiser.
Auctioneer.
Banker.
Bookseller.
Broker.
Business Corres.
Cashier.
Collector.
Commis. Mer.
Conductor.
Druggist.
Expressman.
Importer.
Insurance.
Landlord.
Merchant.
Principal.
Publisher
Salesman.
Shipping Clerk.
Speculator.
do., Real Estate.
Superintendent.
Trader.

Retail Dealer.
Wholesale do.
Dealer in —
Boots, shoes.
Leather.
Cattle, horses.
Coal, lumber.
Dry-goods.
Fancy Articles.
Grain, groceries.
Hardware.
Implements.
Jewelry.
Marketing.
Useful Articles.

Professional.
Actor.
Author.
Bishop.
Clergyman.
Conveyancer.
Correspondent.
Editor.
Elocutionist.
Governor.
Governess.
Historian.
Judge.
Lawyer.
Lecturer.
Literature.
Linguist.
Officer.
Poet.
Politician.
Professor.
Proof-reader.

Reporter.
Teacher.
Writer.

Mechanical.
Baker.
Blacksmith.
Boss Workman.
Builder.
Carpenter.
Chandler.
Compositor.
Contractor.
Cooper.
Dairyman.
Dentist.
Dressmaker.
Farmer.
Finisher.
Gardener.
Gunsmith.
Gas Fitter.
Inventor.
Laborer.
Locksmith.
Machinist.
Mason.
Miller.
Milliner.
Paperer.
Plumber.
Printer.
Tailor.
Tanner.
Tinsmith.
Turner.
Seamstress.
Stonecutter.

Shipbuilder.
Upholsterer.
Manufacturer of —
Boots, shoes.
Fancy Articles.
Furniture.
Trunks, harness.
Useful Articles.

Scientific.
Anatomist.
Captain.
Chemist.
Commander.
Engineer.
Geologist.
Manager R. R.
do., of Workmen.
Miner.
Naturalist.
Phrenologist.
Physician.
Representative.
Secretary.
Surgeon.
Surveyor.
Statesman.

Miscellaneous
Fisherman.
Housekeeper.
Livery Keeper.
Matron.
Nurse.
Restaurant.
Teamster.
Waiter.
Watchman.

MARRY one ___ In Size ___ Height ___ Blonde ___ Brunette

Figure 2.5. Business Adaptations and Chart of Faculties, recording Fowler's delineation of Moetley's character, from O. S. Fowler (1868), *The Practical Phrenologist: A Compendium of Phreno-Organic Science.*

(again, like Moetley) also "experience the greatest solicitude for the welfare of friends" (p. 100). Each description also contains specific recommendations for restraining or cultivating particular faculties. For example, to restrain excitability, Fowler recommended that Moetley "fulfill all health conditions, so as thereby to allay all false excitement, . . . [take] air, water, exercise, and sleep [freely], . . . if in trouble, banish it, and make yourself as happy as possible. Take lessons of Quakers" (p. 48). Similar recommendations to cultivate continuity include "dwell on, and pore over, till you complete the thing in hand; make thorough work; and never allow your

Top table (Conditions 17–42):

CONDITIONS.	7 Very Large	6 Large	5 Full	4 Average	3 Moderate	2 Small	Culti-vate	Re-strain	Marry one having
17. Conscientious	112	112	113	113	114	114	114	114	
18. Hope	115	115	116	116	116	117	117	117	*6*
19. Spirituality	117	118	118	118	118	118	118	119	
20. Veneration	119	120	121	121	121	121	121	121	
21. Benevolence	122	123	123	123	123	123	123	124	
SELF-PERCEPTIVES.	124	124	124	124	124	125	125	125	
22. Constructiveness	125	125	125	125	126	126	126	127	
23. Ideality	127	127	127	128	128	128	129	129	
24. Sublimity	129	129	130	130	130	130	130	130	
25. Imitation	130	131	131	132	132	132	132	132	
26. Mirthfulness	133	133	133	134	134	134	134	134	
INTELLECTUALS.	136	135	135	135	135	135	135	136	
PERCEPTIVES.	136	136	136	137	137	137	137	137	
27. Individuality	137	138	138	139	139	139	139	139	
28. Form	139	139	140	140	140	140	140	140	
29. Size	141	141	141	141	141	141	141	142	
30. Weight	142	142	142	142	143	143	143	143	
31. Color	143	143	144	144	144	144	144	144	
32. Order	144	145	145	145	145	145	146	146	
33. Calculation	146	147	147	147	147	147	147	147	
34. Locality	147	147	148	148	148	148	148	148	
LITERARY FACULTIES.	148	148	149	149	149	149	149	149	
35. Eventuality	149	149	150	150	150	151	151	151	
36. Time	151	151	151	151	152	152	152	152	
37. Tune	152	152	152	153	153	153	153	153	
38. Language	153	154	154	155	155	155	155	156	
REFLECTIVES.	156	156	156	156	156	156	156	156	
39. Causality	157	157	158	158	158	158	158	158	
40. Comparison	159	159	160	160	160	160	160	160	
41. Human Nature	161	161	161	161	161	161	161	162	
42. Agreeableness	162	162	162	162	162	162	162	162	

Bottom table (Size of Brain, Vital/Motive/Mental Power, Conditions 1–16):

CONDITIONS.	7 Very Large	6 Large	5 Full	4 Average	3 Moderate	2 Small	Culti-vate	Re-strain	Marry one having
Inches. / Size of Brain,	PAGE 6	7	7	7	8	8			
Organic Quality	16	17	17	17	17	17	17	18	
Health	21	21	21	21	22	22	22	22	
Vital Power,	25	25	26	26	26	26	26	27	
Breathing Power	28	28	29	28	29	29	29	29	
Circulatory Power	30	30	30	30	30	30	30	31	
Digestive Power	31	31	31	31	31	32	32	33	
Motive Power,	34	35	35	35	35	35	35	36	
Mental Power,	39	40	41	41	41	41	41	41	
Activity	46	46	46	46	46	47	47	47	
Excitability	47	48	48	48	48	48	48	48	*average 4*
DOMESTIC GROUP.	66	66	66	66	66	66			*anxious 4*
1. Amativeness	67	68	69	69	70	70	71	71	
2. Conjugality	72	72	72	72	73	73	73	73	
3. Parental Love	74	74	75	75	75	75	76	76	
4. Friendship	76	77	77	78	78	78	78	78	
5. Inhabitiveness	79	79	79	80	80	80	80	80	
6. Continuity	80	80	81	81	81	81	82	82	
SELFISH GROUP.	83	82	83	83	83	83	83	83	
7. Vitativeness	84	84	84	84	84	84	84	84	
8. Combativeness	85	85	86	86	87	87	87	87	
9. Destructiveness	88	88	89	89	89	89	90	90	
10. Alimentiveness	91	91	91	91	91	91	92	92	
11. Acquisitiveness	94	94	96	96	96	96	96	96	
12. Secretiveness	97	97	97	98	98	98	99	99	*medium 3*
13. Cautiousness	99	100	101	101	101	101	102	102	
14. Approbativeness	102	103	103	103	104	104	104	104	
15. Self-Esteem	105	106	106	106	106	107	107	107	
16. Firmness	108	108	109	109	109	109	109	109	
MORAL GROUP.	110	110	110	111	111	111	111	111	

Figure 2.5. (Continued)

thoughts to wander, or attention to be distracted, or indulge diversity or variety in anything" (p. 82) and to cultivate spirituality include "muse and meditate on divine things, the Deity, a future existence, the state of man after death, immortality, and that class of subjects; and especially, follow your innermost impressions or presentiments in everything, as well as open your mind to the intuitive perception of truth" (pp. 118–119).

This volume also contains extensive penciled annotations, as Fowler underlined and highlighted his recommendations for action. But Moetley himself went further, and where Fowler had recommended he seek a spouse with average excitability and amativeness (see Figure 2.6), his own marginal notations read "Ella?" One wonders who Ella was and if Moetley took Fowler's advice.

PHRENOLOGICAL GUIDANCE

Careful review of such delineations can help early-21st-century observers generalize about the phrenologists' practice and about the vocational guidance, marital counseling, and child-rearing advice they offered their clients. The Fowlers also often used the *American Phrenological Journal and Miscellany* to report especially interesting examinations, to publicize their successes, and to reprint letters from delighted clients. Their reports of repeat consultations often emphasize such satisfaction, and although these obviously do not embody a random sample of responses to their work, they do provide evidence that phrenology did mean much to many mid-19th-century people in the United States. So, too, do the many cases reported in the phrenologists' memoirs—especially Sizer's (1882) *Forty Years in Phrenology*, which reprints many accounts from the phrenological press—and these also shed light on phrenological practice and advice.

Vocational Guidance

In providing vocational guidance, the phrenologists based their advice on their reading of an individual's faculties. For example, they advised those with large eventuality to become lawyers, those with large constructiveness to become mechanics, and those with large perceptive faculties to become physicians. Sizer's (1882) memoirs reported his examination of "a natural merchant seven years old" with especially "large acquisitiveness and secretiveness, good practical judgment, and great hope, energy, and ambition . . . just the right kind of head for a merchant or a banker" (pp. 297–298). Sizer prided himself on being able to distinguish "off-hand, quick businessmen—ready, smart, successful, apt as traders and speculators" from others "sound in judgment, but slow in reaching conclusions," for whom

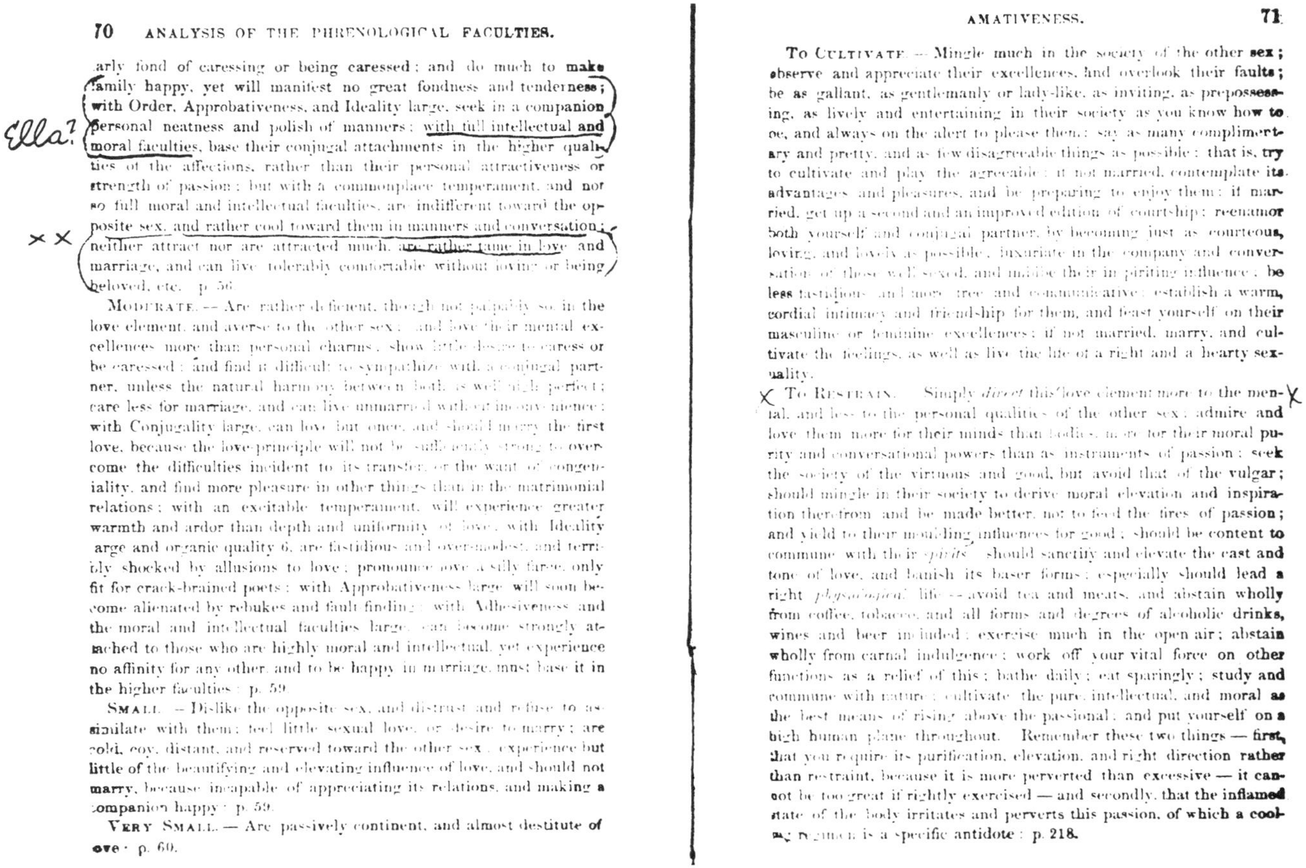

To Cultivate.—Mingle much in the society of the other sex; observe and appreciate their excellences, and overlook their faults; be as gallant, as gentlemanly or lady-like, as inviting, as prepossessing, as lively and entertaining in their society as you know how to be, and always on the alert to please them; see as many complimentary and pretty, and a few disagreeable things as possible; that is, try to cultivate and play the agreeable if not married; contemplate its advantages and pleasures, and be preparing to enjoy them; if married, get up a second and an improved edition of court-ship; reanimate both yourself and conjugal partners by becoming just as courteous, loving, and lovic as possible; luxuriate in the company and conversation of those well-loved, and induce them in getting influence, be less fastidious and more free and communicative; establish a warm, cordial intimacy and friendship for them, and feast yourself on their masculine or feminine excellences if not married, marry, and cultivate the feelings, as well as live the life of a right and a hearty sexuality.

To Restrain.—Simply direct this love element more to the mental, and less to the personal qualities of the other sex; admire and love them more for their minds than their forms; value them more for their moral purity and conversational powers than as instruments of passion; seek the society of the virtuous and good, but avoid that of the vulgar; should mingle in their society to derive moral elevation and inspiration therefrom and be made better, not to feed the fires of passion; and yield to their moulding influences for good; should be content to commune with their spirits; should sanctify and elevate the vast and tone of love, and banish its baser forms; especially should lead a right physiological life—avoid tea and meats, and abstain wholly from coffee, tobacco, and all forms and degrees of alcoholic drinks, wines and beer in dieed; exercise much in the open air; abstain wholly from carnal indulgence; work off your vital force on other functions as a relief of this; bathe daily; eat sparingly; study and commune with nature; cultivate the pure intellectual, and moral as the best means of rising above the passional, and put yourself on a high human plane throughout. Remember these two things—first, that you require its purification, elevation, and right direction rather than its excess, because it is more perverted than excessive—it cannot be too great if rightly exercised—and secondly, that the inflamed state of the body irritates and perverts this passion, of which a cool aperient is a specific antidote. p. 218

arly fond of caressing or being caressed; and do much to make family happy, yet will manifest no great fondness and tenderness; with Order, Approbativeness, and Ideality large, seek in a companion personal neatness and polish of manners; with full intellectual and moral faculties, base their conjugal attachments in the higher qualities of the affections, rather than their personal attractiveness or strength of passion; but with a commonplace temperament, and not so full moral and intellectual faculties, are indifferent toward the opposite sex, and rather cool toward them in manners and conversation, neither attract nor are attracted much, do rather tame in love and marriage, and can live tolerably comfortable without loving or being beloved, etc. p. 56

Moderate.—Are rather different, though not perfectly so in the love element and averse to the other sex, and love their mental excellence more than personal charms, show little desire to excess or be caressed, and find it difficult to sympathize with acquired partner, unless the natural harmony between both is while perfect; rare less for marriage, and can live unmarried without any sex nature; with Conjugality large, can love but once, and should among the first love, because the love principle will not be sufficiently strong to overcome the difficulties incident to its transient, or the want of congeniality, and find more pleasure in other things than in the matrimonial relations; with an excitable temperament, will experience greater warmth and ardor than depth and uniformity of love; with Ideality large and organic quality, are fastidious and over-scrupulous, and terribly shocked by allusions to love; pronounce any silly farce, only fit for crack-brained poets; with Approbativeness large will soon become alienated by rebukes and fault finding; with Adhesiveness and the moral and intellectual faculties large, can become strongly attached to those who are highly moral and intellectual, yet experience no affinity for any other, and to be happy in marriage must base it in the higher faculties. p. 59

Small.—Dislike the opposite sex, and distrust and refuse to assimilate with them; feel little sexual love, or desire to marry; are cold, coy, distant, and reserved toward the other sex, experience but little of the beautifying and elevating influence of love, and should not marry, because incapable of appreciating its relations, and making a companion happy. p. 59

Very Small.—Are passively continent, and almost destitute of love. p. 60

Figure 2.6. Amativeness, from O. S. Fowler (1868), The Practical Phrenologist: A Compendium of Phreno-Organic Science, pp. 70–71.

he recommended other careers less dependent on intuition (pp. 289–291). He also described urging a farmer with good business sense but tendencies "to conjure up dangers and difficulties" and to fear "to act until the favorable opportunity had passed" to "act at once." He also bragged that, two years later, the successful farmer returned to have his sons' "business adaptations" delineated (pp. 287–288).

As this chapter argues, the phrenologists' ability to read their clients' faculties itself derived from a blend of several skills. But in many ways their advice combined 19th-century common sense and what the early 21st century calls self-fulfilling prophecies. They urged "drinking men" to reform or face failure at any job, and Sizer often advised men "remarkable for nervous excitability" to give up coffee and tobacco. More generally, Lorenzo Fowler urged his clients to take as their motto "self-made or never-made" and to work toward their goals. As he advised many individuals, once you "find out your peculiarities of mind . . . decide at once on the profession or business you wish to pursue . . . then cultivate the faculties that are necessary to qualify you for success in the . . . calling you have chosen" (cited in Stern, 1971, pp. 38–39, 53). No wonder his brother Orson advised Randolph Moetley to cultivate his faculties of continuity, acquisitiveness, and self-esteem to support a career as an elocutionist, a lawyer, or a politician.

Marital Counseling

The phrenologists' marital counseling likewise combined common sense and self-fulfilling prophecies but, as Stern (1971) continually emphasized, the Fowlers' view of marriage contrasted sharply with those of many of their contemporaries. As she noted, the Fowlers actively campaigned against "prudery, false modesty, and ignorance" in marriage, and they urged their clients to take the practicalities of married life seriously and to avoid marrying in haste. Indeed, they often reminded them that "getting married is the *most responsible act we can do*" (pp. 42–46, emphasis in original). Sizer (1882) thus condemned the young man who sought a bride with "all the graces and $20,000" (pp. 59–61). In emphasizing practicalities, the Fowlers advertised *Wedlock; Or the Right Relations of the Sexes* as a guide to "mutual obligations, privileges and duties" (cited in Stern, 1971, p. 209). Most generally, the phrenologists stressed both the seriousness of a choice of a spouse and the potential impact of different temperaments on the course of married life. As such, they emphasized the need for "compatibilities of organic development," especially with respect to amativeness; Orson Fowler thus urged Moetley to restrain his large amativeness and very large excitability and to seek a spouse with average (rather than small) developments of these traits. But the Fowlers also warned that "persons of the same temperament, especially if on *the extreme* of that temperament should never be united" (cited in Stern, p. 44, emphasis in original). They spoke especially against marriage of two individuals with very large faculties of excitability and, in general, they recognized the complexities involved. Sizer even recommended that a woman with "very strong firmness and conscientiousness" and "stability, dignity, calm courage, and good moral power" leave a husband who exhibited "a very excitable temperament . . . immense firmness and self-esteem, large secretiveness [and] acquisitiveness [and] . . . low conscientiousness." As Sizer (1882) concluded, "no person with less wisdom than Solomon, or less patience than Job, would be likely to avoid disagreement if brought into contact with him" (pp. 293–294).

On the other hand, Sizer's (1882) advice to the husband of a woman with "very large combativeness, destructiveness and adhesiveness, and a feeble intellect" called for him to "never, when becom[ing] angry, to talk to the angry side of the other's character, but to say nothing, or else talk through loving-kindness to the feelings of love and kindness in the other." And Sizer bragged that, three years later, the couple "bless[ed] the day they met with phrenology and a phrenologist" (pp. 75–76). Sizer's memoirs also describe how potential fathers-of-the-bride often asked him to delineate the characters of their daughters' suitors. These accounts usually emphasize the daughters' expectations and often bore suspiciously uniform titles such as "A Lady's Fortunate Escape," "A Young Girl's Narrow Escape," and "An Elopement and Its Consequences" (pp. 184, 271–272, 336–337). These similarities indicate the tone of the reports that Sizer typically provided to doubting prospective fathers-in-law. They also suggest that he actively cultivated the well-paying clientele of fathers of potential heiresses, who sought to protect their daughters' legacies and reputations.

Child-Rearing Advice

Parents also often sought the phrenologists' guidance about their children and how they should be raised, and their child-rearing advice again differed markedly from that of contemporaneous ministers, physicians, and other authorities. Indeed, they typically advised parents (in Sizer's 1882 words) to "spare the rod and *save* the child" (pp. 301–303). They emphasized this principle even when parents sought counsel about particularly disobedient and headstrong children, and at times they blamed such character traits on parents' reliance on child-rearing advice not based on phrenology. In describing, for example, "A Spoiled Child and How It Was Done," Sizer quoted a mother's confession that, in raising her daughter, she "began early to make her toe the mark, and I used to train and whip her for every little offense or neglect. She has become very peevish and violent of temperament," and Sizer indeed found the child's organs of "destructiveness and combativeness very largely developed." As Sizer concluded, "too much strictness and severity in the training ruins the temper and makes a vixen to torture the next generation." Both Sizer and the child's mother thus feared for her future. But both had high hopes for her sister, described as "easily managed," because she was being raised in accordance with phrenological principles (pp. 73–75). A similar case occurred when parents of a "headstrong, proud, positive, self-willed, and forcible" child—whom they described as "obstinacy itself"—sought Sizer's advice. They told him that "they literally could do nothing" with him, and Sizer "found [his organs of] firmness, self-esteem, combativeness, and destructiveness enormously developed." Feeling pity for the boy, Sizer thus characterized him as "A Child with a Load to Carry." In answer to his parents' question "what can we do with him?" Sizer replied, "Be patient, wise, considerate, firm, but kind. Do not provoke him. . . . Badger him and he will defy restraint and guidance" (pp. 315–316). Sizer did not relate whether his parents accepted this advice. But another father—of a boy "possessed of a fearless and ferocious disposition" and thus "very disobedient and ungovernable"—followed Sizer's advice "to use mild measures in his training, to keep his own temper and ignore the whip." And as Sizer proudly recounted, several years later "the father told me with tremulous voice and moistened eye that Phrenological light had saved his boy and himself a world of trouble and anxiety" (pp. 303–305). As other accounts entitled "Good Advice Neglected" and "They Followed Directions" (pp. 317–318) suggest, the phrenologists never shied from advertising (or at least claiming) their successes.

Although parents most often sought phrenological guidance about stubborn and obstinate children, at times they called on the phrenologists for recommendation with respect to especially timid and shy children. These proved harder to examine and treat, often because they were too withdrawn to submit to a phrenological examination. Sizer indeed once described his treatment of a timid boy as "a great test." He related how he did not have to examine the child to recognize his large cautiousness. He continued by describing in some detail how—during the course of a long visit to the child's home—he "did everything to allay that feeling, and to awaken curiosity and excite his judgment, imagination, and affection." As he concluded, "to urge him to pay attention to the strangers [and to be] coaxed by every one that calls . . . defeats its own purpose" (pp. 63–66).

PHRENOLOGICAL PRACTICE

But how did the phrenologists prepare analyses and offer advice and guidance that meant anything to those whom they examined? How did they (in their terms) identify their clients' phrenological organs and delineate their faculties? Although (with Leek's death) no active phrenologist remains alive to answer these questions, the documents they left provide many clues. Indeed, a review of this record suggests that, in their practice, the phrenologists actively used and combined the abilities of Sherlock Holmes, Phineas T. Barnum, and Clever Hans.

Sherlock Holmes

Why Sherlock Holmes? Remember that Holmes could determine a man's occupation by the calluses on his hands, tell what he had been eating by the stains on his shirt, and discover where he had been walking by the kind of dirt on his shoes. Most Sherlock Holmes tales highlight these skills simply by having Dr. Watson exclaim "Extraordinary!" to which Holmes often replied, "Elementary!" But chapter 2 of *A Study in Scarlet*—the first Sherlock Holmes novel—makes this point especially explicit by presenting a relatively long excerpt from Holmes's own *Book of Life*:

> From a drop of water a logician could infer the possibility of an Atlantic or a Niagara without having seen or heard of one or the other. So all life is a great chain, the nature of which is known whenever we are shown a single link of it. Like all other arts, the Science of Deduction and Analysis is one which can only be acquired by long and patient study, nor is life long enough to allow any mortal to attain the highest possible perfection in it. Before turning to those moral and mental aspects of the matter which present the greatest difficulties, let the inquirer begin by mastering more elementary problems. Let him, on meeting a fellow-mortal, learn at a glance to distinguish the history of the man, and the trade or profession to which he belongs. Puerile as such an exercise may seem, it sharpens the faculties of observation, and teaches one where to look and what to look for. By a man's fingernails, by his coat-sleeve, by his boots, by his trouser-knees, by the callosities of his forefinger and thumb, by his expression, by his shirt-cuffs—by each of these things a man's calling is plainly revealed. That all united should fail to enlighten the competent inquirer is almost inconceivable.

And like Holmes, the phrenologists also self-consciously developed their powers of observation. After all, they had great opportunities to practice these powers on the individuals they examined. They spent a fair amount of time with their subjects, often in close physical contact. They spoke with these clients—and, especially, listened to them—as they introduced themselves and took in their accents and use of words. They shook their hands and felt their calluses. They observed their dress, and noted its style, and cleanliness, and usage. They observed their subjects' carriage as they entered and walked around the examining room and read their "body language." They stood over and behind them as they moved their hands about their heads. And in a less clean age, they especially noted their subjects' odor. At a time when dress, and speech, and carriage, and personal habits revealed much, the phrenologists had much to observe. No wonder they could quickly identify "drinking men," and those "remarkable for nervous excitability," and those with "immense firmness." In the same way, the phrenologists could recognize almost immediately stubbornness and timidity in children, at times even without the formality of a detailed examination. No wonder their clients, like Dr. Watson, marveled at their insight.

Much evidence exists to support this claim. Stern (1971), for example, quoted an 1866 comment by Rutherford B. Hayes, later president of the United States, about Samuel R. Wells, a phrenologist with close ties to the Fowlers; he married Charlotte and was Orson's business partner. Hayes was a good practical politician and thus a good observer of individuals himself, and he wrote to his uncle that Wells

> really gets his impressions [of others] just as you and I do, from their manners, conduct, and conversation. He is evidently not influenced a particle by temperament or head or features. . . . [His work] shows the impression that a tolerably good observer gets on a short acquaintance. (pp. 217–218)

Although Hayes may have been biased against phrenology, the phrenologists themselves at times admitted their reliance on Holmesian powers of observation. Sizer's (1882) memoirs provide much insight into phrenological practice, as he wrote that the phrenologist

> takes into account the Temperament (or physical constitution) as the basis of quality and health; he studies all that face, form, motion, and expression may reveal. In fact, all there is to a man from head to foot are servants of the brain and mind, and character is the result. The mode of reading character is thus founded in the human constitution itself. (pp. 9–10)

These memoirs, indeed, go even further. They tell how he tried to learn as much as he could about a town before he visited it, including such details as its political party preferences, its largest employers, and its largest churches. He readily determined this last point by comparing the heights of the steeples he saw as he rode into town, and he regularly used this information in reading character. He reported how he carefully observed his subjects' dress and often found that the best dressed belonged to the largest church. He talked with them and listened for what he called the "pet words" of each church, or party, or occupation, and he used the information to tell his subjects something about themselves (Sizer, 1882, p. 30). He summarized this point by describing a public reading where his audience—like many others—tried to trick him. They had the town's richest man, who owned a factory, dress in rough clothing and come forth covered with dirt. Sizer heard the audience giggle as the subject came forward, felt that his subject's hands lacked calluses, saw that the dirt did not extend past his collar, heard his unfamiliarity with the rough language he tried to use, and identified his subject as the factory owner (pp. 31–35).

This point does not imply, of course, that the phrenologists used fraud and deceit as they read their subjects' characters. After all, if pressed, they would argue that the faculties whose development they delineated in examining their clients' skulls determined all of the other traits they noted as they spoke with them and observed their actions. In all, much evidence exists that most phrenologists, at least, honestly believed in the power of their system.

Phineas T. Barnum

But if they avoided fraud, how could one claim that the phrenologists practiced the skills of Phineas T. Barnum? After all, did he not assert that a sucker is born every minute and that nobody ever got rich overestimating the intelligence of the U.S. population? This claim refers, however, to what 21st-century clinical psychologists call the Barnum effect, a diagnosis so vague and general that it could apply to almost all people. Such diagnoses often stress the positive and just hint at anxiety, self-doubt, or other concerns, and modern clinical training strongly warns psychologists to avoid such vagueness. Early-21st-century psychology professors often illustrate the Barnum effect for students by having them complete a questionnaire, telling them that each questionnaire will be scored individually and used to provide a detailed individual psychological profile of each student, returning to all students identical profiles, polling the students to find that 80% of them find their profiles accurate and, finally, having the students compare profiles. In the late 1940s, in defining the phenomenon for his colleagues and alerting them to it, eminent clinical psychologist Donald Patterson (see Marks & Seeman, 1962; Meehl, 1956) set forth the classic Barnum effect character reading. Some excerpts include the following:

> You are above average in intelligence . . .; you have a tendency to worry at times, but not to excess. You do get depressed at times, but couldn't be called moody . . .; you are strongly socially inclined [and] like to meet people . . .; you are ambitious, and deserve credit for wanting to be well thought of by your family, associates, and friends. (Patterson, 1951, p. 47)

Such vague positiveness bothers few of those diagnosed in this way, which is why modern clinical psychologists know they must avoid this problem. But the phrenologists did not, and many of the phrenological character readings available today demonstrate this tendency. Most delineations, of course, often stressed the positive, and this fact suggests a major reason why the phrenologists' clients accepted them so readily. Fowler's reading of Moetley, for example, stressed his cautiousness and benevolence, and Sizer's reading of Worcester's Mayor Gillson scored him very large, large, and full in all faculties except continuity, spirituality (often seen as a feminine trait), and self-esteem. Phrenologists often told of a blindfold examination of a boy that led the phrenologist to cry out, "why this boy could grow up to be President of the United States," and the boy was Ulysses S. Grant (Stern, 1971, pp. 314–315). But about how many boys did phrenologists make the same statement? After all, it was true for most young White U.S. males, and the examiner could readily tell the boy's race by his hair texture.

Many phrenologists admitted the positive bias of their readings but claimed that this slant had many useful consequences. Lorenzo Fowler, for example, once compared character readings with epitaphs: "write your own; make it as flattering and eulogistic as possible; then spend the remainder of your life endeavouring not only to reach the standard . . ., but to go far beyond it" (cited in Stern, 1971, p. 188). (This advice meshed well, of course, with the principle embodied in "self-made or never-made.") Sizer (1882) also made a similar point when he conceded that phrenologists "have often not been as severe as the truth required." But he also argued that, "if the same ideas were given in rough language of the angry scold," their delineations and advice would probably have had less impact on their subjects (pp. 270–272).

Although character readings often did include some less-than-positive statements, most of these could be applied to almost all of the phrenologists' clients. In this way, Fowler's advice to Moetley urged him to develop his self-esteem and spirituality, and the phrenologists often found a tendency toward melancholia, the 19th-century equivalent of today's anxiety. Many were even more general and reported, for example, that particular individuals sometimes failed to finish all they set out to do, tended at times to daydream, and at times rushed into things without considering the consequences. In the same way, many of the phrenologists' critical statements reflected common psychological insight; for example, beating a disobedient child will only make him more disobedient, and constant overwork will cause more trouble than it will prevent.

More generally, and perhaps most important, as this type of advice suggests, the phrenologists knew the type of person who was apt to seek their advice. Their clients often were individuals striving to better themselves economically and socially in a society that still cared deeply about social status but that was more open than many that preceded it. The phrenologists knew the traits of such individuals, and what mattered to them, and that they cared deeply how they appeared in their own eyes and in the eyes of prospective spouses or employers. The phrenologists tailored their delineations and advice to fit their audience, and many mid-19th-century subjects found much of value in the phrenologists' readings. Employers often looked to phrenologists' recommendations, and young men often spoke of learning cautiousness from phrenologists. For example, Simon Newcomb (1903), later head of the U.S. Naval Observatory, once described phrenology "as good a moral tonic as I can imagine to be placed in the hands of youth" (p. 16). Other young men, who wondered how their examiners knew they had been leading dissipated lives, took the phrenologists' warnings to heart and reformed.

Clever Hans

Who was Clever Hans, and what were his skills, and how did the phrenologists use them? Perhaps surprisingly, Clever Hans was a horse who lived in early-20th-century Berlin with its owner Wilhelm von Osten, a retired school teacher. What made Hans clever was that von Osten claimed—and demonstrated to others and believed beyond doubt—that his horse could communicate with humans. He had taught Clever Hans to associate each letter of the alphabet with a number; then to tap out with a front hoof numbers corresponding to letters; and then to string letters together to form words, to combine words into sentences, and in this way to answer his master's questions (Krall, 1912). Needless to say, Clever Hans and his ability to answer questions attracted much scientific attention. In 1907, Oskar Pfungst, then a graduate student in psychology at the University of Berlin, published an analysis of "the Clever Hans phenomenon" that (most past and current comparative psychologists agree) effectively explains the horse's actions. After long and detailed study of Clever Hans and his master, Pfungst concluded that the horse had learned to start tapping his hoof when a speaker's voice carried with it the inflection of a question and—more spectacularly—to stop tapping only when von Osten gave one or another unconscious signal, usually a barely noticeable twitch of his facial muscles or a nod of perhaps a fifth of a millimeter.

The claim here is not that the phrenologists resembled von Osten, who never realized that he signaled his horse, and never accepted Pfungst's conclusions, and never ceased believing that Clever Hans could communicate. The claim, instead, is that the phrenologists resembled Clever Hans and learned to sense barely perceptible, and usually completely unconscious, movements on the part of their subjects. After all, the phrenologists usually worked in close physical contact with their clients, presenting their readings as they moved their hands over the subjects' heads. As the subjects reacted, consciously or unconsciously, to each part of the reading, the phrenologists soon learned to read the reactions and redirect the thrust of their delineations in response to them. For example, when a subject instinctively tensed his neck muscles in response to a phrenologist's incorrect statement, the examiner immediately sensed the tension, knew that he had made a mistake, and corrected his error.

Even more subtly, the phrenologists also probably developed the ability to fine-tune their at-first crude delineations of their subjects' character and to provide gradually, during the course of their examinations, increasingly more detailed information about their subjects and their lives. Most likely, phrenologists learned this skill as unconsciously as their subjects responded to their readings. Indeed, they often claimed that the ability to use certain examining techniques emerged only with experience. Sizer's (1882) memoirs, for example, describe how he learned to stimulate a drunkard's odor by rubbing the proper mental "organ": "I can't tell you *how* it smells, but you . . . will never forget [the odor] of a man who drinks heavily" (p. 204). And as Sizer learned consciously to stimulate organs and identify his subjects' pet words, such skills gradually became automatic, and he came to practice them unconsciously. The phrenologists and their clients thus had good reason to believe in the power of their system.

THE DECLINE OF PHRENOLOGICAL PRACTICE

But if phrenology worked so well, why did it lose its authority and nearly disappear from the U.S. scene? Earlier attempts to explain this decline have proved unsatisfactory, and no generally accepted thesis has yet emerged. Most probably, however, an effective explanation would relate the decline of practical phrenology to the evolution of the reform spirit in the United States before and after the U.S. Civil War. Before the war, abolition embodied this spirit, as antislavery crusaders used moral suasion to try to convince individual slaveholders to abandon their evil practices. But abolition failed, and the war came, and after the war reformers abandoned moral suasion to seek legislative remedies for social ills. That is, they refocused their attention from the individual to the society at large and tried to pass laws rather than change people (see Frederickson, 1965). Historians have explained this transition by reference to the failure of suasion-based abolition, to the fading of evangelicalism (with its concern for individual salvation) among mainline Protestant thinkers and its replacement by the social gospel, and to the growth of power of the state itself that resulted from its mobilization for the war. Whatever the cause of this transition, in its archetypal form it led reformers to abandon temperance for Prohibition. Although practical phrenology had much to say to individuals seeking to reform themselves, it had little to say—despite the claims of the Fowlers and other phrenologists—to legislators trying to set public policy. These ideas require further elaboration before they deserve much further consideration.

CONCLUSION

This study leads, however, to several other conclusions. Most simply, practical phrenology gave mid-19th-century people in the United States a scientific technique for psychological diagnosis, prognosis, and counseling. Although early-21st-century people in the United States find no reasonable basis for its claims, the phrenologists' advice often meant something to those whom they examined. This point should not be too surprising; after all, as many of today's clinical psychologists readily admit, nearly any form of psychotherapy can work effectively in a setting to which it is especially well adapted.

More generally, as others have argued, phrenology provides an example of a highly effective body of knowledge that was almost totally socially constructed. That is, in today's philosophical terms, phrenology had no "positive truth value" nor "correspondence with reality" and, despite Sybil Leek, rational people in the United States today do not use phrenology to chart the course of their lives. To be sure, this example does not support claims that all (or most) technologies derive their authority solely (or primarily) through the construction and elaboration of some sort of implied social contract. But the case of practical phrenology demonstrates that historians and others cannot explain the success or failure of any science or technology simply by an appeal to its positive truth value or how well it works. They must also consider the richness of its social and cultural context.

But as this chapter also tries to demonstrate, any claim for the social construction of science or technology must look beyond the written discourse of that body of knowledge to examine its practice and determine just how its practitioners created their "knowledge." In many ways, past analyses of socially constructed science and technology that emphasize their creators' discourse at the expense of their practice simply miss the point. Their authors, perhaps, share much with a magician's audience, which attends closely to his flamboyant patter designed to distract his spectators and ignores all he does with his hands. Like phrenologists, magicians actually use their hands to create their illusions. This point, of course, explains why this chapter goes beyond the programmatic writings of Gall and his immediate followers and of those who (in Great Britain and the United States) based their calls for reform on appeals to phrenology. The Fowlers and Sizer may not have been systematic thinkers, but they probably influenced more individuals directly than did most other 19th-century phrenologists.

Even more generally, and perhaps most importantly, the case of phrenology demonstrates just how any understanding of any past science or technology requires the careful analysis of how the practitioners of that science or technology actually worked. Certainly past histories of phrenology provide suggestions as to why the phrenologists' character readings meant something to mid-19th-century people in the United States. But unless one can explain just how these phrenological examiners arrived at the readings they offered to their clients, these suggestions remained undeniably incomplete. Sherlock Holmes, Phineas T. Barnum, and Clever Hans thus prove surprisingly useful in helping delineate not only the course of phrenology but also of the evolution of U.S. reform and of the history of U.S. science and technology.

REFERENCES

Bakan, D. (1966). The influence of phrenology on American psychology. *Journal of the History of the Behavioral Sciences, 2*, 200–220.

Cooter, R. (1986). *The cultural meaning of popular science: Phrenology and the organization of consent in nineteenth-century Britain*. Cambridge, England: Cambridge University Press.

Cooter, R. (Comp.). (1989). *Phrenology in the British Isles: An annotated bibliography and index*. Metuchen, NJ: Scarecrow Press.

Fowler, O. S. (1868). *The practical phrenologist: A compendium of phreno-organic science*. New York: Eugene W. Auston.

Frederickson, G. (1965). *The inner civil war: Northern intellectuals and the crisis of the union*. New York: Harper & Row.

Hopkins, M. (1873). *An outline study of man; or, The mind and body in one system. With illustrative diagram and a method for blackboard teaching*. New York: Scribner's.

Krall, K. (1912). *Denkende Tiere* [Thinking animals] (2nd ed.). Leipzig, Germany: Friedrich Engelmann.

Leek, S. (1970). *Phrenology*. New York: Collier Books.

Marks, P. A., & Seeman, W. (1962). On the Barnum effect. *Psychological Record, 12*, 203–208.

Meehl, P. E. (1956). Wanted: A good cookbook. *American Psychologist, 11*, 263–272.

Newcomb, S. (1903). *Reminiscences of an astronomer*. Boston: Houghton-Mifflin.

Patterson, D. G. (1951). *Counseling and psychology*. New York: Prentice-Hall.

Risse, G. (1976). Vocational guidance during the depression: Phrenology versus applied psychology. *Journal of the History of the Behavioral Sciences, 12*, 130–140.

Sizer, N. (1882). *Forty years in phrenology; Embracing recollections of history, anecdote and experience*. New York: Fowler & Wells.

Stern, M. B. (1971). *Heads and headlines: The phrenological Fowlers*. Norman: University of Oklahoma Press.

Walsh, A. A. (1972). The American tour of Dr. Spurzheim. *Journal of the History of Medicine and Allied Sciences, 27*, 187–205.

3

SEALING OFF THE DISCIPLINE: WILHELM WUNDT AND THE PSYCHOLOGY OF MEMORY

KURT DANZIGER

Wilhelm Wundt's (1832–1920) role in the genesis of modern psychology was paradoxical. During the discipline's earliest years, toward the end of the 19th century, he was the world's best-known exponent of experimental psychology, his highly productive laboratory was the mecca for those seeking to immerse themselves in the procedures of the new science, and his monumental textbook was the indispensable reference work for a new generation of practitioners. Yet, within a few years, at the beginning of the 20th century, his whole approach was repudiated by most of those who at that time represented the discipline, including many who had studied with him (Danziger, 1990a). Instead of founding a disciplinary tradition, Wundt became a focus of controversy, and in its wake, of gross misrepresentation. Twentieth-century psychology emerged as a different species from anything that Wundt thought he was launching. In terms of worldly success, Wundt's version of a discipline of psychology was clearly a failure.

Is it not a waste of time to pay much attention to history's failures? That depends on what one hopes to gain from historical studies. If the task is essentially describing the march of scientific progress, then yes, the failures only need to be mentioned to show how wrong they were. But if one hopes for some understanding of the reasons why history took one path rather than another, one must look carefully at the turns that represented blind alleys. There were always alternatives, and to understand why psychology became the kind of discipline it is, one must look for the factors that favored one variant over another. The danger in restricting the historical account to the perspective of the successful variant is that many of the most significant factors will remain invisible because they are simply taken for granted. The contrasts provided by alternative perspectives illuminate these hidden factors and make it possible to analyze them.

For the question of discipline formation, Wundt's case is particularly interesting because he had a coherent vision of the kind of discipline that psychology ought to become, a vision that certainly included the systematic use of experimentation. Yet this vision was obviously not viable in the long run. Why was this? What did other versions of the disciplinary project get right that Wundt got wrong? There can be several answers to this question, but in this chapter I focus on one aspect that I believe to be crucial, namely, the relationship among the concepts, language, and practices of the discipline and the world outside of the discipline for which they must ultimately be relevant. The emergence of a scientific discipline involves the gradual formation of a boundary between what goes on within the discipline and what goes on outside of it. This boundary is usually contested and, especially in the early stages, different views exist about where and how this boundary should be drawn. Wundt's ideas, as well as his practice, had implications for the formation of the boundaries of scientific psychology that proved to be unworkable. An examination of these implications therefore provides valuable clues to the conditions of possibility for the transformation of psychology into a modern discipline.

The question of what belongs inside a discipline covers many things, including topics or content areas. For example, does parapsychology belong inside or not? In the early days of a discipline's formation the number of such controversial topics is far greater than it is later. But not only topics are affected; distinctions must be made between acceptable and unacceptable methods or practices. For example, does the territory of scientific psychology extend beyond the territory of experimental psychology? Then there is the question of language. A scientific discipline is distinguished, among other things, by its use of a specialized language of terms with technical meanings familiar only to insiders. What is the relationship between the terms of such a language and corresponding terms in everyday language? This is particularly important for psychology, a science that finds it difficult to do without terms that are also used intensively in everyday life. Closely connected with the question of language is the question of concepts. Just as the concepts of the physical sciences have to prove their worth by being applied to the physical world, the concepts of psychological science have to prove themselves in the human world. But the human world lies largely outside of the discipline itself, so this is a boundary question, too. At some point, the concepts of a scientific psychology have to reach into the world outside, and this has consequences for what happens inside the discipline.

THE STUDY OF MEMORY

The psychology of memory provides illustrations for all of these issues. Memory is one of the few truly ancient psychological categories, having been in more or less continuous and recognizable use since the time of Plato and Aristotle. Memory is very much part of everyday psychological talk, and ideas about it as well as practices directed at it (mnemotechnics) have a long history of popular use. A scientific psychology might be expected to take up such a topic and to make it its own. Indeed, this is what happened in due course, although that was not because of Wundt. On the contrary, memory was one of Wundt's more conspicuous failures, even at the height of his fame. Certainly his contribution did not establish memory as a core topic of the new scientific psychology; the credit for that development belongs to the much younger Hermann Ebbinghaus (1850–1909), who had neither laboratory nor research students to back him up. Why was this so?

In the traditional historiography of psychology this curious fact is interpreted in terms of Ebbinghaus's invention and Georg Elias Müller's development of a special technique for the experimental study of memory, namely, the learning and forgetting of lists of nonsense syllables. The implication is that Wundt had nothing useful to say about memory because he had no *effective*—the word is Boring's (1950, p. 343)—experimental technique for investigating it. This perspective makes it possible to see the history of scientific psychology as one of cumulative progress brought about by the improvement of empirical methods. In that case a simple explanation exists for the emergence of psychology as a scientific discipline: The advent of "effective" techniques of empirical investigation was responsible for the flourishing of scientific psychology, and where such techniques were not available or recognized, psychology could not flourish.

There is no denying the historical importance of empirical methods, but in this account they seem to be understood simply as technologies. That is to say, they are treated as means toward the achievement of ends that are fixed and taken for granted. In the case of memory research, it makes sense to say that Ebbinghaus had an effective method for investigating memory, whereas Wundt did not, if we assume that the term *memory* has a fixed meaning and that Wundt, Ebbinghaus, and the modern reader would all agree as to what it covers. However, that is not something to be taken for granted but something to be examined in the light of historical evidence.

Relatively few of the many empirical studies supervised by Wundt were explicitly identified as dealing with the psychology of memory. However, some studies in his laboratory dealt with empirical topics that would later be classified as part of the psychology of memory, although that is not how Wundt saw them (Scheerer, 1980). This applies particularly to work on what Wundt called the "span of consciousness" and the "focus of attention." Such work was in many respects similar to some of the later work on short-term and working memory. That Wundt did not see it as a contribution to the psychology of memory suggests that he may have had a notion of memory that was different from that of many 20th-century psychologists. In other words, the historical changes may be conceptual as much as empirical.

Here it becomes necessary to distinguish between *technique* and *practice*. The former abstracts procedures from the goals they serve and from the effects they produce; the latter refers to a fusion of goals, procedures, and effects. The former is typically taught by the use of explicit how-to manuals; the latter always contains significant elements that remain implicit. In their approach to the topic of memory, Wundt and Ebbinghaus differed not only on the level of technique but, more importantly, on the level of practice. They used different procedures because they pursued different goals, and that entailed different effects.

This becomes clearer if we compare Ebbinghaus's experimentation with that of Wundt's. An early example is provided by one of Wundt's American students, H. K. Wolfe (1886), who presented the experimental subject with a standard tone and subsequently with comparison tones at varying intervals of time after the standard tone. In each case the subject had to judge whether the pitch of the standard and the comparison tone was the same or different. The proportion of correct judgments could then be plotted as a function of the time that had elapsed between the presentation of the standard and the comparison tones. This information was used not as a measure of correct performance but as an indication of the gradual decay in the conscious experience of a past sensation.

There is a sharp contrast between the goals pursued and the effects produced here and what happened in experiments that followed Ebbinghaus's paradigmatic procedures involving the learning of nonsense syllables. For Ebbinghaus, and those who followed in his footsteps, memory was not to be studied as an aspect of conscious experience but as an objective achievement. Memory became a matter of task performance made possible by the operation of mechanisms defined by their functions, not by their mental qualities. In Ebbinghaus's memory experiments it was not a question of reproducing a conscious experience but of achieving a certain objective result.

Because "memory," as used outside of scientific boundaries, is such a broad category, potentially implicated in nearly every cognitive or behavioral phenomenon, one has to perform a conceptual reduction if the psychology of memory is to become scientifically manageable. Both Wundt and Ebbinghaus clearly saw the need for such a reduction, and they both distinguished between something they called "memory proper" (*das eigentliche Gedächtnis*) and other phenomena that might be included under memory in ordinary use but need to be excluded in a more rigorous scientific use. However, they had different conceptions of what was to be considered memory proper. For Wundt this always involved the renewal of a set of conscious contents, especially self-consciousness, and it finds its characteristic expression in the phenomenon of reminiscence or recollection (Wundt, 1887, pp. 396–397). His notion of what constituted memory in the true sense was actually quite close to the notion of episodic memory introduced much later.

In the published version of his celebrated monograph on memory, Ebbinghaus gave few clues to the thinking that lay behind the procedures he adopted. But in an 1880 unpublished draft he is more explicit (Ebbinghaus, 1983). The complexity of the phenomena of conscious memory, he said, is due to the fact that they are affected by "reminiscence" (*Erinnerung*), which is neither simple nor elementary and which resists "experimental investigation." Apart from reminiscence, although there is "mere retention, true (or proper) memory" (*das blosse Behalten, das eigentliche Gedächtnis*; Ebbinghaus, 1983, p. 70), this entity, memory defined as mere retention, is susceptible to precise scientific investigation, provided that one does not focus on the conscious experience of memory that is uncontrollably corrupted by reminiscence. Ebbinghaus's experimental practice was designed to achieve precisely this effect.

Wundt and Ebbinghaus agreed on the need for a distinction between memory in the wide sense and memory in the true sense. They also agreed that on one side of this distinction lies *Erinnerung*. But for Wundt this side of the distinction represents memory proper; for Ebbinghaus it represents dross that must be removed to get to memory proper, defined as "mere retention." The latter was a purely functional notion with no necessary reference to consciousness, let alone self-consciousness.

The similarity of their starting point and the wide divergence in the conclusions of these two key figures shows a scientific boundary in the making. Agreement exists that a restricted conceptual space must be created within which a scientific psychology of memory can operate. But disagreement exists about the appropriate criteria for constructing such a space. For Ebbinghaus, the criterion of what one might call "experimentability" was paramount. If memory were to yield to scientific investigation, it had to be defined in a way that allowed for the identification, experimental manipulation, and objective measurement of relevant variables.

This was not possible for the phenomena of *Erinnerung,* and so these had to be set aside. Wundt, however, believed that the range of psychological phenomena that were amenable to experimental investigation was actually quite restricted, and so experimentability could never become a criterion for defining psychological categories. If memory in the true sense did not yield to experimentation, it simply joined a long list of other psychological phenomena for which this was the case.

This did not exclude all experimentation on the aftereffects of previous experience, provided that the aftereffects studied in such experiments were those that involved consciousness, such as the waning memory of a tone sensation. The experimental effect Ebbinghaus was after was quite different. Here it was a question of comparing some product of the subject's activity, the number of nonsense syllables correctly recalled, with an external standard, the complete list as presented. The difference between the two approaches was not that the one had a more effective technique than the other; they differed on the goals of their investigations. This divergence makes it meaningless to compare their methodologies in terms of their effectiveness. Wundt's methods were as effective for pursuing his goals as Ebbinghaus's methods were in pursuing different goals.

A QUESTION OF RELEVANCE

Sharp differences in the effectiveness of the two approaches did emerge, but only when the issue became one of recrossing the disciplinary boundary to the world outside. Wundt's approach neither sought nor achieved any applications outside of the narrow confines of the psychological laboratory. His was an encapsulated vision of psychological science. Ebbinghaus's approach, on the other hand, constituted a template for establishing the kinds of empirical regularity that were in demand among many potential consumers of psychological knowledge (Danziger, 1990a). Research on memory treated as mere retention might have large-scale practical applications in, for example, a school system already dedicated to promoting the learning of masses of information and testing their recall. However, not all kinds of memory research would have this practical relevance. The kind favored by Wundt did not. Memory phenomena taken purely as a form of conscious experience were neither here nor there when it was a question of improving the efficiency of objective memory performance. Needed was knowledge cast in the form of empirical regularities linking techniques of learning and objective measures of recall, exactly what Ebbinghaus's functionalization of memory research provided.

In Germany, the topic of memory was being addressed in a pedagogical context. Ebbinghaus was himself a former teacher with practical experience of memory work in schools. Two years after the publication of

Ebbinghaus's work on memory, educationist Franz Fauth (1888) published a 350-page text, *Memory. A Pedagogical Study on the Basis of Current Physiology and Psychology*. By the early years of the 20th century, there was a flood of studies of memorizing and remembering in the context of what was called "experimental pedagogics." This field even had its own journal.

A leading role in these developments was taken by Ernst Meumann, who had served as Wundt's assistant for 6 years but who made a deliberate break with that tradition when he went into educational psychology. He clearly recognized the need for a different kind of research practice, indicating that psychological processes like memory must be studied not in terms of inner experience but in relation to their "intended or prescribed success" (1912, p. 240). They ought to be studied in terms of "psychological economy" or how the desired success might be achieved with the least expenditure of time and energy. Meumann's post-Wundtian orientation is accurately reflected in the title of his 1907/1913 major work, translated into English as *The Psychology of Learning: An Experimental Investigation of the Economy and Technique of Memory*.

The research practices most suited to the pursuit of such goals were those pioneered by Ebbinghaus and were not those associated with Wundt's laboratory. The latter had never been intended to have applications beyond the narrowly drawn boundaries of a discipline envisaged as a kind of empirical philosophy. By the beginning of the 20th century, this was not a viable project. Instead, the investigative practices of the discipline would have to carry the promise of practical relevance outside the psychological laboratory.

SCIENTIFIC PSYCHOLOGY AND EVERYDAY LANGUAGE

Not only did Wundt's psychology provide no scope for the functionalization of the concept of memory, he was distinctly reluctant to use the concept at all. This strange reluctance was not because of any distaste for the topic but was the result of a more general conviction that a scientific psychology needed to erect barriers against everyday psychological language. In the first edition of Wundt's 1874 foundational textbook, the only explicit mention of memory as a psychological category is in the introduction. There Wundt noted that ordinary language provides certain terms for classifying psychological events, for example, feeling, understanding, sensibility, and also memory which, in prescientific psychology, are taken to identify distinct faculties or mental powers. Such ordinary-language psychological categories have, at best, the status of descriptors that explain nothing and have no place in a scientific psychology. Not only do they have no place, they also are dangerous for the project of a scientific psychology because they are the carriers of a legacy of confusing description and explanation.

"This concept (of) memory," Wundt stated in his introductory textbook *Outlines of Psychology*, "originated in popular psychology and was then carried over into the now abandoned faculty-psychology" (1896/1907, p. 277). For Wundt's version of scientific psychology, "popular psychology" was something that had to be avoided. At times he refers to it as "vulgar psychology." Apart from its tendency to confuse description and explanation popular psychology is scientifically useless because it treats complex and heterogeneous categories as though they were psychologically unitary and homogeneous. Memory is a good example. For Wundt, "memory and all processes of recollection are complex results . . . analogous to a large number of other forms of mental work, such, for example, as reading, writing, counting, and using numbers for complex processes of calculation" (1896/1907, pp. 281–282). So memory is no more a core category of psychology than is reading or counting. To use an analogy that I think Wundt would have agreed with, the phenomena of memory stand in about the same relation to scientific psychology as the phenomenon of rain does to scientific physics.

It is therefore not surprising that Wundt did not devote much attention to memory as a distinct psychological topic. Even when, in later editions of the *Grundzüge*, he found himself obliged to devote a few pages to the topic, he carefully began the discussion by saying that terms like *memory* have a purely descriptive role. Then he went further and limited that descriptive role to the area of individual differences, which was an aspect of psychology to which, notoriously, he attached no great significance.

Clearly, Wundt was out of tune with subsequent developments that established the psychology of memory as a demarcated area of inquiry and attributed a distinct identity to memory systems separate from other cognitive processes. In view of the fact that the merits of this development are now being questioned (Toth & Hunt, 1999), it is interesting to note that in his time Wundt's negative views about memory as a psychological category would not have seemed particularly strange to those of his readers who were at all psychologically sophisticated. Herbart, who was by far the most influential writer on psychological topics for much of the 19th century (see also Benjafield, chap. 5, this volume), had been critical of memory as a psychological category many years before Wundt. These criticisms were well known.

In his early and influential work on the principles of education, Herbart dismissed the topic of memory with these words, "I avoid here all psychological development of the phenomena, stamped with the names of memory, power of recollection, etc., as if they presupposed a particular activity or even power of the mind" (1806/1977, p. 202). Later, in his systematic treatise on psychology, he asserted that the concept of memory has no place in a scientific psychology. He always insisted that if psychology was to become scientific it had to root out the legacy of faculty psychology lock, stock, and barrel, and memory as a psychological category was part of that legacy. Faculty psychology, according to Herbart, deals in empty abstractions that cannot provide the framework for a scientific psychology. He illustrated his point with an analogy: Because people have cognitions and desires, should psychology be divided into the study of a cognitive and a conative faculty? That is like saying that because triangles have lines and angles there should be two divisions of trigonometry, one dealing with lines the other with angles (1824/1890, p. 197). For Herbart such divisions made as little sense in psychology as in mathematics.

Memory Herbart regarded as an empty abstraction that was unsuitable as a core concept of psychology. As soon as one turns to actual cases of memory, he pointed out, the concept shatters into a multitude of sub-categories: memory for places, for names, for numbers, for concepts, for judgments, for sensations, for desires, for volitions. The list goes on and on—a striking example of memory in action being revenge. In each case a multitude of conditions determine the actual course that memory takes: intentions, interests, qualities of feeling, time relationships, and so forth. By the time one has taken all this into account, said Herbart, one will come to realize "that all that remains of so-called memory is an empty name" (1824/1890, pp. 198, 203).

Wundt's position, although similar, goes beyond Herbart in making explicit something that had only been implicit in the latter's critical comments. The 19th-century critics of faculty psychology spoke in the name of a self-consciously scientific psychology thought to be profoundly different from the psychology of the streets. Not only did faculty psychology represent an old academic tradition, it was also implicit in the use of psychological terms in everyday life. In its avoidance of the categories of faculty psychology, scientific psychology was also drawing a boundary between itself and popular psychology. Such a boundary constituted one of the conditions for the emergence of a scientific psychology. Because everyone was a psychologist of sorts, the science of psychology had to distinguish itself clearly from lay psychology. To a large extent this was accomplished on procedural grounds, mathematization in the case of Herbart and laboratory experimentation in the case of Wundt. But conceptual differentiation also seemed to be important. The ill-defined and fluid categories of popular faculty psychology were regarded as unsuitable for providing the kind of explanatory account demanded by an exact science.

When Wundt complained that in popular use memory is used in both a descriptive and an explanatory sense he said that this use does not distinguish between the function of the same category as an explanandum to be explained and as an explanans, which does the explaining. Scientific psychology, however, must operate on the basis of a clear separation between categories of observed phenomena to be explained and theories that do the explaining. Memory is unsuitable for use on either side of this divide. It is unsuitable as an explanation because to refer to a mental faculty of memory is no explanation at all. But it is also unsuitable as an explanandum, because the phenomena of memory constitute such a heterogeneous collection. There is no science of memory, just as there is no science of roundness.

However, not all the phenomena covered by the global term *memory* are unsuitable for scientific investigation. One phenomenon that Wundt did think worthy of scientific analysis was what he called the "reproduction of ideas," the reappearance in consciousness, without sensory stimulation, of mental content that was previously experienced. This is an undeniable psychological phenomenon, and in his attempt at explaining it Wundt had to confront the ancient metaphor of storage that had become embedded in everyday talk about memory.

THE METAPHORICAL LEVEL

The relationship between everyday psychological language and the discourse of scientific psychology must be considered on two levels. First, there is the more obvious level of the categories used to identify psychological phenomena and explanations. Memory is such a category. But beyond this there is the level of the metaphors embedded in everyday speech as much as in scientific discourse. Everyday talk involves more than implicit classifications; it also metaphorically assigns certain characteristics to that which it identifies. Such metaphors function as pervasive, and some would say indispensable, vehicles of human understanding (Johnson, 1987). When people share similar metaphorical understandings of a topic they are able to exchange information on that topic with relative ease, but divergent metaphors make for misunderstanding, especially when the divergence is not recognized (Danziger, 1990b). Just as scientific psychology can take over or reject the categories of everyday psychology, it can take over or reject the metaphors of everyday psychology. Most of the time the taking over of well-established metaphors occurs without any reflection, and this undoubtedly enhances the intelligibility of psychological theories. But this was not Wundt's way. In the course of sketching his own theory of mental reproduction he subjected the traditional metaphorical understanding of memory to critical examination and found it unacceptable.

What Wundt rejected was the metaphor of memory as a container in which past experience and knowledge was preserved, like pieces of furniture in a house, coins in a purse, or birds in a cage. Such metaphors are associated with Western discourse about memory virtually from its beginnings in classical antiquity, an association that only seems to have broadened and deepened with time (Carruthers, 1991). Indeed, it became difficult to talk about memory at all without invoking such storage metaphors, explicitly or implicitly (Draaisma, 2000). The pioneers of modern psychology readily took over such metaphors from popular discourse. William James (1890, I, p. 654), for example, suggested that "we make search [sic] in our memory for a forgotten idea, just as we rummage our house for a lost object." Twentieth-century psychology continued this ancient tradition, often incorporating metaphors of spatial storage in its models of how memory works (Koriat & Goldsmith, 1996; Roediger, 1980).

Wundt's critical comments focused on attempts to account for mental reproduction by assuming that the mind contained distinct entities that were traces or copies of past conscious contents and that could reoccupy a place in consciousness. At the time, the latest incarnation of this model was found in the theories of Herbart. So, although Wundt had agreed with Herbart in rejecting the category of memory and substituting the phenomenon of mental reproduction as a more appropriate explanandum, he parted company with him on the question of how to explain this phenomenon. For Herbart, the reappearance of mental content in consciousness was the result of an interaction among ideas, each of which had an inherent tendency to occupy a place in consciousness where the number of available places was limited. He regarded the mind as a depository of mental units called ideas and postulated the continued, subterranean existence of ideas when they were temporarily absent from consciousness.

Surely, this is a latter-day version of the ancient storage metaphor, with the significant modification that the stored elements are not passive but highly active and interactive. Perhaps this was merely a return to the earliest form of the metaphor, Plato's suggestion that the contents of memory were like birds in a cage—entities that are contained but definitely active. Wundt did not object to this modification; he objected to the implication, common to all versions of the storage metaphor, that mental contents should be thought of as distinct objects that merely change their location but not their identity. Whatever the aftereffects of previous experience, it was misleading to think of them in terms of some kind of continued existence, as trace or copy, of the original mental content.

At the beginning of his scientific career Wundt still accepted the Herbartian notion that ideas temporarily absent from consciousness continued to exist unconsciously, but by the time he took up his life's work at Leipzig his views had changed (1874, pp. 689–693). From then on he made a clear distinction between two theories of mental reproduction, the trace theory and the theory of dispositions. *Trace theory*, in which he included that of Herbart, accounts for the reappearance of previous mental contents by postulating their unconscious survival. *Dispositional theory*, favored by Wundt, rejects this model and claims that all that need be assumed is a disposition for previously experienced mental content to be reproduced.

No doubt, said Wundt, there is a physiological basis for such a disposition, but this must be clearly distinguished from the functional disposition itself. What psychology must be concerned with are the conditions under which a disposition to remember becomes transformed into an actual memory, and this depends on conscious activity at the time of recollection. There are no idea entities striving to return to consciousness, as Herbart believed, only reproductive dispositions interacting with the current assembly of conscious experience. Wundt's attention was devoted to the latter. He considered it unfruitful to speculate about the psychological nature of reproductive dispositions.

Although the establishment of a scientific discipline always requires the erection of a boundary between itself and lay discourse, the question of what falls outside and what inside the boundary remains open. This is because neither the categories of lay discourse nor conceptions of scientificity are forever the same—on the contrary, they are both subject to historical change. Moreover, they influence each other over time: The categories of current lay discourse often reflect the science of an earlier period, and the scientific respectability of concepts is subject to swings of fashion that are underdetermined by strictly intrascientific factors. Therefore, what is banished from science and what is seen as admissible can change over the years. Such a change can be observed in the case of Herbart and Wundt. Although they agreed that the category of memory was not scientifically acceptable, Wundt also rejected a model for psychological retention that had seemed scientifically viable to Herbart. But this extreme stance served to isolate Wundt from several significant developments outside of the boundaries of academic psychology that were opening up vast new territories for the psychology of memory and taking it in directions quite different from those he had favored.

THE CHANGED STATUS OF MEMORY

To put the views of Herbart and Wundt in proper perspective one must see them in the context of much broader changes that affected the concept of memory during the latter part of the 19th century. Although the topic of memory had attracted considerable attention at various times in the past, the recognition of its importance did not follow a smooth path. Compared to some earlier periods, there was not much interest in the topic during the 18th and early 19th century. In many quarters memory was regarded as merely a popular name for the association of ideas. Elsewhere it was dissolved into various separate functions, as in Gall's phrenology, which counted six different kinds of memory.

Wundt was born in 1832, and the first edition of his foundational textbook was published in 1874. For someone of his generation there was really nothing remarkable or idiosyncratic in adopting a dismissive stance toward the general topic of memory. His misfortune was to have reached the height of his career just as the topic was about to undergo a decisive change in its fortunes. During the last quarter of the 19th century, memory became interesting again, and there was a new readiness to assign it an importance and significance not given during the immediately preceding period. In William James's 1890 textbook, published only 16 years after Wundt's, there is a nearly 50-page chapter on memory that makes no mention of the strictures on the concept by the likes of Herbart and Wundt but certainly mentions the work of Ebbinghaus. There is also a readiness to broaden the category of memory to include phenomena that were also discussed by Wundt, but not as examples of memory. In this connection James uses the notion of "primary memory," the progenitor of concepts such as immediate, short-term, and working memory (Waugh & Norman, 1965). By the closing years of the century the topic of memory was attracting too much serious attention for Wundt's dismissal of it to carry any weight. His strategy of erecting a hermetic seal around the scientific discipline of psychology was not paying off. For the new discipline to flourish it would have to show itself responsive to changing interests, fashions, and requirements in the world outside.

In the case of memory, several interacting developments converged to produce an upsurge in its appeal toward the end of the 19th century. At the broadest level one can discern a pervasive cultural preoccupation with a past that becomes estranged as modernity triumphs (Terdiman, 1993; Shore, chap. 4, this volume). This is surely connected with the pathologizing of memory that is so noticeable during this period (Hacking, 1995; Leys, 1996; Roth, 1989). Both of these aspects have been studied extensively and require no further comment here. There is, however, another development that is perhaps less well known and that is of special significance for psychology—the biologization of memory.

In the late 19th century the drawing of analogies between biological and psychological phenomena became a popular intellectual pastime that transformed the meaning of several psychological concepts. Intelligence and learning are notable examples. Memory, too, was caught up in this tide. The term *memory*, being already elastic, was easily stretched to cover any change in physiological function as a result of exercise, while still retaining its accustomed reference to phenomena of conscious recall. The suggestion was that memory in the traditional, psychological sense was simply one manifestation of a more fundamental biological process. In the late 19th century this was often referred to as "organic memory," or sometimes "unconscious memory," and it became a topic that attracted considerable interest, being popularized by such well-known writers as Samuel Butler (1880). An early and influential version of the idea had been publicized by the eminent physiologist Ewald Hering (1870/1902), in 1870 when he addressed the Imperial Academy of Sciences in Vienna on "memory as a universal function of organized matter." Essentially, what Hering proposed was an enormous expansion in the meaning of memory so that it could cover everything from visual recall to the inheritance of acquired characteristics, instinct, habit, and the effects of exercising a muscle. This was a crucial move in transforming memory into an essentially biological category, a transformation that was simultaneously being fostered by early medical studies of memory defects associated with brain lesions. The result was a complete change in the status of memory: From having been degraded to "a mere name" early in the century, memory had risen to the status of a fundamental property of living matter by the end of the century.

WHAT THE DISCIPLINE NEEDED

It so happened that the emergence of the new discipline of psychology coincided with the change in the fortunes of memory. Not that the new discipline was in any way responsible for initiating the change; it came too late and was still too weak for that. Rather, the new interest in questions of memory presented the representatives of the discipline with a situation they had to come to terms with for, whatever else it might be, the concept of memory still had undeniable psychological connotations. A science of psychology that had nothing to contribute to the new interest in questions of memory would have been a considerably diminished science. Nor did Wundt's conceptually critical contribution meet these expectations. Being told that memory was not a scientifically viable category was not what people wanted to hear at the end of the 19th century. For conceptual illumination one might look to philosophy, provided it preserved the importance of memory (e.g., Bergson, 1896/1911), but a science of psychology had to deliver what sciences were expected to deliver, that is, facts and empirically grounded explanations. The tradition of experimental memory research initiated by Ebbinghaus undoubtedly provided facts, even if it was a bit weak on the explanatory side.

Of course, Wundt's laboratory had also provided facts. The difference was that Wundt steadfastly refused to describe these facts in terms of the category of memory. He could give a precise, experimentally grounded meaning to terms such as "span of consciousness" or "reproduction of representations," but he could not do the same for memory. So memory was not a significant category for his scientific psychology.

Ebbinghaus was not so fastidious. Although, as I have indicated, he recognized the need for a conceptual reduction of the everyday concept of memory, he believed that it contained a clear core meaning, simple retention, which referred to a phenomenon that he could study experimentally. This maneuver made it possible to import an increasingly popular category of everyday life into scientific psychology. That was a crucial move in establishing a science that could claim to have some relevance for the solution of psychological problems outside the laboratory. In the early stages of the discipline's formation the plausibility of its claims to social relevance was almost entirely based on the fact that the same psychological categories were used to cover observations made in daily life and observations gathered under experimental conditions. Whether these sets of observations had anything significant in common except their name was a question that was left for later generations to sort out. In the meantime, psychology flourished on the basis of an unrecognized leap of faith.

Boundary formation was particularly important in the establishment of a scientific discipline of psychology because, as the saying goes, everyone was a psychologist. The science of psychology had to distinguish itself clearly from lay psychology, and it certainly did so on the basis of its methodology. But there is another side to this issue. The boundary, once established, had to be permeable, because, if not, the new psychology would never be able to address the concerns of the lay psychologists speaking their own lay psychological language. Yet, ultimately, the science depended on the goodwill of lay psychologists. If these could see no possible benefits from a scientific psychology, how dependable would their goodwill be? Wundt might well have answered that one could not have it both ways. The boundary between scientific and lay psychology had to be impermeable, or there would be no scientific psychology. If this entailed a field with no practical applications, then so be it.

The younger generation of psychologists found such views unacceptable, and the discipline that they built was one that had no compunctions about working with everyday psychological categories. Whether it was memory or intelligence, personality or motivation, scientific psychology would make them the objects of its investigations. That meant it could address the lay public in terms the latter could understand. In this way psychology was quite different from the physical sciences, which were able to establish their usefulness without having to import the categories of lay beliefs about the physical world (Baker & Hacker, 1982).

At the same time, scientific psychology did maintain a clear boundary between itself and folk psychology on methodological grounds. As a result, it was able to work with concepts that had a relatively precise meaning in restricted investigative contexts. For example, Ebbinghaus-type experiments created a special context within which memory could be given a fairly precise although restricted meaning. The relationship of this strictly local use of memory to the various uses of the term outside of the psychological laboratory was, however, highly problematic. Nevertheless, the implication that psychological memory experiments had any relevance for real-life memory depended significantly on the maintenance of a fundamental ambiguity in the deployment of the term.

Wundt failed here because he attempted to secure the new field of experimental psychology by unrealistically tight and impermeable boundaries that were intended to demarcate its domain from physiology and logic (Kusch, 1999) as much as from any kind of real-life application and folk psychology. But this turned out to be no more than the elitist dream of an old-style academic mandarin of imperial Germany (Ringer, 1969). It soon became apparent that, to be successful, the discipline of psychology must operate within boundaries that were permeable rather than impermeable.

This entailed psychological categories that presented a Janus face, one turned outward to the ordinary world of lay psychological problems and concerns, the other turned inward to the sheltered world of disciplinary investigative practices. On the one hand, "the conceptual bedrock of psychology is made of common-or-garden concepts" (Maraun, 1998, p. 454), on the other hand, the scientific terms of psychology refer not simply to a particular fragment of the life world but to "a systematically disambiguated and transformed version of such a fragment" (Rommetveit, 1998, p. 229). At first sight it seems that these claims cannot both be true. But of course they are. The contrast between Wundt's and Ebbinghaus's approach to memory illustrates that psychological concepts had to maintain their link both to the life world and to the laboratory for the new discipline to be viable.

REFERENCES

Baker, G. P., & Hacker, P. M. S. (1982). The grammar of psychology: Wittgenstein's *Bemerkungen über die Philosophie der Psychologie*. *Language & Communication, 2,* 227–244.

Bergson, H. (1911). *Matter and memory.* New York: Macmillan. (Original work published 1896)

Boring, E. G. (1950). *A history of experimental psychology* (2nd ed.). New York: Appleton-Century-Crofts.

Butler, S. (1880). *Unconscious memory.* London: D. Bogue.

Carruthers, M. (1991). *The book of memory: A study of memory in medieval culture.* New York: Cambridge University Press.

Danziger, K. (1990a). *Constructing the subject: Historical origins of psychological research.* New York: Cambridge University Press.

Danziger, K. (1990b). Generative metaphor and the history of psychological discourse. In D. E. Leary (Ed.), *Metaphors in the history of psychology* (pp. 331–356). New York: Cambridge University Press.

Draaisma, D. (2000). *Metaphors of memory: A history of ideas on the mind.* Cambridge, England: Cambridge University Press.

Ebbinghaus, H. (1983). *Urmanuskript "Ueber das Gedächtnis" 1880* [Original manuscript: On memory]. Passau, Germany: Passavia.

Fauth, F. (1888). *Das gedächtnis. Studie zu einer Pädagogik auf dem Standpunkt der heutigen Physiologie und Psychologie* [Memory. A pedagogical study on the basis of current physiology and psychology]. Gütersloh, Germany: Bertelsmann.

Hacking, I. (1995). *Rewriting the soul: Multiple personality and the sciences of memory.* Princeton, NJ: Princeton University Press.

Herbart, J. F. (1890). Psychologie als Wissenschaft [Psychology as science]. In K. Kehrbach (Ed.), *Joh. Fr. Herbart's sämtliche Werke* [J. F. Herbart's collected works] (Vol. 5). Langensalza, Germany: Hermann Beyer. (Original work published 1824)

Herbart, J. F. (1977). The science of education. In D. N. Robinson (Ed.), *Significant contributions to the history of psychology 1750–1920* (Series B, Vol. 1). Washington, DC: University Publications of America. (Original work published 1806)

Hering, E. (1902). *On memory.* Chicago: Open Court. (Original work published 1870)

James, W. (1890). *Principles of psychology* (Vol. 1). New York: Holt.

Johnson, M. (1987). *The body in the mind: The bodily basis of meaning, imagination, and reason.* Chicago: Chicago University Press.

Koriat, A., & Goldsmith, M. (1996). Memory metaphors and the real-life/laboratory controversy: Correspondence versus storehouse conceptions of memory. *Behavioral and Brain Sciences, 19,* 167–228.

Kusch, M. (1999). *Psychological knowledge: A social history and philosophy.* London: Routledge.

Leys, R. (1996). Traumatic cures: Shell shock, Janet, and the question of memory. In P. Antze & M. Lambek (Eds.), *Tense past: Cultural essays in trauma and memory* (pp. 103–145). New York: Routledge.

Maraun, M. D. (1998). Measurement as a normative practice: Implications of Wittgenstein's philosophy for measurement in psychology. *Theory & Psychology, 8,* 435–461.

Meumann, E. (1912). *Abriss der experimentellen Pädagogik* [Outline of experimental pedagogics]. Leipzig, Germany: Teubner.

Meumann, E. (1913). *The psychology of learning: An experimental investigation of the economy and technique of memory.* New York: Appleton. (Original work published 1907)

Ringer, F. K. (1969). *The decline of the German mandarins.* Cambridge, MA: Harvard University Press.

Roediger, H. L. (1980). Memory metaphors in cognitive psychology. *Memory and Cognition, 8,* 231–246.

Rommetveit, R. (1998). On human beings, computers and representational–computational vs. hermeneutic–dialogical approaches to human cognition and communication. *Culture and Psychology, 4,* 213–233.

Roth, M. S. (1989). Remembering forgetting: Maladies de la memoire in nineteenth century France. *Representations, 26,* 49–68.

Scheerer, E. (1980). Wilhelm Wundt's psychology of memory. *Psychological Research, 42*, 135–155.

Terdiman, R. (1993). *Present past: Modernity and the memory crisis.* Ithaca, NY: Cornell University Press.

Toth, J. P., & Hunt, P. R. (1999). Not one versus many, but zero versus any: Structure and function in the context of the multiple memory systems debate. In J. K. Foster & M. Jelicic (Eds.), *Memory: Systems, process, or function?* (pp. 232–272). New York: Oxford University Press.

Waugh, N. C., & Norman, D. A. (1965). Primary memory. *Psychological Review, 72*, 89–104.

Wolfe, H. K. (1886). Untersuchungen über das Tongedächtnis [Investigations of tonal memory]. *Philosophische Studien, 3*, 534–571.

Wundt, W. (1874). *Grundzüge der physiologischen Psychologie* [Principles of physiological psychology]. Leipzig, Germany: Engelmann.

Wundt, W. (1887). *Grundzüge der physiologischen Psychologie* (3rd ed.) [Principles of physiological psychology]. Leipzig, Germany: Engelmann.

Wundt, W. (1907). *Outlines of psychology.* London: Williams & Norgate. (Original work published 1896)

4

PSYCHOLOGY AND MEMORY IN THE MIDST OF CHANGE: THE SOCIAL CONCERNS OF LATE-19TH-CENTURY NORTH AMERICAN PSYCHOLOGISTS

MARLENE SHORE

At a time when psychology was gaining disciplinary autonomy in North America by moving toward laboratory investigation, it was recognized—for the first time ever at an international fair—as an official exhibit at the World's Columbian Exposition held in Chicago in 1893. Leading American psychologists regarded the exposition as a prime opportunity to introduce their work to a wider public, hoping to gain increased professional acceptance as well as to counter continuing popular interest in superstition, mysticism, and other forms of what they considered pseudoscience (Burnham, 1987, pp. 9, 34, 41, 86).

Psychology's scientific turn, partly manifested in its adoption of experimental investigation in the late 19th century, facilitated its public display more easily than had been the case when it was primarily linked to philosophy. Indeed, the use of experiment won institutional and popular

I wish to acknowledge the support of the Social Sciences and Humanities Research Council of Canada and its Standard Research Grants Program.

support for psychology in North America. Nevertheless, as this chapter shows, the discipline's turn toward experimental methods in the late 19th century can be explained by more than the growing ascendancy—and authority—of science in the West. It is also attributable to the preeminence of the visual sense in Western culture, where one of the strongest tendencies has been to reify thought—to externalize and objectify interior states (Scarry, 1985, pp. 4, 5, 13–22, 179). Psychology was shaped not only by this trend but also by the increasing speculation in the late 19th century about sight itself, particularly about the trust that could be placed in vision —in what the eye actually saw—in a period of rapid, economic, technological, and social change, when much of the familiar past was disappearing. Linked to that, psychologists also began to take an interest in investigating memory in an era when others were expressing concern about the past's erasure.

All of these complex and often conflicting dimensions of psychology's 19th-century development were evident in its representation at the World's Columbian Exposition—both in the official psychology exhibits and as the subject of discussions at the international academic congresses held in tandem with the fair. At the exposition, one could see in microcosm many of the different strains of thought—popular and academic—that had played a role in shaping the multifaceted nature of psychology by the end of the 19th century. Ostensibly scientific, psychology was still linked in the public's mind—even among those who were educated—with phrenology; ostensibly representing detached laboratory investigation, psychology was being called on to solve social problems while at the same time providing the foundation for the shaping of an industrial workforce. For all of these reasons, this examination of psychology's representation at the exposition provides a window on the beginnings of modernist culture and the ways in which it simultaneously buttressed and reflected the uncertainties that accompanied modernization. By the late 19th century, psychology was a mirror of that emerging culture.

SETTING THE STAGE:
THE WORLD'S COLUMBIAN EXPOSITION

The World's Columbian Exposition was the culmination of a series of world's fairs held in the 19th century after the success of London's Crystal Palace Exhibition of 1851 (Rydell, 1984, pp. 4, 8; Seager, 1995, p. 94). Chicago won the competition to host the exposition—the 15th world's fair and one that was intended to honor the 400th anniversary of Columbus's discovery of the New World (Burg, 1976, p. xiii; Cronon, 1991, p. 341). Vaster in scope than previous fairs, the exposition was primarily inspired by the Parisian Exposition Universelle of 1889, which had marked the centenary of the French Revolution. The Paris fair highlighted the enormous technological innovations and social changes that France had experienced over the previous 100 years by displaying the material technologies that had moved the country into a competitive position with other European nations. Accordingly, at the Paris fair, major inventions of the 19th century took center stage—the bicycle, telephone, telegraph, new lighting systems, and photographic and printing techniques (Weisberg, 1989, pp. 1–3). The Eiffel Tower, of course, stood as the primary symbol of new systems of technology and communication (Levin, 1989, p. 12).

Like the Exposition Universelle, the World's Columbian Exposition was intended to show the public the advancement of civilization and humanity's march toward the promise of modernity. Both fairs were essentially idealized consumer cities, held in walled-off grounds, displaying a future where everything was manmade; both used electricity extensively to convey the triumph of modern technology. In fact, the Chicago fairgrounds had more lighting than any city in the United States at the time, and lighting made the immense Ferris wheel popular at night (Nye, 1990, pp. 33–34; Trachtenberg, 1982, p. 215). By outdoing the spectacle at Paris, Chicago fair organizers intended to proclaim America's greatness before the world. They hoped that the depiction of an urban, industrial United States, involved in the world's economy and politics, adapting its traditional institutions to widespread economic and social change, would demonstrate that leadership had passed from the Old World to the New and that in the United States—"the first new nation"—the mission and vision of Columbus had been realized (Badger, 1979, p. 21; Commager, 1950, p. 41; Cronon, 1991, p. 341). Despite these optimistic overtures, the fair took place during a period of intense social unrest and economic depression.

The elaborately designed fair, attended by almost 30 million people, was built on the reclaimed swamplands of the shores of Lake Michigan, 7 miles south of the downtown loop. The exhibit grounds were constructed in the neoclassical style of Beaux Arts architecture replete with domes and columns. Approximately 400 buildings made of a mixture of plaster and jute fiber over steel skeletons covered 700 acres filled with canals, lagoons, fountains, plazas, promenades, and a preserve of woods (Rydell, 1984, p. 39; Trachtenberg, 1982, pp. 208–209). Known as "The White City," the exhibit grounds were meant to symbolize the allegedly advanced culture of the Western world, standing in sharp contrast to the "honky-tonk" section of the fair—the Midway Plaisance—a mile-long strip of amusements, sideshows, and entertainment facilities. Here, the supposedly inferior peoples of the world were put on display in temporarily constructed villages hierarchically arranged: The villages of European ethnic groups were located closest to the White City, whereas those of the non-White, non-Christian peoples were farthest away. In featuring these displays of ethnic and racial groups from many parts of the globe, organizers of the Chicago fair were following the example of the earlier Paris exposition, where the installation of people from France's colonies had been a popular attraction. By such means, however, the fair also promoted notions of racial hierarchy, ironically at a time when American anthropology was in a transitional stage, moving from a hierarchical view of human nature to one more pluralistic (Cotkin, 1992, pp. 55, 60; Rydell, 1984, pp. 5, 5n11; Seager, 1995, pp. xiv–xxvii; Trachtenberg, 1982, pp. 220–221). These notions of racial hierarchy were also ones that American psychologists attempted to eschew in their own official exhibit.

Smithsonian Assistant Secretary G. Brown Goode, who was responsible for classifying all of the fair's exhibits, conceived of the World's Columbian Exposition as an opportunity "to educate and formulate the modern" and intended that it would show the evolution of knowledge in all fields as a catalogue in the progress of civilization—"an illustrated encyclopedia of humanity" (1895, pp. 5–7; see also Rydell, 1984, p. 45). Consequently, buildings in the formal part of the Exposition—the White City—were organized according to an encyclopedic plan that encompassed fields of knowledge as they were then understood by the fair's organizers—into such categories as agriculture, machinery, transportation, liberal arts, electricity, and so on. In these so-called "temples of intelligence and industry," inventions from 36 nations and all the American states and territories were displayed.

The World's Columbian Exposition featured more than just exhibits. The idea that a world's fair should also concentrate on and express the progress of humanity in intellectual, moral, and spiritual realms began receiving support after the London Fair of 1851, which had been devoted primarily to manufacturing and to the display of British industries. This was partly an extension of the argument that a world's fair should have as one of its major objectives the exchange of knowledge necessary for facilitating mutual understanding among all nations and peoples of the world. The French gave the nonmaterial special emphasis in their world's fairs, and it was they who instituted, beginning in 1889, a series of intellectual and religious congresses held concurrently with international expositions—to these were invited leading figures in various fields of knowledge and cultural activity (Badger, 1979, p. 9; Seager, 1995, p. xix).

At the World's Columbian Exposition, the formal center of the fair was devoted to art and culture. The organized spaces, buildings, and exhibits were intended to convey the fair's message about "the progress of civilization," but so, too, were the religious, educational, and scholarly events of the World's Congress Auxiliary—20 departments whose conventions met throughout the summer. These international congresses were conceived of as a "summer university" in which the progress of all disciplines could be studied (Bonney, 1892, pp. 166–167); ultimately, 6,000 delegates presented papers that would have filled an estimated 50 volumes of 600 pages each (Seager, 1995, p. xx). These events and academic meetings evoked the motto of the fair, "Not Matter, But Mind, Not Things, But Man." While the fair's exhibits displayed matter and things, the congresses reflected on what they symbolized (Trachtenberg, 1982, p. 213).

A persistent theme in the opening addresses of the International Congress of Education was the expression of wonderment at what the World's Columbian Exposition represented and uncertainty about what might transpire when it ended and the buildings were demolished. In his address of welcome, Dr. Selim H. Peabody, chief of the exposition's Department of Liberal Arts, described the Chicago World's Fair as "the wonder of the present age," recalling that when he first saw it under construction two years earlier, "it was simply a succession of sand hills, separated by a stream of water, and a marsh." But then the engineer brought in his instruments, the dredge followed and gathered up the sands from a portion of the area and elevated the surface of the remainder. The architect followed, covering the whole surface "with structures whose magnificence has never been surpassed" (Peabody, 1893, p. 23). He continued,

> the sculptor has adorned these edifices, and painting has glorified them. The Acropolis, the Duomo of Florence, the buildings of the Champs de Mars, the Trocadero, and the multitudes of others have gathered themselves together on the Banks of a new Venice, and produced what we call "the White City." Its beauty, its glory have come up like hallucinations of a dream, and we mourn that in a few months we shall have only the barren surface when these buildings are gone. (p. 24)

Nevertheless, what was contained therein, Peabody concluded, "were the material illustrations of every occupation, of every science, of every art of mankind at the close of this nineteenth century" (p. 24).

In another address of welcome, Albert Lane, president of the National Educational Association and superintendent for public instruction for the City of Chicago, proclaimed,

> after the magnificent architectural structures of the White City have been removed, the thoughts and ideas, the social, economic, and educational problems which have been discussed from these halls, will find realization in the lives of people and will culminate in history. (1893, p. 31)

When he stepped up to the podium, University of Michigan President and Professor of Modern Languages James B. Angell (father of psychologist James Rowland Angell), who was the permanent chairman of the sessions, told of his experience walking enchantedly through the splendid architecture of the White City. He described the tears that had been brought to many eyes by the "inexpressible pathos of the thought" that in a few months, the collection of works of industry and art from all parts of "the civilized and from many parts of the uncivilized world" will have vanished.

Wondering whether they would vanish forever "like the unsubstantial fabric of a vision, leaving not a rack behind?" Angell (1893) reassured his audience that

> the intelligence which has formed them, the genius which has fashioned them, the great ideas which are incorporated in them—these shall abide forever and forever; and it is to these that you and I and every teacher address our work day by day. We work in that which is eternal and which shall never pass away. (p. 34)

MEMORY AND RECOLLECTION IN LATE 19TH-CENTURY SOCIAL THOUGHT

In many respects, the rhetoric permeating the opening addresses of the World's Columbian Exposition revealed a deep concern in the late 19th century about memory and its functioning—a concern shared by many of the first generation of experimental psychologists in North America. To argue that they were interested in memory and furthermore, that it reflected a deep social concern underlying their work, does not, however, deny that late 19th-century North American psychologists undertook other types of investigation, nor does it suggest that the nature of their experimental investigations was shaped by a unified and coherent project. They took an increasing interest in memory during the 1890s for a variety of reasons. As Kurt Danziger suggests (chap. 3, this volume), it partly grew out of an increased awareness that "memory," while once considered too broad a category for psychological investigation, nevertheless had popular appeal. Systems of memory training—*mnemonics*—continued to hold the public's fascination, and popular publications in memory training flourished, as in many other areas of self-help (see Samuel, 1994, pp. 3–25, on popular memory). A certain sensitivity to what held popular attention was especially important to the first generation of experimental psychologists in America, particularly at a time when they were attempting to win acceptance for their discipline in institutions of higher learning and when they were also determined to displace the amateurs—among them, spiritualists and phrenologists—who had captured public attention with their supposed insights into the functioning of the human mind (see Sokal, chap. 2, this volume). This does not mean that their interest in memory was totally calculated for public consumption, even though the venues where memory was the subject of discussion were public ones—International Congresses of Psychology, round table sessions at meetings of the National Educational Association (NEA), and exhibits of the World's Columbian Exposition. It is nevertheless the case that experimental psychology, like the discipline of history, was shaped in the late 19th century by widely expressed concerns that economic and social concerns were threatening to a society's recollection of its past and, accordingly, to its stability.

By the late 19th century, rapid changes arising from urbanization and industrialization had placed society's connection with the past under pressure. Although similarly tense relationships with the past had characterized other eras, many historians have noted that the experience from the late 18th century to about 1920—what is known as "the long 19th century" —was particularly traumatic. The leap in the productive power of human labor resulting from the introduction of machines, which facilitated the rapid replication and dissemination of commodities, promoted much reflection on the impact of technology and economic and social systems that were increasingly dependent on it. One of the results was the emergence of what the Frankfurt School labeled "the consciousness industry"—all the activities involved in the institutionalization of cultural memory through such things as national political ceremonies like world's fairs and the construction of civic monuments. Growing out of the same ethos were increased efforts to conserve the past in archives—through the collection and storage of written documents—so that remembering the past was not merely reliant on memory but aided through other mechanisms and institutions. The late 19th century also saw the establishment and proliferation of museums, which were preserving the material evidence of former societies, and art galleries, which were displaying pictures whose symbolism bore cultural memories. Moreover, the emergence of the discipline of anthropology and its study of belief systems embedded in ritual dances, religious ceremonies, songs, and myths, as well as a concomitant interest in the primitive and the exotic, constituted part of this interest in recovering and preserving the past (Fara & Patterson, 1998, p. 3; Matsuda, 1996, p. 12; Terdiman, 1993).

It is not surprising that under these circumstances, history itself grew as a dominant mode of inquiry in the late 19th century and became quickly organized into a professional discipline throughout Europe and North America. Whereas in the 18th century, philosophy had staked its claim as the queen of the disciplines, by the middle of the 19th century, history began to enjoy preeminence: Historical paintings and the historical novel acquired importance, and the study and criticism of the arts were recast as the history of art or the history of literature. Moreover, much urban architecture adopted the styles of earlier eras, as if to lend ballast to modern constructions of railway stations, banks, houses of parliament, and city halls. As historian Carl Schorske argued, historicism in culture arose as a way to come to grips with modernization by marshaling the resources of the past in what was also an era of growing nationalism, when collective identities were being redefined (1998, p. 4).

By the late 19th century, modernism arose in reaction to much of these developments, as intellectuals in many realms of thought attempted to confront modernity on its own terms. But these were actually two sides of the same coin. As Schorske argued,

> to master modernity by thinking *with* history, to master modernity by thinking *without* history, these are not simply antitheses but rather successive phases in the same effort to give shape and meaning to European civilization in the era of industrial capitalism and the rise of democratic politics. (1998, p. 5, emphasis in original)

The late 19th-century concern with memory was a product of the same apparent contradictions: The era saw almost an obsession with memory across disciplines and cultures; memory itself became an object of study, with many techniques developed for investigating how it functioned (Fara & Patterson, 1998, p. 3).

In their investigations of memory, late 19th-century psychologists worked with no one specific definition. Instead, they seemed to share the era's fascination with memory in its multiple meanings and connotations wherein memory could refer to the ability to remember the past and thus represent a function generally attributed to the brain, or it could connote something more abstract—a feeling, a person, or an event remembered. Of course, these were closely intertwined. One historian of late 19th-century European intellectual history argued that memory was conceived in that era as "a framing of experiences and observations in a language of disappearance and change, moments, movements, and multiplicities" (Matsuda, 1996, p. 84). Such ideas, for instance, were evident in Charles Baudelaire's famous celebration of "*le transitoire, le fugitif, le contingent*" (the transitory, the fleeting, the contingent); they could also be seen in the works of the Impressionist painters, whose art depicted the spectacles of daily life in a world transformed by urbanization, commerce, transport, and communications. At the end of the 19th century, writers on the brain used similar kinds of images. Many referred to the brain's ability to accumulate an incalculable number of ideas (Matsuda, 1996, p. 85).

There was another important dimension to the late 19th and early 20th centuries' concern with memory. As suggested above, memory was linked with the rise of nationalism and ethnic identity, in which the issue of history's location—as a vestige or remnant of the past both within a people's memory and in physical landscapes and territory—was central. In Europe, such issues underlay drives of territorial expansion and imperialism. For this reason, historian Laura Otis (1994) called the period between 1870 and 1918, the era of "organic memory" because of the theory's intimate relationship with nationalism. Although it is important to note that Ewald Hering first formulated the concept of organic memory as a scientific hypothesis in 1870, this does not suggest that all psychologists adhered to his ideas, particularly that memory and heredity represented the same basic function of organic matter. (Indeed, the North American figures at the center of this chapter refuted it.) Moreover, the organic memory theory was by no means the only way of looking at memory in the late 19th and early 20th centuries. William James, for example, believed that people could remember only because they could form associations—the same associations that enabled them to form habits. The more associations they formed with a particular memory, the greater its persistence. However, James also argued that the human ability to locate memory in the past and to associate it with a context that one could identify as part of "self" was memory's most essential feature, and he did not link it to heredity.

In effect, concern with memory in the late 19th century drew together many unknowns and was used almost metaphorically. It this way, memory served as a means by which scholars in a variety of fields explored extremely controversial problems, such as the relationship between the individual and society or the mental and the physical; it also was a way in which they investigated the mechanism of heredity or the roles that heredity and environment played in shaping the individual.

PSYCHOLOGY'S EXHIBIT AT THE WORLD'S COLUMBIAN EXPOSITION

In many respects, the representation of psychology at the World's Columbian Exposition in 1893 reflected all the late 19th-century developments, concerns, and questions traced above, many of them also issues treated in other parts of this volume.

The classification of knowledge that framed the organization of buildings and exhibits at the World's Columbian Exposition categorized topics in science so that anthropology, neurology, and psychology were grouped together in one department—Department M, Ethnology. This assemblage of anthropology, psychology, and neurology in one building would seem to stem from the public's—and therefore, the fair organizers'—fascination with phrenology and with the notions of racial hierarchy, from which professional psychologists were attempting to distance themselves. The idea that racial superiority could be biologically validated through the measurement of skulls was linked in psychology, to Francis Galton's work in anthropometry (see Fancher, chap. 1, this volume). Although they were not entirely happy with their exhibit's location at the Columbian Exposition, American psychologists conceded that it was better treatment than psychology had received at previous world's fairs, when it had been ignored (Baldwin, 1893, pp. 303–304). Moreover, for the leading practitioners of experimental psychology in the United States, the timing of the exposition was propitious because they had spent the previous couple of years attempting to win professional and curricular acceptance for their approaches to the discipline. In 1892, American psychologists made their first showing at the International Congress of Psychology held in London; that same summer, a small group of psychologists, including G. Stanley Hall of Clark University, James Mark Baldwin of the University of Toronto, James McKeen Cattell of the University of Pennsylvania, and Joseph Jastrow of the University of Wisconsin, met to form the American Psychological Association (APA), which was dedicated to "the advancement of psychology as a science," and to bringing the discipline to the public's attention (see Cadwallader, 1992, p. 31; Fernberger, 1932, pp. 2–3; "Preliminary Meeting," 1894, pp. 1–2; Sokal, 1992, p. 46; Spielberger, 1992, p. xi).

In the summer of 1892, Jastrow was already working as an assistant to Frederick Ward Putnam, director of Harvard's Peabody Museum of Archaeology, who had been put in charge of collecting material for the Columbian Exposition's Department M. Accordingly, at the founding meeting of the APA, Jastrow invited his colleagues to participate in the Chicago fair, and they took up the offer, recognizing that the event was a prime opportunity, as Jastrow put it, "to render visible to the public" the nature of the problems that psychologists were considering (1961, p. 142). As a subfield of philosophy for much of the 19th century, as other chapters in this volume discuss, academic psychology had not been popularly accessible, with the result—to the psychologists' dismay—that the public continued to be fascinated with phrenology, mesmerism, hypnotism, and spiritualism (Burnham, 1987, p. 46). So prominent was psychical research in the late 19th century that in many circles, Jastrow once complained, a psychologist meant "a spook hunter." In fact, when plans were being laid for the meeting of the International Congress of Psychology in London in 1889, the only official association of psychology that organizers could identify in the United States was the Society of Psychical Research—a matter of embarrassment for the new generation of experimental psychologists (Jastrow, 1961, p. 158; Sokal, 1992, p. 45).

In their objective to use the Chicago World's Fair to attract public interest to psychology, the group was successful. Magazines and newspaper reports on the fair applauded the psychological laboratory, which contained the largest collection of instruments and appliances ever brought together in America, as the exposition's greatest educational contribution (Johnson, 1897, p. 425). One report observed that the use of the techniques and instruments of the laboratory had allowed for "the diagrammatic and material representation" of the discipline (Editor's Table, 1893, pp. 125–126); the graphs and charts, James Mark Baldwin noted, facilitated the presentation of psychologists' investigations in "a form easily taken in by the eye" (1893, pp. 303–304).

Appointed to the Columbian Exposition's Committee on Awards, Baldwin was responsible for writing the report on psychology for the U.S. Congress. He used the opportunity to trace the discipline's history and development up to the time of the exposition. In his report, he argued that it was unfortunate that in earlier years, the social, moral, and theo-retical sciences, being "abstract" and "immaterial," had not been able "to show their work to the eye" and thus had appeared at world's fairs only as results incorporated in education and other social institutions. As he saw it, this meant that popular instruction had been rendered defective pre-cisely in those sciences that essentially embodied "the more ideal and spir-itual aspects of a nation's life"; he concluded that these were things that should not have been omitted in the "surveys of civilization" that fairs were supposed to represent (1901, pp. 383, 404).

One of the leading members of the new generation of North Amer-ican psychologists, Baldwin believed that modern knowledge was charac-terized by its adoption of the methods of scientific procedure. This "modern transformation," as he described it, was most evident in psychology, which had essentially applied scientific procedure to philosophy and which, in its use of the methods of laboratory investigation, had also allowed its results to be made visible and displayed in graphic—or quantitative—form (1901, pp. 365–366, 377, 389, 393). The psychology exhibits at the World's Co-lumbian Exposition gave expression to this conviction. Although there were a few psychology exhibits at the fair—some of them mounted by private instrument makers and another, for example, put on by Harvard University in the Educational Building—in the official psychology exhibit housed in the Ethnology Building, instruments and apparatus used in ex-periments and contributed by numerous universities the world over were arranged in topical displays. Included among them was a kymograph, chronoscopes, and instruments for work in the field of vision (Baldwin, 1893, pp. 303–304). On the walls hung numerous charts and graphs show-ing research results from university laboratories. The exhibit also included a working laboratory set up, not to conduct research—although photo-graphs of numerous university research laboratories were displayed on the walls—but as a testing room where, for a small fee, fairgoers could have their sense capacities and mental powers tested (Baldwin, 1901, pp. 384, 398–399).

As the first attempt to introduce psychological tests to the American public, the testing room was used to demonstrate the methods experimental psychologists were then using to test the range, accuracy, and nature of what they called "some elementary mental powers" and also to collect data for a larger study of the ways in which such factors as age, education, gender, race, environment, social status, and physical development could affect those powers. An army of graduate student volunteers brought to Chicago for the occasion tested thousands of the fair's visitors. However, as Jastrow, who was responsible for their administration, conceded, the greatest value of the tests was educational because the noise, commotion, distraction, and time constraints at the fair were not conducive to scientific accuracy. More reliable results were expected from data obtained from the same tests administered to American college students before the fair opened (Baldwin, 1901, p. 384).

The Ethnology Building also included a section on physical anthropology where Franz Boas, employed as another of Putnam's assistants, directed a program of anthropometric measurements on visitors to the fair, including as many foreigners as possible, as well as on the Native groups,[1] who had been brought to Chicago for an outdoor ethnographic exhibit (Jastrow, 1961, p. 149; Sokal, 1987, p. 31). Putnam, Boas, and Jastrow saw no reason to limit the program to physical anthropology and extended it to include mental tests, resulting in the testing laboratory described above.

Jastrow had written to Francis Galton in 1892, asking for suggestions about procedures and apparatus, and at the Chicago fair, he used a schedule of tests resembling Galton's (Jastrow, 1961, pp. 141–142). Galton had used reaction-time experiments in a series of trial tests at the International Health Exhibition in London in 1884. There, he set up an Anthropometric Laboratory: a small fenced-off area of hall with a long table staffed by three attendants where over 9,000 visitors—for a fee of 3 pence—were voluntarily tested and measured for 13 characteristics, including reaction times, keenness of sight and hearing, color discrimination, ability to judge length and weight, and breathing power and capacity (Fancher, 1996, pp. 216–218; Hunt, 1993, p. 209). Although Jastrow created a virtual replica of Galton's Anthropometric Laboratory at the Chicago fair, his interest in Galton's testing methods was only in their potential use as a way to measure the duration of mental states. For him, testing the range of human capacity was important, quite apart from its use as a means to compare individuals on a scale of performance (Jastrow, 1961, p. 156). To that degree, his ideas were also influenced by James McKeen Cattell, Galton's greatest follower in North America, whose research program on mental tests and measurements ignored the simple measurements of bodily dimensions included in Galton's program and concentrated instead on procedures to examine both physiological and psychological characteristics. As historian Michael Sokal (1987, pp. 22, 26, 30) argued, Cattell was interested in measuring individual differences without considering what inferences could be drawn from the results. What Jastrow and his colleagues hoped could result from the tests, once the so-called normal capacity had been ascertained in whatever power was being tested, was some indication of what types of faculties developed earlier and which later; to what extent their growth was conditioned by age, education, race, and environments; the differences between the sexes at various ages; the relationship of physical development to mental; the correlation of one form of mental faculty with others; and the effects of special kinds of training (Baldwin, 1901, p. 384).

---

[1]Anthropologists brought groups of indigenous peoples to the Columbian Exposition for the outdoor ethnographic exhibit.

Perhaps because of their apparent social utility for education and for solving other social problems, the psychological tests used at the World's Columbian Exposition drew substantial attention. The popularity of the fair's Anthropometric Laboratory precipitated a vogue for testing in American psychology, which lasted for a brief period before waning and re-emerging in the 20th century. The tests, set up on a series of tables, included: judgment of lengths by finger movements, judgment of weights and touch, and judgment of surfaces by feeling and rapidity of movement. In a pain sensitivity test developed by Cattell using Fechner's principles, gradually increasing pressure was applied on the tip of the forefinger of the subject's left hand, and he or she was asked to indicate the moment at which the pressure first became painful. There were also simple reaction tests on touch, hearing, and sight in which the chronoscope was used, as well as tests of complex reaction. There were tests judging accuracy of aim and quickness of perception: In the latter, there appeared for 1/20th of a second behind a photographic shutter a card bearing a series of black dots —or dots of different colors—or words. The subject had to remember the number, and the quickness of his or her perception was estimated according to the correct number of answers. In a memory test, a series of printed words appeared behind an opening in a screen. As soon as the series was completed, the subject was asked to write down as many as possible in their proper order: The number correctly recalled without regard to order was regarded as an indication of range of memory or "memory span." In an association test, the amount of time needed to think and write down an association of each of 10 given words was measured. In picture and word tests, the rapidity with which a given 10 words or pictures could be found among 40 was determined—this was supposed to be an indication of mental alertness and also an indication of memory, the power to recall, and the power to recognize (Baldwin, 1901, p. 384; Jastrow, 1961, p. 142). Memory tests of the sort described above had never been part of Galton's program, and they attest to the increasing interest which North American psychologists took in memory.

The testing room in the official psychology exhibit at the Chicago World's Fair also included a series of optical tests of the range and accuracy of form and color vision. The proliferation of studies in color vision in the last quarter of the 19th century among physicians, psychologists, and anthropologists was prompted by a concern about safety in certain occupations, stemming partly form a major railroad accident that occurred in Sweden in 1876 when a color-blind employee misperceived a signal, and subsequent tests revealed that he was not the only railroad worker suffering from color blindness (Kuklick, 1991, pp. 146, 174). However, the growth of interest in color vision was also related to the era's fascination with the visual and with the individual as observer—already the subject of investigation in the first few decades of the 19th century, when much study in the empirical sciences centered on subjective vision and the role of the body in the apprehension of the visual world (Crary, 1991, pp. 71, 79). Much of this investigation occurred in the discipline of physiology in mid-19th-century Europe, especially Germany, where physiology rose to prominence in part because of its creation of instruments that allowed one to see inside the body (Coleman & Holmes, 1988, pp. 3–4, 8). The new physiological optics, for instance, was dedicated to exposing the idiosyncrasies of the so-called normal eye by studying retinal afterimages, peripheral vision, binocular vision, and thresholds of attention (Crary, 1991, p. 16).

PSYCHOLOGY AND THE CULTURE OF MODERNISM

Experimental psychology's investigation of such phenomena as attentiveness and reaction time, its use of equipment and photographs, and even its liberal use of photographic displays on the walls of the official psychology exhibit at the World's Columbian Exposition evinced its connections with the beginnings of modernist culture. It shared in the late 19th-century fascination with the visual, seeking to understand and display the results of investigations into the mind and consciousness in material terms. However, it was also shaped by that era's increasing concern about the reliability of vision, raising questions—which perhaps harbored doubts—about what was taken in by the eye (Crary, 1991, pp. 10–19; Jay, 1992, p. 179). All of this was essentially undergirded by a concern with how knowledge was obtained and retained in a society being transformed by economic, social, and technological change.

Experimental psychologists' effort to give material expression to their investigations, their use of instruments and apparatus to study the workings of the mind, and even their conceptualization of consciousness and mental states as the product of sensorimotor connections all reflected the importance that Western culture attached to the visual. The West's faith in sight was a legacy that Renaissance thinkers attributed to the culture of ancient Greece; the Renaissance also exalted the visual, producing the theoretical and practical development of perspective in the visual arts. Nevertheless, as historian Martin Jay (1994, pp. 32–34, 44, 69, 71) argued, the modern era privileged sight in a way that differentiated it from other eras: The 19th century was one of the most visual periods in Western culture, as ideals of precise observation were exalted in the sciences and were evident in literary and popular fascination with spectacle. All of this was evident in the world's fairs. The growth of commodity capitalism was undeniably at root. As social theorist Guy DeBord noted, "in societies where modern conditions of production prevail, all of life presents itself as an immense accumulation of spectacles" (1983, pp. 1, 5). By the late 19th century, fascination with the visual involved speculation about sight itself, for not only had technology produced evidence of visual change within urban landscapes, it had also created changes in the capacity to see—the introduction of electricity, for instance, meant that there was more to be seen after dark. These new visual experiences, however, also introduced uncertainty about what the eyes saw and led to an increased interrogation of vision. Although some scholars have linked this speculation about human sight to the introduction of the camera and photography, the role that the individual played as "observer" was already being subjected to investigation in the first few decades of the 1800s (Crary, 1991, pp. 7–10, 14–16, 19).

The deep-rooted propensity in Western culture to externalize and objectify interior states, evident in the efforts of experimental psychologists to give material expression to the conceptualization of consciousness and mental states through the use of instruments and apparatus, was borrowed from physiology. The study of visual phenomena such as optical illusions was already having an impact on the development of experimental psychology by the mid-19th century. In the 1850s and 1860s, physiologist and physicist Hermann von Helmholtz paid particular attention to the apparent imperfections, physical and psychological, of the visual sense by studying the eye as an imperfect optical instrument and by investigations of color sensation as determined by the trichromatic sensitivity of the retina and not just the physical nature of light; he also conceived of optical illusions as examples of "unconscious inference" (Fancher, 1979/1996, pp. 120–127).

Many of the developments described above clearly linked psychology to the central tenets of the emerging culture of modernism. Recent scholarship in cultural and intellectual history sees modernism as a set of beliefs, values, and modes of perception that came into being in the late 19th century as part of the processes associated with modernization—industrialization, technology, rationalization, and efficiency—as well as in response to new findings in the biological and physical sciences, which ultimately led to the collapse of linear conceptions of time and space and to the development of such notions as streams of consciousness. This interpretation differs from earlier treatments of modernism, which linked it to modernity in general or identified it with the avant garde movement of artists and intellectuals who expressed hostility to modernization or else— particularly with regard to the American scene—regarded it as a celebration of technology. Nevertheless, although it might be the case that modernism was a culture inseparable from the processes of scientific and economic rationalization occurring throughout the West, it cannot simply be identified with them. There was a fundamental ambivalence at the center of modernism: Whereas in some senses it buttressed technology, rationalization, and efficiency, modernism was also concerned about the potentially corrosive impact that these developments were exerting on community, history, and memory at the same time as it emphasized flux and contingency.[2]

It is common to identify as the first example of cultural modernism in North America the New York Armory Exhibit of 1913. In fact, intellectual developments in such fields as physics, biology, philosophy, psychology, and the social sciences had already established forerunners of modernist thought in North America before that. Already in the late 19th century, a group of social thinkers in the universities, connected with the fledgling social sciences, among whom some of the early experimental psychologists must be counted, were asking questions about human nature and the workings of society that much resembled what later came to be called modernism. Their ideas could no longer be said to belong to a Victorian outlook which, generally speaking, was grounded in a belief in a predictable universe; an accompanying conviction that humans were capable of arriving at a unified and fixed set of truths about all aspects of life; and an insistence on a dichotomy that separated that which was deemed animal and that which was regarded as human, thereby polarizing so-called "civilized" societies from "primitive" ones (Singal, 1987, pp. 7–26). In several different ways, these social thinkers were beginning to question the notion of the fixed and the final and, in so doing, were beginning to abandon 19th-century positivism in exchange for a view of a more open universe governed by change and chance (see, e.g., Shore, 1987, pp. 68–120). Along with that went the concern about memory and its operation: Historians wrote about the nation as a way to provide common links to an imagined collective past, while psychologists took an interest in individual memory. At the same time, research in neurology sought to discover whether the mind—and memory—had an organic basis (see, e.g., Rosenfield, 1988).

Many of these themes were echoed in the World Congresses held in conjunction with the Chicago World's Fair. As historian Richard Seager (1995, p. 164) noted in his study of the religious congresses at the World's Columbian Exposition, the texts of the meetings of the international congresses that met in Chicago throughout the summer of 1893 represented "crowning statements in an encyclopedic system of knowledge generated at the turn of the century, which aimed to be global or universal in scope and progress and disposition" (p. xx). In effect, they present insight into modern American thought at the point when the United States was on the verge of joining, if not overtaking, Britain, France, and Germany as a leader of the modern industrial society.

---

[2]The literature on modernism is vast. In addition to the titles in the references, see, for example, S. Kern, *The Culture of Time and Space, 1880–1918* (Cambridge, MA: Harvard University Press, 1983); D. Harvey, *The Condition of Postmodernity: An Enquiry Into the Origins of Cultural Change* (Oxford, England: Blackwell, 1989); and F. Karl, *Modern and Modernism: The Sovereignty of the Artist, 1885–1925* (New York: Atheneum, 1985).

The Congresses in Rational Psychology and Experimental Psychology were among the most highly attended sessions of the academic meetings organized in conjunction with the World's Columbian Exposition. These sessions were held during the meetings of the International Congress of Education, under the auspices of the NEA. The sessions of the International Congress of Education treated all levels of education from kindergarten to university training, as well as instruction techniques and teacher training, educational publications, and the application of rational and experimental psychology to education (Badger, 1979, p. 9). The Congress in Experimental Psychology was presided over by G. Stanley Hall, then President of Clark University, while James McCosh, the influential philosophy professor at Princeton who initiated the curricular transition from philosophy to psychology, presided over the Congress in Rational Psychology (Buchner, 1896, p. 590).

PSYCHOLOGY AND THE INTERNATIONAL CONGRESSES

It is significant that by the 1890s, psychology was able to claim the attention of international gatherings of this sort. Indeed, it is almost possible to see the growth of interest in the discipline itself in the history of these international psychological congresses. The First International Congress of Psychology, held in Paris in 1889—the Congress of Physiological Psychology—was primarily occupied with the study of hypnosis and telepathic hallucinations. The second international meeting, held in London in 1892—the Congress of Experimental Psychology—reflected the increasing importance that the experimental approach had gained by that point (Buchner, 1896, p. 588). It also reflected the efforts that had been made to move psychology away from the issues that interested the French—hallucinations, hypnotism, and the abnormal mind. The 1892 congress, which lasted for four days, was attended by eminent figures, including French psychologist Théodule Ribot, German experimental psychologist Hermann Ebbinghaus, Italian criminologist and physician Cesare Lombroso, English scientist Francis Galton, French physician and psychologist Pierre Janet, and psychologist Edward Bradford Titchener. Hermann von Helmholtz also attended, arriving to have a look at experimental psychology before continuing on to a physics meeting in Edinburgh. It was estimated that over 300 people, coming from all parts of Europe, North America, and Australia, attended the London congress. At the close of the London meeting, consideration was given to holding an Extraordinary Session of the Congress in the United States in 1893 to accord with the timing of the World's Columbian Exposition, but the committee set up to investigate the possibility decided against it. As originally planned, the next

International Congress was held in Munich in 1896 (*Reports of Proceedings of the 2nd International Congress of Psychology*, 1892, pp. iii–iv).

At the same time in North America, psychology had come to figure in the meetings of the NEA, beginning in 1891. Indeed, this was a sign of psychology's rapid acceptance in educational circles and institutions. At the NEA meeting held in Toronto in 1891, psychology was the subject of a round table session, "The Study of Children," presided over by G. Stanley Hall. Hall summarized results of observations made on school-age children in Russia, Denmark, Germany, France, England, and the United States in studies dealing with health, growth, mental power, and attainment and in another project that dealt with practical methods in the study of children, including anthropometry. He also described psychological tests on memory, association, will, and "the contents of children's minds" (1891, pp. 829–831).

At the NEA conference of 1892, held in Saratoga Springs, New York, officers of the organization met to make plans for the association's sessions at the Chicago World's Fair. There, it was decided to include congresses on psychology under the NEA's umbrella because the association was already doing so much in the area ("Report on the World's Educational Congress," 1892, pp. 117–118). That summer, at the first annual meeting of the APA, the question of the APA itself holding a Psychological Congress in connection with the World's Congress was discussed. Consideration was given to the APA's possible cooperation with the anthropological, philosophical, and educational congresses or to the idea that the organization might hold a separate congress. In the end, the decision was made to leave the members free to place their allegiances wherever they thought best rather than attaching the APA to one or other of the congresses (Sokal, 1992, pp. 50–51).

Eminent scholars in almost every field attended the World's Congresses in Chicago in the summer of 1893, although the conditions were far from favorable. The meetings were held 7 miles from Jackson Park in a building—the Memorial Art Palace—which, although newly constructed, directly abutted a noisy railroad and was often filled with smoky and dusty air from the locomotives and nearby factory chimneys. A reporter from *The Nation* commented that the whole scene was often too much for human endurance (Editor's Table, 1893, p. 126; "W. H. D.," 1893, pp. 186–187).

The Congress on Rational Psychology, which featured papers by James McCosh, Josiah Royce, Jacob Gould Schurmann, and philosophy professor John Watson of Queen's University in Kingston, Ontario, Canada, was devoted to considering "transient and permanent characteristics of mind" as part of the effort to discover what distinguished "mind" from mere biological phenomena. Papers explained what psychology was supposed to be, how and why it developed, and its links to religion and philosophy.

The Congress of Educational Psychology was devoted to questions of child study in physical, emotional, intellectual, and volitional aspects and included reports of investigations on physical development, stuttering, imagination in childhood, children's language, children's religious beliefs, and ear and eye mindedness, to name only a few. Reports covered work being carried out throughout the world, with several more showing the relationship of this sort of work to educational theory and practice. Prominent in these discussions was the issue of the degree to which education had changed in the past couple of decades, especially with the introduction of kindergarten, manual and art training, technological instruction, and business education. The necessity of psychology helping to ease the effects of this transformation was emphasized.

Papers made frequent references to the explosion of knowledge that had occurred in a short span of years and to the ability of students to take in all the changes (and requisite information) that accompanied the emergence of new disciplines and new modes of inquiry. As Charles Bonney (1893), president of the World's Auxiliary Congress commented,

> modern science itself is a new word, created within the living memory of men. In all the old branches of learning there has been a wonderful increase of knowledge; more of natural science; more of political and social science; more of moral and intellectual science . . . than can be mastered during the school years. (pp. 17–18)

He saw this as an "emergency" with respect to the degree of information that could be absorbed—cramming had been tried and abandoned as worse than useless. Like many others, Bonney was hopeful that the introduction of practical psychology would give teachers and students "knowledge of the mind, its constitutions, faculties, and operations." Without that, he warned, serious errors could not be avoided (p. 19).

Although papers in educational congresses were supposed to deal with psychology in education, they also focused on issues and concerns that highlight much of what this chapter argues regarding the nature of late 19th-century psychology—that it evinced its links with modernist culture in its concern with perception and memory and especially in relation to the question of how memory was retained in a society experiencing enormous change. Papers that dealt with fatigue conveyed the same concerns. A paper on "mental waste and economy" among school children, for instance, asserted that the key to averting waste lay in the retention of memory. It also expressed concern about the amount of knowledge that had to be absorbed in the modern age by contrast with the limited amount of time available (Patrick, 1893, p. 725). The author, G. T. W. Patrick, of the State University of Iowa, argued that the educational system should find ways to strengthen retentive powers as much as it had strengthened perceptive, discriminative, and volitional powers of mind. This neglect, he argued, taken together with conditions of modern life, was leading gradually to the weakening of retentive ability, and it meant that an immense amount of nervous energy and time would be wasted in relearning what had been forgotten. "If students have slovenly memory," he commented, "they will forget most of what they learned" (p. 728). Patrick conceded that there would be objections to his statement because it defied the then-popular position in education—a reaction against the old form of memory education, which had been led by John Locke, Jean-Jacques Rousseau, and Johann Heinrich Pestalozzi. But he thought that the pendulum of reform had swung too far in the contempt for memory culture. And he reminded the audience that the great men of the world had been ones with strong memories—because they did not have to waste nervous energy and time relearning what they had forgotten, they were able to move steadily forward and "accumulate intellectual wealth" that others acquired and then lost (pp. 728–729).

Another presenter noted that experimental psychology had been helpful in fashioning a well-constructed school curriculum. Experiments in association had shown the importance of coordinating studies, not only as a means to save time and energy but to secure stronger "mental products," while experiments in the localization of cerebral function revealed that there were "many memories instead of one," and this had modified methods of instruction. The result was that ear-minded, eye-minded, tactile, or muscular-minded children were less frequently misunderstood (Shimer, 1893, pp. 444–445).

Such concerns about waste and fatigue, evident in a number of other papers presented to the educational congresses, demonstrated the degree to which the cult of efficiency was on the rise in the late 19th century and would give way to ideas of scientific management. Within this context, the concern with memory cut two ways—it was expressive of fears of erasure of the past, but it was also recognized as a key element in the creation of efficient men and women for the industrial work force.

Discussions about memory clearly affected the discipline of psychology just as it had many other realms of thought in late 19th-century North America. It is evident that much of the attention grew out of concerns about the potentially negative impact of rapid industrialization and technology. At the same time, late 19th-century psychology's experiments—especially those used by North American psychologists and displayed at the World's Columbian Exposition that dealt with vision, reaction time, and memory (or the power of recall)—were related to the productive tasks requiring attentiveness in the work force. Ultimately, along with physiology, psychology would become the basis of efforts to mould individuals suited to the needs of economic modernity (see Rabinbach, 1990). In the early 1890s, however, during the period under discussion here, just the beginnings of that trend were discernible.

CONCLUSION

This chapter's examination of psychology's representation at the World's Columbian Exposition of 1893 has illustrated the state of the discipline by the end of the 19th century and many of the influences that shaped and buffeted it. The exposition was one of the major events of the fin de siècle: During the months that it was held, it received extensive and almost daily news coverage throughout the world. The fact that psychologists were given an official exhibit there for the first time at an international fair demonstrated that the discipline was finally conceded popular recognition. In no small way, this development was attributable to hard work and lobbying efforts by its North American practitioners to give it recognition, just as they had endeavored to win curricular acceptance in institutions of higher learning for their disciplinary approaches.

However, it was evident from the ways in which psychology was exhibited and discussed at the Chicago World's Fair, that it stood for a myriad of things by the close of the century, mirroring the jumble of intellectual, cultural, and political messages and symbols that the fair itself had reflected and promoted. The use of instruments and laboratory techniques might have promoted psychology as a "scientific" discipline; the graphs and charts displaying the results of research investigations might have placed it firmly as part of the quantitative revolution. But it was also caught up with popular ideas not entirely acceptable to its practitioners, such as notions of racial hierarchy. And what they already had experienced in their efforts to institute the discipline in North America grew even more apparent: Psychology would not be a discipline characterized wholly by scientific detachment. There were demands to which the North American psychologists readily responded—to deal with pressing social concerns and provide solutions to economic and social problems, rife during the last decade of the 19th century. More than just a response to such conditions, psychology was, in numerous ways, a product of these concerns and of many of the intellectual and cultural currents that accompanied them.

REFERENCES

Angell, J. B. (1893, July). Address of welcome to the second general session. *National Education Association, Proceedings of the International Congress of Education of the World's Columbian Exposition, 32,* 34–40.

Badger, R. (1979). *The great American fair: The World's Columbian Exposition and American culture.* Chicago: Hall.

Baldwin, J. M. (1893). The Columbian Exposition: Psychology. *The Nation, 26,* 303–304.

Baldwin, J. M. (1901). Historical and educational report on psychology. In *Report* of the Committee on Awards of the World's Columbian Commission: Special reports upon special subjects or groups (Vol. 1, House Report No. 4374, pp. 357–404). Washington, DC: U.S. Government Printing Office.

Bonney, C. G. (1892). The World's Congress of 1893. *National Educational Association, Journal of Proceedings and Addresses, 31,* 166–174.

Bonney, C. G. (1893, July). Address of welcome. *Proceedings of the International Congress of Education of the World's Columbian Exposition, 32,* 17–20.

Buchner, E. F. (1896). The Third International Congress of Psychology. *Psychological Review, 3,* 589–602.

Burg, D. (1976). *Chicago's White City of 1893.* Lexington: University of Kentucky.

Burnham, J. C. (1987). *How superstition won and science lost: Popularizing science and health in the United States.* New Brunswick, NJ: Rutgers University Press.

Cadwallader, T. C. (1992). The historical roots of the American Psychological Association. In R. B. Evans, V. S. Sexton, & T. C. Cadwallader (Eds.), *The American Psychological Association: A historical perspective* (pp. 3–41). Washington, DC: American Psychological Association.

Coleman, W., & Holmes, F. L. (Eds.). (1988). *The investigative enterprise: Experimental physiology in nineteenth-century medicine.* Berkeley: University of California Press.

Commager, H. S. (1950). *The American mind.* New Haven, CT: Yale University Press.

Cotkin, G. (1992). *Reluctant modernism: American thought and culture, 1880–1900.* New York: Macmillan.

Crary, J. (1991). *Techniques of the observer: On vision and modernity in the nineteenth century.* Cambridge, MA: MIT Press.

Cronon, W. (1991). *Nature's metropolis: Chicago and the Great West.* New York: Norton.

DeBord, G. (1983). Society of the spectacle (reprint ed). Detroit, MI: Black & Red.

Editor's Table: Science at the Columbian Exposition. (1893, November). *Popular Science Monthly, 44,* 123–126.

Fancher, R. (1996). *Pioneers of psychology* (3rd ed.). New York: Norton. (Original work published 1979)

Fara, P., & Patterson, K. (1998). Introduction. In P. Fara & K. Patterson (Eds.), *Memory* (pp. 1–9). Cambridge, UK: Cambridge University Press.

Fernberger, S. W. (1932). The American Psychological Association: A Historical Summary, 1892–1930. *Psychological Bulletin, 29,* 2–89.

Goode, G. B. (1895, January). America's relation to the advance of science (from "What Has Been Done in America for Science," address delivered before the Philosophical Society of Washington, 24 November 1894). *Science,* pp. 5–7.

Hall, S. (1891). Round Table Conference: The Organization of Higher Education [conducted by Nicholas Murray Butler]. *National Educational Association, Journal of Proceedings and Addresses, 30,* 829–831.

Hunt, M. (1993). *The story of psychology*. New York: Doubleday/Anchor Books.

Jastrow, J. (1961). Joseph Jastrow. In C. Murchison (Ed.), *A history of psychology in autobiography* (pp. 135–162). New York: Russell & Russell. (Original work published 1939)

Jay, M. (1992). Scopic regimes of modernity. In S. Lash & J. Friedman (Eds.), *Modernity and identity* (pp. 178–195). Oxford, England: Blackwell.

Jay, M. (1994). *Downcast eyes: The denigration of vision in twentieth-century French thought*. Berkeley: University of California Press.

Johnson, R. (Ed.). (1897). *History of the World's Columbian Exposition* (Vol. III, Exhibits). New York: Appleton.

Kuklick, H. (1991). *The savage within: The social history of British anthropology, 1885–1945*. Cambridge, UK: Cambridge University Press.

Lane, A. (1893, July). Address of welcome. *Proceedings of the International Congress of Education of the World's Columbian Exposition, 32*, 30–32.

Levin, M. R. (1989). *When the Eiffel Tower was new: French visions of progress at the centennial of the revolution*. South Hadley, MA: Mount Holyoke College Art Museum (Amherst). (Distributed by University of Massachusetts Press)

Matsuda, M. K. (1996). *The memory of the modern*. New York: Oxford University Press.

Nye, D. (1990). *Electrifying America: Social meanings of a new technology*. Cambridge, MA: MIT Press.

Otis, L. (1994). *Organic memory: History and the body in the late nineteenth and early twentieth centuries*. Lincoln: University of Nebraska Press.

Patrick, G. T. W. (1893, July). Mental waste and economy. *Proceedings of the International Congress of Education of the World's Columbian Exposition*, pp. 725–730.

Peabody, S. H. (1893, July). Address of welcome. *Proceedings of the International Congress of Education of the World's Columbian Exposition*, pp. 23–25.

"Proceedings of the American Psychological Association: I. Preliminary meeting." (1894). In *Proceedings of the American Psychological Association* (pp. 1–2). New York: Macmillan.

Rabinbach, A. (1990). *The human motor: Energy, fatigue, and the origins of modernity*. Berkeley: University of California Press.

"Report on the World's Educational Congress." (1892). *National Educational Association, Journal of Proceedings and Addresses, 31*, 117–118.

Reports of Proceedings of the 2nd International Congress of Psychology (2nd Sess., pp. iii–iv). (1892). London: International Congress of Experimental Psychology.

Rosenfield, I. (1988). *The invention of memory*. New York: Basic Books.

Rydell, R. (1984). *All the world's a fair: Visions of empire at American international expositions*. Chicago: University of Chicago Press.

Samuel, R. (1994). *Theatres of memory. Vol. 1: Past and present in contemporary culture*. London: Verso.

Scarry, E. (1985). *The body in pain: The making and unmaking of the world*. New York: Oxford University Press.

Schorske, C. E. (1998). *Thinking with history: Explorations in the passage to modernism*. Princeton, NJ: Princeton University Press.

Seager, R. H. (1995). *World's parliament of religion: The east/west encounter, Chicago 1893*. Bloomington: Indiana University Press.

Shimer, E. D. (1893, July). The candidate for the degree of pedagogy should be able to make original investigations in experimental psychology. *Proceedings of the International Congress of Education of the World's Columbian Exposition*, pp. 444–445.

Shore, M. (1987). *The science of social redemption: McGill, the Chicago School, and the origins of social research in Canada*. Toronto, Ontario, Canada: University of Toronto Press.

Singal, D. (1987). Towards a definition of American modernism. *American Quarterly, 39*, 7–26.

Sokal, M. (1987). James McKeen Cattell and mental anthropometry: Nineteenth-century science and reform and the origins of psychological testing. In M. Sokal (Ed.), *Psychological testing and American society, 1890–1930* (pp. 21–45). New Brunswick, NJ: Rutgers University Press.

Sokal, M. M. (1992). Origins and early years of the American Psychological Association: 1890 to 1906. In R. B. Evans, V. S. Sexton, & T. C. Cadwallader (Eds.), *The American Psychological Association: A historical perspective* (pp. 43–71). Washington, DC: American Psychological Association.

Spielberger, C. D. (1992). Foreword. In R. B. Evans, V. S. Sexton, & T. C. Cadwallader (Eds.), *The American Psychological Association: A historical perspective*. (pp. xi–xiii). Washington, DC: American Psychological Association.

Terdiman, R. (1993). *Present past: Modernity and the memory crisis*. Ithaca, NY: Cornell University Press.

Trachtenberg, A. (1982). *The incorporation of America: Culture and society in the Gilded Age*. New York: Hill & Wang.

Weisberg, G. (1989). Introduction. In M. R Levin (Ed.), *When the Eiffel Tower was new: French visions of progress at the centennial of the revolution* (pp. 1–10). South Hadley, MA: Mount Holyoke College Art Museum (Amherst). (Distributed by University of Massachusetts Press)

"W. H. D." (1893). The Columbian Exposition—VII: Science. *The Nation, 57*, 186–187.

5

THE PSYCHOLOGY OF MATHEMATICAL BEAUTY IN THE 19TH CENTURY: THE GOLDEN SECTION

JOHN G. BENJAFIELD

The relation between mathematics and psychology has a long and complex history. One of the mathematical ideas that figures prominently in this history is the *golden section*, which is the proportion that obtains between two quantities when the smaller is to the larger as the larger is to the sum of the two. The golden section is an irrational proportion that has a value of approximately .618. Figure 5.1 shows a line divided in golden sections. As Howat (1983) put it,

> C is the golden section of the line AB, with the longer portion lying to the left; D is the opposite golden section of AB, with the shorter portion to the left. The special property of the golden section is that D also divides the portion AC in the golden section. The system can

Thanks are due to Prof. John Michielsen and Heidi Klose for translating Zeising's (1884) article. I am also grateful to Prof. Roger Herz-Fischler for allowing me to see part of his forthcoming book. Special thanks are due to Kurt Danziger, Ray Fancher, Chris Green, Marlene Shore, and Thomas Teo for their useful comments on a previous version of this chapter.

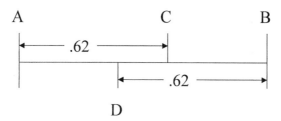

Figure 5.1. A line divided in its golden sections.

be further filled in or extended, forming a network of golden sections and symmetrical divisions—something no other ratio will do—and this is accepted as the main reason for the ratio's importance in the structure of organic forms and for its repeated appearance through many epochs of art. (p. 69).

The golden section appears in Euclid (Heath, 1956, p. 267) and has intrigued many architects, artists, mathematicians and musicians, both an-cient and modern, amateur as well as professional. Part of the reason for their admiration is the fact that one can nest golden section relations within one another, as Howat's example shows. The best-known 20th-century golden section advocate was probably Le Corbusier (1951), who intention-ally used it as an aid to design, based on the assumption that the golden section was a natural way of dividing the human body. However, the most controversial area of research concerns those cases in which there is no evidence that someone intentionally used the golden section. Rather, its use is inferred from an analysis of someone's creative products. For example, one study measuring the lengths of parts of Mozart's compositions claimed that he had used the golden section to organize his work (May, 1996).

By the time psychologists began studying the golden section in the 19th century, they were doing so against a very rich historical background. In fact, it was precisely this history that appealed to Romantics such as Adolph Zeising (1810–1876), who saw in the golden section a universal "law of proportion" (Höge, 1995, p. 134) that, among other things, gov-erned aesthetic judgment. The widespread acceptance of Zeising's claims inspired Gustav Theodor Fechner (1801–1887; see his 1876) to try to evaluate them experimentally. This chapter describes the developments that eventuated in Fechner's attempt to bring aesthetic judgment under the aegis of the emerging psychological science. We conclude that the methodology that Fechner used was surprisingly similar to more "objective" methods that became standard only much later in the history of psychology.

THE GOLDEN SECTION BEFORE THE 19TH CENTURY

One of the most attractive features of the golden section is its rela-tionship to the Fibonacci numbers, named after the 13th-century mathematician who also introduced the Arabic number system into Europe. The Fibonacci numbers begin with 0 and 1, and each subsequent number is the sum of the two preceding numbers. Thus, the series goes 0, 1, 1, 2, 3, 5, 8, 13, 21, 34, 55, 89, and so on. The relationship between the Fibonacci numbers and the golden section is as follows: As the successive numbers in the Fibonacci series increase, the ratio of any two successive numbers gets closer and closer to the golden section. Thus, $1/2 = .500$, $2/3 = .667$, $3/5 = .600$, $5/8 = .625$, $8/13 = .615$, and so on. There are two things to note about this list of approximations. First, the series rapidly generates excellent approximations to the golden section. Second, the successive approximations are alternately greater than and less than the eternally elusive value of the golden section. D'Arcy Thompson (1929) argued that the Fibonacci series was too simple and its properties too interesting for it not to have been known by ancient Greek mathematicians.

The relationship between the golden section and the Fibonacci numbers might be little more than a mathematical curiosity but for the fact that, for centuries, features of naturally occurring forms have been understood in terms of Fibonacci numbers. The example usually used to illustrate this point is spiral phyllotaxis in plants, many of which may easily be perceived as having a leaf arrangement that instantiates the Fibonacci series. Stevens (1974, p. 160) gave good examples of the fact that the number of spirals shown by pinecones, pineapples, daisies, and sunflowers are almost always members of the Fibonacci sequence.[1]

The spirals observed in plants can be fit by the curve in Figure 5.2. This curve is drawn within a so-called *golden rectangle*, the sides of which are in golden section proportion. (This particular rectangle was an object of study by 19th-century psychologists, as we shall see.) If one draws a square at one end of a golden rectangle, then the remainder is also a golden rectangle. This procedure can be repeated indefinitely, as illustrated in the figure. Drawing a curve tangent to each square yields the kind of spiral that is also traced out by the growth of many shells and horns. As Thompson (1942/1992, p. 754) pointed out, this shape "may be conceived of as growing continuously without ever changing its shape the while," which means that each part reflects, in miniature, the structure of the whole. It is this feature of the spiral that has endeared it to so many natural philosophers throughout the ages.

The golden section has consistently been experienced as what William James (1902/1958, p. 327), in his discussion of mysticism, called a

---

[1]Many important figures in the history of science have had a special place in their hearts for the golden section and Fibonacci numbers. One of the best known is Kepler (e.g., 1619/1997, p. 406), who regarded the golden section as one of the "two treasures" of geometry (Herz-Fischler, 1987/1998, pp. 173–175). Kepler (1611/1966) also theorized about Fibonacci phyllotaxis: "It is in the likeness of this self-developing series that the faculty of propagation is, in my opinion, formed; and so in a flower the authentic flag of this faculty is flown" (p. 21).

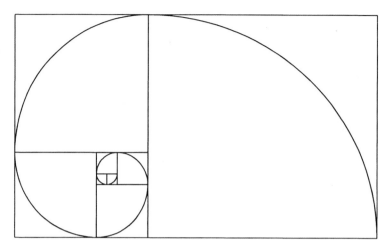

Figure 5.2. A golden rectangle containing a golden spiral.

"window through which the mind looks out upon a more extensive and inclusive world." The golden section is a simple idea, easy to understand, and has been applied to an enormous range of phenomena in both nature and culture. Indeed, to some it has appeared to explain virtually everything (e.g., Cook, 1914/1979; White, 1970/1984). As Richards (1995, p. 125) pointed out, "old mathematics never dies," and the golden section is certainly old mathematics. Those who rediscover the golden section often feel that they belong to an ancient tradition of enthusiasts that includes Pythagoras, Johannes Kepler, and Jakob Bernoulli (e.g., Huntley, 1970).

This attitude was perhaps best realized in the Renaissance. Wittkower (1960, p. 202) outlined the influence of "the Pythagorean–Platonic notion . . . that beauty resides in certain fundamental and universally valid proportions." The Renaissance was a period before mathematics was separated from aesthetics, in which mathematics still had many "extra-scientific connotations," and aesthetic phenomena were not yet regarded as "irrational phenomena of subjective sensibility" (p. 202). There were certainly those in the Renaissance who associated the golden section with ancient and divine wisdom. They pointed to passages, such as the one describing the "divided line" (*Republic*, 509 D6-8), in which Plato used terms that were often taken to refer to the golden section (Des Jardins, 1975). The Renaissance attachment for the golden section is best illustrated by Luca Pacioli's (1509) *Divina Proportione*, for which Leonardo da Vinci made drawings. In a passage typical of the kind of thinking that has often found the golden section attractive, Pacioli sang the praises of the golden section as follows:

> Just as in the divine there are three persons in the same substance: Father, Son and Holy Ghost, likewise a proportion of this kind always involves three kinds. . . . Just like God cannot be properly defined, nor

can be understood through words, likewise this proportion of ours cannot ever be designated through intelligible numbers, nor can it be expressed through any rational quantity, but always remains occult and secret, and is called irrational by the mathematicians. (cited in Herz-Fischler, 1987/1998, pp. 171–172)

Such thinking illustrates why the golden section has been used to articulate the relationship between macrocosm and microcosm. If an artist wished to represent the divine harmony, the golden section would certainly have been a possible compositional tool. Art is sometimes regarded as potentially wielding a magical influence on the spectator, and so it would be important to design one's work so as to exert the most benevolent influences on those who experienced it. In this way, the divine harmony above would be instantiated here below, and the spectator brought more closely into alignment with heavenly forces (Panofsky, 1955, p. 91). This attitude is still, in one form or another, behind many instances of the use of the golden section in 19th- and 20th-century art.

THE GOLDEN SECTION AND THE HISTORY OF MATHEMATICS

As Richards (1995) observed, although the polarity of *nature versus society* works well as an analytic tool in the history of science (e.g., Latour, 1993), it is less directly applicable to the history of mathematics. As an analog for the nature pole, she suggested "mathematical experience," which is the title of a popular treatment of this subject by Davis and Hersh (1982). We are concerned with the aesthetic aspect of mathematical experience, and Davis and Hersh observed that many mathematicians have felt that "the aesthetic rather than the logical is the dominant aspect in mathematical creativity" (p. 168). However, they went on to argue *against* the notion that there are universal principles that inform the aesthetic experience in mathematics. Rather, they regarded aesthetic judgment as something that "can be cultivated, can be passed from generation to generation, from teacher to student, from author to reader," but tends "to vary with cultures and with generations" (p. 170). Thus, for Davis and Hersh,

aesthetic judgments may be transitory and may be located within the traditions of a particular mathematical age and culture. Their validity is similar to that of a school or period of art. It was once maintained that the most beautiful rectangle has its sides in the golden ratio. Such a statement would not be taken seriously today by a generation brought up on nonclassical art and architecture, despite experiments of Fechner . . . or of Thorndike . . . which are said to bear it out. (p. 170)

Thus, Davis and Hersh saw the aesthetic aspect of mathematical experience as determined by social context and not by any general laws. In reaching this conclusion they are dismissive of evidence from psychological science, but let us turn to the possible role of psychological science in investigations of the aesthetic aspect of mathematical experience.

HERBART, ZEISING, AND THE GOLDEN SECTION

The 19th century was the golden age of the golden section. Indeed, as far as we can tell, the name "golden section" was first used in the beginning of the 19th century. The *Oxford English Dictionary* (1992) gives 1835 as the first published source, but Herz-Fischler (1987/1998, p. 168) presented evidence that the name was not made "up on the spot and that it had gained at least some, and perhaps a great deal of currency by 1835." Herz-Fischler (p. 169) also considered the possibility that the term may have been part of an oral tradition that existed "among artisans and engineers, outside the general school system."

Whereas neo-Platonism provided the context for the interest in the golden section during the Renaissance (Wittkower, 1960), it is J. F. Herbart's (1776–1841) mathematical psychology (see Boudewijnse, Murray, & Bandomir, 1999) that provided the background for the golden section revival in the 19th century. Herbart's (1891/1966) general approach to psychology rested on the assumption that all mental life is the "result of the action and interaction of elementary ideas" (Ward, 1910, p. 337). By elementary ideas, Herbart meant "entirely simple concepts or sensations— e.g., red, blue, sour, sweet, etc." (1891/1966, p. 395). He suggested that some ideas *facilitate* each other, whereas other ideas *inhibit* each other. As he saw it, consciousness tended to consist of a set of ideas that mutually facilitate each other. For Herbart it was the relations between ideas that mattered rather than the intrinsic properties of ideas themselves. As Danziger (chap. 3, this volume) observes, Herbart believed that the content of mental life was too evanescent to be a part of a scientific psychology.

Herbart's (1808/1931, 1831/1931) psychology leads naturally to the view that the relations between the various parts of an experience determine how beautiful or ugly it will be (Gilbert & Kuhn, 1953/1972, p. 515). Herbart was regarded as a founder of *formalism*, which held that aesthetics was exclusively concerned with relations. As a formalist, Herbart was careful to distinguish between the aesthetic value of a work and any associations we might have to it. The meaning of a work is irrelevant to its beauty.

> Works of art are expected to have a meaning . . . and the artists are glad to oblige. . . . But music is *music* and to be beautiful need mean nothing. . . . What did the old masters mean to *express* who developed the possible forms of the fugue, or those still older whose industry differentiated the possible orders of column? Nothing. (1831/1931, p. 156, italics in original)

Herbart (1808/1931, p. 152) argued that true aesthetic judgment was immediate and involuntary (Gilbert & Kuhn, 1953/1972, p. 513) and occurred in response to "objects of art and nature taken as wholes."

> Each element of the approved or distasteful whole is, in isolation, indifferent; in a word the material is indifferent, but the form comes under the aesthetic judgment. The simplest instances are here the best. What, for instance, in music is a third or fifth or any interval of definite musical value? Obviously neither of the single tones, whose relation composes the interval, has by itself, in the least degree, that character which attaches to it when they sound together. Consequently taste is not a faculty strictly of conferring approval or disapproval; rather those judgments which are commonly conceived under the name of taste, to distinguish them as a class from other mental manifestations, are the results of the perfect apprehension of relations formed by a complexity of elements. (p. 153)

The Herbartian program involved searching "for relations, indefinite in number, of variable elements. This procedure would be completed, if the empirical accumulation should finally yield a series of mathematically definable ratios" (Gilbert & Kuhn, 1953/1972, p. 514). As Herbart put it,

> aesthetic philosophy, as the establishment of *aesthetic principles*, would properly be bound not to define or to demonstrate or to deduce, nor even to distinguish species of art or argue about existing works, but rather to *put us in possession of all* the single relations, however many they be, which in a complete apprehension of anything produce approval or distaste. (1808/1931, p. 154, italics in original)

Thus, one could contribute to the formalist program by finding mathematically definable ratios that automatically gave rise to aesthetically pleasing experiences. At first this seems like an enormous task, but it would be simplified considerably if there were one relation that was the most beautiful of all. This is where the golden section came in, and the German philosopher Adolph Zeising was its champion.

Zeising (1854) is usually characterized as a follower of Herbart's (Gilbert & Kuhn, 1953/1972, p. 515). However, he did not simply follow Herbart's program but instead blended it with "the Romantic philosophy of nature that had been prominent one generation before. Schelling's (and Goethe's) influence can easily be detected in his conception of natural shapes as being led by ideas rather than material processes" (van der Schoot, 1998, p. 407). More than anyone else, Zeising was responsible for the creation of what has been called *golden numberism* (Herz-Fischler, 1994, p. 1580), which is the doctrine that the golden section regulates both natural phenomena and cultural products.

Zeising came to public attention with the publication in 1854 of *Neue Lehre von den Proportionen des menschlichen Körpers* [A New Theory of the

Proportions of the Human Body]. However, perhaps his most widely cited work has been *Der goldne Schnitt* [The Golden Section] (see Huntley, 1970, p. 62; van der Schoot, 1998, p. 180). It was published posthumously in 1884 under the auspices of the Leopold–Carolingian Academy, of which Zeising was a member.

Zeising (1884/1998, p. 1) realized that, although ancient mathematicians had been aware of the importance of the golden section, interest in the golden section had declined since the Renaissance. He lamented the fact that the properties of the golden section were not appreciated as much as they should be and believed that one of his tasks was to enable people to appreciate once again "the profound and extensive meaning of . . . the Golden Section in morphological as well as in aesthetic terms" (p. 4). One can see in Zeising's conception of his task an attitude similar to von Goethe's (1840/1970), who believed that "an understanding of . . . natural phenomena comes through a long process in which truth is fitfully expressed, obscured and re-expressed" (Sepper, 1990, p. 193). von Goethe had sought "the eternal laws of form" (Lenoir, 1987, p. 17), and it was Zeising's project to make people aware once again that the golden section is such a law.

In the *Neue Lehre*, Zeising argued that the golden section was a basic law of proportion that was "as important in its own way as the laws of logic" (Höge, 1995, p. 134). Indeed, for Zeising, once an observer realized how important the golden section really was, then it could be found virtually everywhere one looked. One of Zeising's (1854, p. 178) best-known analyses, which has been imitated many times since (e.g., Ghyka, 1977, p. 102), attempted to show how the human body can be divided in golden section relations, all nested within one another. For example, the forefinger can be partitioned at the knuckles into three parts. The length of each part is supposed to bear a golden section relation to its neighbor.

At the same time that Zeising's (1854) work was becoming well known, Friedrich Röber (1855) suggested that the golden section had been a regulating idea in the construction of some of the Egyptian pyramids (Fischler, 1978). Zeising regarded these "findings" as further support of the more general "law of the golden section" which he had discovered (Herz-Fischler, in press). For Zeising, an artist or architect did not need to intentionally choose to use the golden section in order for it to find its way into a work. It could occur of necessity, in the same way as the law of gravity. Thus, people were quite capable of using the golden section without knowing that they were doing so (Herz-Fischler, in press). Although Zeising certainly believed that the golden section was a morphological law, its range of application was far broader.

Zeising's (1884/1998) list of sites in which the golden section could be found included the entire formation of the human body, the construction of many exceptional animals by means of an excellent evolution, the fundamental type of many plant forms, in particular the leaf arrangements, . . . the proportions of the most world renowned beautiful architectural works and sculptures, in short, the most accomplished creations in nature and art [as they exist in both] normal and ideal relationships. (p. 5)

Zeising (pp. 29–30) rhapsodized about the golden section as a vehicle for representing "inner unity and harmony of infinity and finiteness, of universality and uniqueness, ideality and reality, . . . general and individual characteristics." Much like Pacioli, Zeising (p. 30) believed that the golden section had a "creative, extended meaning," which allowed us to understand the way in which "the individual is based on a shaping of general types into infinite different individual creations." The golden section may be found in the most basic relationships, including "the inorganic and organic, vegetative and animal, animal and human" and regulated such polarities as "severity and pleasantness, the dignified and the graceful" (p. 30). The general idea underlying Zeising's work was that the various parts of virtually any whole bear golden section relations to one another. The whole could be the human body, or it could consist of elements of human experience, like the pleasant and the unpleasant (van der Schoot, 1998, p. 407). In the case of a dichotomy, such as the pleasant and the unpleasant, a follower of Zeising would claim that pleasant experiences should constitute 62% of the whole, in order to follow the law of the golden section. Although this may sound ludicrous initially, some contemporary psychologists have taken this idea seriously. For example, in a variety of situations it has been repeatedly found that the percentage of positive judgments that people make is a good approximation to the golden section (Benjafield & Adams-Webber, 1976; Gross & Miller, 1997; Lefebvre, 1985; Ronan & Kendall, 1997; Schwartz, 1997).

Others took up Zeising's analyses with enthusiasm. By the end of the 19th century, Zeising's work had become a standard source, cited alongside that of such giants as Ernst Mach (see Winston, chap. 6, this volume) in discussions of the way in which "geometry is implicitly exhibited in nature," responsible for aesthetically pleasing forms that give "the impression of equilibrium and harmony" (e.g., Emch, 1901, p. 63). Even by the 1860s, when Fechner began his work on the golden section, it had become almost "common sense" to believe in the importance of the golden section as a regulating idea in both nature and culture.

FECHNER'S GOLDEN SECTION INVESTIGATIONS

Given his mystical predilections, it seems natural that Fechner would take on the golden section as a research problem, and his experimental work on the golden section has in fact generated a large body of research (Green, 1995). Fechner began his studies of the golden section when he was in his 60s, after his psychophysical researches. According to Boring (1950, p. 281), Fechner finally could study something of interest to him without worrying about whether or not it would advance his career. Although Fechner (1876/1997, p. 122) thought that Zeising's work "had interest and merit," he also thought that Zeising might have "overemphasized" the aesthetic importance of the golden section (Höge, 1997b, p. 235). Fechner (1876/1997, p. 122) did not reject Zeising's work, but he concluded that "the aesthetic advantage of the golden section" had not been established to the degree that "Zeising makes us believe." Fechner simply felt that Zeising's work had not settled the matter and that experimental investigations might help reduce the uncertainty that remained. Fechner's use of the experimental method was a way of subordinating aesthetic experience, a typically Romantic subject matter, to the methods of the emerging psychological science.

Of course, the use of an experimental method to investigate aesthetic experiences usually characterized by such terms as *the sublime* or *the beautiful* is not a straightforward matter. Fechner believed that such terms were too polysemous to form the basis of experimental investigations (Höge, 1997b, p. 236). He chose instead to use simple *pleasingness* as an index of "beauty." In Fechner's (1876/1997, p. 116) terms, the relevant experimental question was which formal relationship is the most pleasing relative to "other relations *regardless of purpose and meaning*" (emphasis added). In putting the question this way, Fechner was giving an experimental twist to Herbart's formalist program.

Fechner called his approach *experimental aesthetics*, and he anticipated several objections to it. His main concern was that such investigations would be seen as yielding trivial results, far removed from real-world applications. His answer to this objection has become the standard answer of experimental psychologists ever since: Experiments with simple stimuli can uncover basic laws that can later be transposed to more complicated situations, in which one could assess the contribution of such variables as level of education, age, gender, and "individuality" (Fechner, 1876/1997, p. 119). Having settled to his satisfaction the value of experimental aesthetics, Fechner (p. 120) then went on to propose appropriate methods. He distinguished among the *method of choice*, the *method of production*, and the *method of use*. Fechner used the method of choice in an experiment that has been extremely influential.

One important innovation that Fechner introduced in his aesthetic experiments was the use of several participants rather than relying on the observations of a single subject. He did this because he had

> no means of measuring the intensity of the pleasure response directly, [and so] had to substitute counting for measuring. . . . By testing a great

many observers he could use the number of votes given a particular stimulus as an indicator of the intensity of the pleasure it aroused in the human species as such and in general. (Arnheim, 1986, p. 45)

Fechner provided his participants with 10 rectangles, varying in proportion but equal in area, and asked them to choose the one that made the most pleasurable impression and the one that made the least pleasurable impression without considering the utility of the shape. Fechner's selection of participants was somewhat haphazard. They appear to have been ages 16 and older, not chosen on the basis of having good taste but of having educated backgrounds. One participant was "the blind Dr. v. Ehrenstein, a composer of music," and at least one other participant was tested more than once (Fechner, 1876/1997, p. 125). The experiment went on for several years. Fechner's method of recording the data allowed for interpretation of any doubt or uncertainty that a participant expressed, so that fractional scores could be given to different rectangles. This is a good example of the practice discussed by Danziger (1990, p. 138) whereby the investigator imposes a quantitative scale on the participant's qualitative responses. However dubious this practice may be, Figure 5.3 shows that the results were consistent with the hypothesis that the golden rectangle exhibits the most pleasing proportion.

It is difficult to know what to make of Fechner's experimental findings. They were taken sufficiently seriously that other late-19th-century and early-20th-century psychologists tried to explain them. The list of such

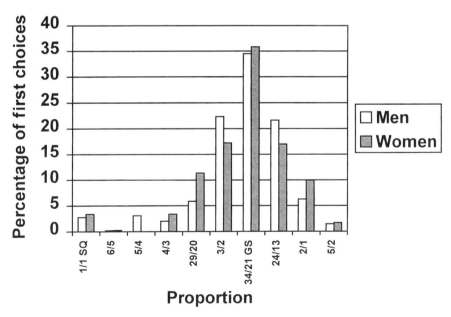

Figure 5.3. Results for men and women from Fechner's experiment with rectangles. SQ = square; GS = golden section.

contributors reads like a who's who of early experimental psychology. Külpe (1893/1895), Wundt (1897/1969), and Titchener (1899) all proposed their own explanations, each trying to make Fechner's results somehow fit in with his own viewpoint. Green (1995), in an exhaustive review of the experimental work done since Fechner, concluded that there was a thread of evidence supporting the notion that the golden section is special, but a more recent attempt to replicate Fechner's experiment as precisely as possible was a failure (Höge, 1997b). However, we are not here concerned with judging the reliability of Fechner's results, but rather to understand the ways in which Fechner himself contextualized his findings. For example, he provided comments from several of his participants, none of whom were supposed to have any knowledge of the golden section and its history. One participant, described as "a well-educated lady" who preferred the golden section, dismissed the square as having "unadventurous satisfaction" (Fechner, 1876/1997, p. 126). Another, described as "a person with very good taste," also preferred the golden section and rejected the thinnest forms as "careless" and the thickest as "common" (p. 126). Among the other comments recorded by Fechner (p. 126) were that thick forms "have no proportions" and are "hypocritical forms," that thin forms "are beautifully slim," and that the golden section was the "noblest" proportion. This latter judgment was attributed to several participants who preferred the golden section. Notice that these remarks use words that are somewhat removed from the simple meaning of pleasingness. However, Fechner did not appear to be bothered by the fact that his participants were apparently perceiving the shapes physiognomically rather than basing their judgments on a sensation of pleasantness.

Although he appeared to be somewhat surprised by the outcome of his rectangle experiment, Fechner (1876/1997, p. 126) nevertheless concluded that people of "good taste" preferred the golden section. This suggested that the uneducated and children would prefer the golden section less, and Fechner went on to report experiments with people he called "tradesmen" that bore this out. He also described an experiment with "little children" to whom he presented a square and the golden section "made out of beautifully colored paper, such as children like" (p. 126). Ever the careful experimenter, Fechner controlled for the side of the table on which each was presented and found that these children showed no preference.

The final section of Fechner's (1876/1997) report contains an account of his exploration of the method of use. Here he described several measurements that he made of common objects. The list is astonishing and is a testament to how seriously Fechner took his empirical work. He measured writing paper, note paper, sales slips, greeting cards, postcards, purses, slates, chocolates, stock cubes, gingerbread, toilet bags, snuff boxes, bricks, playing cards, children's books, scientific books, novels, window envelopes, visiting cards, address cards, picture frames, pillows, cushions, doorways, gateways, and windows. After reviewing all of these cases, Fechner appeared to argue that an object would approximate the golden section to the extent that aesthetic considerations predominated over functional ones. For example, he observed that

> squares . . . are not found in palace gates. Only barn doors are by all appearances approximately quadratic. Here the consideration of pleasantness is no longer decisive. Anyone can realize that such a form of a gate would not be tolerable in a palace. (p. 128)

Thus, preference for the golden section and aversion for the square go along with social class. This is quite a demotion for the golden section. Far from being the *divine* proportion, it had become merely the *noble* proportion.

THE ROLE OF EXPERIMENTATION IN THE STUDY OF MATHEMATICAL BEAUTY

Fechner's experiments operate at a considerable remove from the experience of mathematical beauty that captivated people such as Kepler and Zeising. Davis and Hersh (1982, p. 171) described this experience as one in which "amazement gives way to delight and delight gives way to feelings that the universe is united in a wondrous way." Davis and Hersh suggested that such experiences are borne out of a certain naivete about mathematics, and that, "with study and experience . . . aesthetic delight is possibly diminished and certainly transformed." The Davis and Hersh view, which must surely be shared by most professional mathematicians, is that the surprise and wonder that the novice experiences will eventually be replaced by the more mature, sophisticated understanding of the expert.

Professional mathematicians may resist the notion that the experiences of the amateurs studied by Fechner might be of interest. However, mathematical experience is not solely the property of professional mathematicians. There may be naïve forms of mathematical experience that can be widely shared. The experience of mathematical beauty elicited by the golden section may be one such example. Zeising was trying to reestablish the importance of the golden section as it was understood in an earlier age (Steadman, 1979, pp. 18–19) and wanted to instill in his readers the same awe and wonder that the novice can experience when introduced to the golden section. Zeising, like many others before him, was completely besotted by the golden section. His vision of mathematical beauty led him to see the golden section everywhere. He presented himself as someone who found the truth and wanted everyone to share his vision. By contrast, if Fechner's mystical tendencies (Arnheim, 1986) were aroused by the golden section, he kept them well hidden. He presented himself as someone who was taking a detached and impersonal approach to a topic that Zeising had treated in a naïve, overly enthusiastic manner. Where Zeising had pursued a Romantic science, Fechner wanted a science of the Romantic (C. Green, personal communication, September 22, 1999).

Fechner's experiments were similar in one way to the experiments of Hermann Ebbinghaus (1885/1964; Danziger, chap. 3, this volume) in that the experimental situation was made as meaningless as possible. The participants were not golden section enthusiasts like Zeising, whose attitudes would merely contaminate the experimental situation as Fechner understood it. Fechner played the role of the professional investigator whose participants were intended to be ignorant of the purpose and historical context of the investigation. As such, Fechner's study is unlike many of the early psychological experiments described by Danziger (1990, p. 91) in which both the functions of making observations and of providing data could be carried out by the same person. Indeed, as Danziger (p. 91) observed, Fechner's *psychophysical* experiments were good examples of such investigations. By contrast, Fechner's *experimental aesthetics* is a model for later forms of psychological experimentation in which the roles of investigator and participant were clearly separated (p. 93).

As we observed earlier, professional mathematicians like Davis and Hersh (1982) find experiments like Fechner's to be irrelevant to an understanding of true mathematical experience. Such experiments do not address the richness of the experience of mathematical beauty because they reduce this experience to mere pleasingness. Fechner's experimental aesthetics illustrates the process, well documented by Maraun (1998), whereby "a measurable phenomenon occupies the place previously occupied by a nonmeasurable one" (Wittgenstein, 1967, p. 77e). By counting the number of times a rectangle was judged to be the most "pleasing," Fechner put a simple measure in place of the nonmeasurable experience of mathematical beauty. As Wittgenstein (p. 77e) observed, "in science it is usual to make phenomena that allow for exact measurement into defining criteria . . .; and then one is inclined to think that now the proper meaning has been found." This is what happened with Fechner's definition, which was taken over by subsequent generations of experimenters who measured people's reactions to simple geometric figures (Arnheim, 1986, p. 45). Following Machotka (1995) and Maraun (1998), it is difficult to see how an understanding of the experience of mathematical beauty can be recovered from such studies of pleasingness. This point is similar to that made by Danziger (1990, p. 183), who observed that what was lost in the process of establishing experimental psychology as a discipline was the richness of individual experience, in this case the individual's experience of mathematical beauty.

Despite (or, perhaps, because of) its simplicity, the research program initiated by Fechner has nevertheless been perceived as successful in many quarters. Although professional psychologists are far from agreed on the proper conclusions to be drawn from Fechner's experiments and the ones he inspired (Benjafield, 1985, 2000; Green, 1995; Höge, 1997a; Machotka, 1995), there appears to be a widespread belief among amateur psychologists that the golden section is "inherently pleasing and intrinsic to the human perception of beauty" (Nolen, 1998, p. D5). Although psychologists themselves have generally paid little attention to Fechner's experimental aesthetics (Hilgard, 1987, p. 163), many scholars in other disciplines appear to believe that experimental psychologists have "discovered" that the golden section is psychologically important. One example is the work of Kemp and Rose (1991), whose research on the golden section in ancient Egypt was partly inspired by the work of experimental psychologists. As we saw earlier, it was partly 19th-century work on the golden section in ancient architecture that helped create the enthusiasm for the golden section that eventually led to Fechner's psychological experiments. It turns out that, more than a century later, the research program begun by Fechner has been credible enough to stimulate research in older, more established disciplines.

SUMMARY AND CONCLUSION

The golden section has long been used in a variety of disciplines and is often associated with the experience of mathematical beauty. In the 19th century, great claims were made for the golden section by the formalist Adolph Zeising, who was a follower of J. F. Herbart's. Zeising's "law of proportion" held that the various parts of any whole bear golden section relations to one another. Zeising's work was only crudely empirical, and Fechner attempted to evaluate Zeising's claims from the viewpoint of experimental psychology. In doing so, Fechner not only invented a new methodology for aesthetics but also incorporated aesthetic experience, a typically Romantic subject matter, into the new psychological science.

Fechner's experimental aesthetics should not simply be seen as an example of early empirical work combined with an eager attempt to quantify experience, but rather deserves to be remembered as a prototype for subsequent experimental methods in psychology. As such, it shares both their strengths and weaknesses. Although Fechner attempted to be rigorously objective, his research program can be criticized for paying insufficient attention to the richness of aesthetic experience.

Although it would be hard to argue that Fechner's experimental aesthetics were directly responsible for sending psychology as a whole in a particular direction, his work did become extremely well known in the 19th century and was the impetus for extensive psychological investigation in the late 19th and early 20th centuries (e.g., Martin, 1906). Moreover, Fechner's use of relatively naïve participants was a methodological innovation that prefigured the experimental paradigm in which the roles of investigator and participant were clearly separated. Fechner's faith in experimentation as a way of uncovering basic laws that could later be generalized to more lifelike contexts resonated with generations of experimental psychologists throughout the 20th century. Remembering Fechner's experimental aesthetics gives us the opportunity to "attach more value to our early achievements, and learn some lessons from our past" (Link, 1994, p. 340).

REFERENCES

Arnheim, R. (1986). The other Gustav Theodor Fechner. In R. Arnheim (Ed.), *New essays on the psychology of art* (pp. 39–49). Berkeley: University of California Press.

Benjafield, J. (1985). A review of recent research on the golden section. *Empirical Studies of the Arts, 3,* 117–134.

Benjafield, J. (2000). Dalzell's theorem and the analysis of proportions: A methodological note. *British Journal of Psychology, 91,* 287–291.

Benjafield, J., & Adams-Webber, J. (1976). The golden section hypothesis. *British Journal of Psychology, 67,* 11–15.

Boring, E. G. (1950). *A history of experimental psychology* (2nd ed.). New York: Appleton-Century-Crofts.

Boudewijnse, G.-J., Murray, D. J., & Bandomir, C. A. (1999). Herbart's mathematical psychology. *History of Psychology, 2,* 163–193.

Cook, T. A. (1979). *The curves of life.* New York: Dover. (Original work published 1914)

Danziger, K. (1990). *Constructing the subject.* Cambridge, England: Cambridge University Press.

Davis, P. J., & Hersh, R. (1982). *The mathematical experience.* Boston: Houghton-Mifflin.

Des Jardins, G. (1975). How to divide the divided line. *Review of Metaphysics, 29,* 483–496.

Ebbinghaus, H. (1964). *Memory: A contribution to experimental psychology.* New York: Dover. (Originally published 1885)

Emch, A. (1901). Mathematical principles of esthetic forms. *The Monist, 11,* 50–64.

Fechner, G. T. (1876). *Vorschule der Aesthetik* [Preschool of esthetics]. Leipzig, Germany: Breitkopf & Hartel.

Fechner, G. T. (1997). Various attempts to establish a basic form of beauty: Experimental aesthetics, golden section and square (M. Neumann, J. Quehl, & H. Höge, Trans.). *Empirical Studies of the Arts, 15,* 115–130. (Original work published 1876)

Fischler, R. [R. Herz-Fischler]. (1978). Théories mathématiques de la grande pyramide [Mathematical theories of the great pyramide]. *Crux Mathematicorum, 4,* 122–129.

Ghyka, M. (1977). *The geometry of art and life.* New York: Dover.

Gilbert, K. E., & Kuhn, H. (1972). *A history of esthetics.* New York: Dover. (Original work published 1953)

Green, C. D. (1995). All that glitters: A review of psychological research on the aesthetics of the golden section. *Perception, 24,* 937–968.

Gross, S. R., & Miller, N. (1997). The "golden section" and bias in perceptions of social consensus. *Personality and Social Psychology Review, 1,* 241–271.

Heath, T. L. (Ed.). (1956). *The thirteen books of Euclid's elements* (Vol. 2). New York: Dover.

Herbart, J. F. (1931). Encyclopedia of philosophy. In E. F. Carritt (Ed. & Trans.), *Philosophies of beauty* (pp. 155–158). Oxford, England: Oxford University Press. (Original work published 1831)

Herbart, J. F. (1931). Practical philosophy. In E. F. Carritt (Ed. & Trans.), *Philosophies of beauty* (pp. 151–154). Oxford, England: Oxford University Press. (Original work published 1808)

Herbart, J. F. (1966). A textbook in psychology (M. K. Smith, Trans.). In B. Rand (Ed.), *The classical psychologists* (pp. 395–415). Gloucester, MA: Peter Smith. (Original work published 1891)

Herz-Fischler, R. (1994). The golden number and division in extreme and mean ratio. In I. Grattan-Guinness (Ed.), *Companion encyclopedia of the history and philosophy of mathematics* (pp. 1576–1584). London: Routledge.

Herz-Fischler, R. (1998). *A mathematical history of the golden number.* New York: Dover. (Original work published 1987)

Herz-Fischler, R. (in press). *The shape of the great pyramid.* Waterloo, Ontario, Canada: Wilfrid Laurier University Press.

Hilgard, E. R. (1987). *Psychology in America: An historical survey.* New York: Harcourt Brace Jovanovich.

Höge, H. (1995). Fechner's experimental aesthetics and the golden section hypothesis today. *Empirical Studies of the Arts, 13,* 131–148.

Höge, H. (1997a). Fechner in context: Aesthetics from below, inner and outer psychophysics: A reply to Pavel Machotka. *Empirical Studies of the Arts, 15,* 91–97.

Höge, H. (1997b). The golden section hypothesis—Its last funeral. *Empirical Studies of the Arts, 15,* 233–255.

Howat, R. (1983). Bartok, Lendvai and the principles of proportional analysis. *Music Analysis, 2,* 69–94.

Huntley, H. E. (1970). *The divine proportion.* New York: Dover.

James, W. (1958). *The varieties of religious experience.* New York: New American Library. (Original work published 1902)

Kemp, B., & Rose, P. (1991). Proportionality in mind and space in ancient Egypt. *Cambridge Archaeological Journal, 1,* 103–129.

Kepler, J. (1966). *The six-cornered snowflake* (C. Hardie, Trans.). Oxford, England: Oxford University Press. (Original work published 1611)

Kepler, J. (1997). *The harmony of the world* (E. J. Aiton, A. M. Duncan, & J. V. Field, Trans.). Philadelphia: American Philosophical Society. (Original work published 1619)

Külpe, O. (1895). *Outline of psychology based upon the results of experimental investigation* (E. B. Titchener, Trans.) New York: Macmillan. (Original work published 1893)

Latour, B. (1993). *We have never been modern* (C. Porter, Trans.). Cambridge, MA: Harvard University Press.

Le Corbusier. (1951). *The modulor.* Cambridge, MA: Faber.

Lefebvre, V. A. (1985). The golden section and an algebraic model of ethical cognition. *Journal of Mathematical Psychology, 29,* 289–310.

Lenoir, T. (1987). The eternal laws of form: Morphotypes and the conditions of existence in Goethe's biological thought. In F. Amrine, F. J. Zucker, & H. Wheeler (Eds.), *Goethe and the sciences: A reappraisal: Vol. 97. Boston studies in the philosophy of science* (pp. 17–28). Dordrecht, The Netherlands: D. Reidel.

Link, S. (1994). Rediscovering the past: Gustav Fechner and signal detection theory. *Psychological Science, 5,* 335–340.

Machotka, P. (1995). Aesthetics: If not from below, whence? *Empirical Studies of the Arts, 13,* 105–118.

Maraun, M. D. (1998). Measurement as a normative practice: Implications of Wittgenstein's philosophy for measurement in psychology. *Theory and Psychology, 8,* 435–461.

Martin, L. J. (1906). An experimental study of Fechner's principles. *Psychological Review, 13,* 142–219.

May, M. (1996). Did Mozart use the golden section? *American Scientist, 84,* 118–119.

Nolen, S. (1998, September 29). The science of smiles: Esthetic dentistry. *The Globe and Mail,* p. D5.

Oxford English Dictionary [Compact disk]. (1992). Oxford, England: Oxford University Press.

Pacioli, L. (1509). *Divina proportione* [The divine proportion]. Venice, Italy: Paganinus de Paganinis.

Panofsky, E. (1955). *Meaning in the visual arts.* New York: Doubleday Anchor.

Richards, J. L. (1995). The history of mathematics and "L'esprit humain": A critical reappraisal. *Osiris, 10,* 122–135.

Röber, F. (1855). *Die aegyptischen Pyramiden in ihren ursprünglichen Bildungen, nebst einer Darstellung der proportionalen Verhältnisse am Parthenon zu Athen* [The Egyptian pyramids in their original formation, together with a depiction of the proportional ratios of the Parthenon at Athens]. Dresden, Germany: Franke.

Ronan, K. R., & Kendall, P. C. (1997). Self-talk in distressed youth: States-of-mind and content specificity. *Journal of Clinical Child Psychology, 26,* 330–337.

Schwartz, R. M. (1997). Consider the simple screw: Cognitive science, quality improvement, and psychotherapy. *Journal of Consulting and Clinical Psychology, 65,* 970–983.

Sepper, D. L. (1990). Goethe, colour and the science of seeing. In A. Cunningham & N. Jardine (Eds.), *Romanticism and the sciences* (pp. 189–198). Cambridge, England: Cambridge University Press.

Steadman, P. (1979). *The evolution of designs: Biological analogy in architecture and the applied arts.* New York: Cambridge University Press.

Stevens, P. S. (1974). *Patterns in nature.* Boston: Little, Brown.

Thompson, D. W. (1929). Excess and defect: Or the little more and the little less. *Mind, 38,* 43–55.

Thompson, D. W. (1992). *On growth and form.* New York: Dover. (Original work published 1942)

Titchener, E. B. (1899). *An outline of psychology* (rev. ed.). New York: Macmillan.

van der Schoot, A. (1998). *De ontstelling van Pythagoras* [The Pythagorean disposition]. Kampen, The Netherlands: Kok Agora.

von Goethe, J. W. (1970). *Theory of colors* (C. L. Eastlake, Trans.). Cambridge, MA: MIT Press. (Original work published 1840)

Ward, J. (1910). Herbart, Johann Friedrich. In *Encyclopaedia Britannica* (11th ed., Vol. 13, pp. 335–338). New York: Encyclopaedia Britannica Company.

White, W. E. (1984). Mathematical basis of wave theory. In A. J. Frost & R. R. Prechter (Eds.), *Elliott wave principle: Key to stock market profits* (pp. 177–190). Gainesville, GA: New Classics Library. (Original work published 1970)

Wittgenstein, L. (1967). *Zettel.* Berkeley: University of California Press.

Wittkower, R. (1960). The changing concept of proportion. *Daedalus, 89,* 199–215.

Wundt, W. (1969). *Outline of psychology* (C. H. Judd, Trans.). St. Clair Shores, MI: Scholarly Press. (Original work published 1897)

Zeising, A. (1854). *Neue Lehre von den Proportionen des menschlichen Körpers* [A new theory of the proportions of the human body]. Leipzig, Germany: Weigel.

Zeising, A. (1884). *Der goldne Schnitt* [The golden section]. Halle, Germany: Blockmann.

Zeising, A. (1998). *The golden section* (H. Klose & J. Michielsen, Trans.). Unpublished manuscript. (Original work published 1884)

6

CAUSE INTO FUNCTION: ERNST MACH AND THE RECONSTRUCTION OF EXPLANATION IN PSYCHOLOGY

ANDREW S. WINSTON

By the early 1930s, an extraordinary consensus began to emerge in academic psychology. E. G. Boring, E. C. Tolman, R. S. Woodworth, B. F. Skinner, and others began to describe the basic project of psychological research as the manipulation of independent variables while holding all other conditions constant and observing the effect on dependent variables. Texts and other writings began to identify the independent variables as the "causes" of behavior and to suggest that the functional relationships obtained by experimentation constituted the explanation of phenomena. This construction elevated the manipulation of independent variables to preeminent epistemological status among methods (Winston, 1988, 1990; Winston & Blais, 1996).

In previous articles I described the dissemination of these ideas through the work of R. S. Woodworth and their emergence as universal linguistic practices in psychology. The adoption of these concepts of experiment and explanation in textbooks and journals reflected the development of a crude but pervasive philosophy of science, in which the 2,400-

I thank Laurence D. Smith, Judith Winston, and the contributors to this volume for their helpful comments on earlier versions of this chapter.

year-old discussion of "causality" was settled by a simple methodological dictum. This understanding of "cause," "function," and "experiment" exerted a powerful hold on the way in which psychological questions were asked and answered and thus altered the contours of the discipline.[1]

However, the origins of this development and the history of "functional relations" as a discursive product require further explication. In a discipline whose history is as problematic and multisourced as psychology, changes in the use of terms and categories are particularly important, as Danziger (1990, 1997) has shown. Certainly this shift from cause to function is imbedded in the long history of positivisms, and its stirring is felt in Auguste Comte, John F. W. Herschel, William Whewell, John Stuart Mill, and others. The concept of a function is rooted in the work of Gottfried Leibniz and Peter Gustav Lejeune Dirichlet, a French mathematician who made clear the use of the terms *independent* and *dependent variable* in their modern mathematical sense in the 1830s (Winston, 1988). However, it is in the work of Ernst Mach (1838–1916) that the foundations for this change in psychology are most clearly seen. Starting in 1872, Mach urged the substitution of function for cause as fundamental for progress in science and fundamental for all science.[2]

"Mach exerted a great influence on psychology," said E. G. Boring (1950, p. 392), and this was indeed true for research in sensation, perception, psychophysics, and the discipline as a whole. As William James wrote to his wife after visiting Mach, "I don't think anyone ever gave me so strong an impression of pure intellectual genius" (1882, quoted in Blackmore, 1972, p. 76). So widely admired was Mach that it is sometimes difficult to identify which ideas were specifically taken from him. It is often thought that his influence was primarily exerted through the *Wiener Kreiss*, which was originally known as the Ernst Mach Society (Hanfling, 1981), although Mach's successors departed from his philosophy of science in important ways. Mach's influence on psychology was not primarily through logical positivism, given the complex relationship of that movement with psychology (see Smith, 1986), but through his direct influence on leading psychologists who read and admired his work.

The importance of Mach for the history of psychology had been recognized for some time. In his insightful analysis of "The Positivist Repudiation of Wundt," Danziger (1979) described the critical turning point when Oswald Külpe, Hermann Ebbinghaus, and E. B. Titchener all adopted a fundamentally Machian philosophy of science and showed how this phi-

---

[1]Danziger (1997) provided an excellent discussion of the interplay among linguistic practices, methods, and theory in psychology, particularly in regard to "variables" (pp. 158–180).
[2]The secondary literature on Ernst Mach is large, but the best general sources in English are Blackmore's (1972) excellent biography, as well as Blackmore's (1992) more recent edited volume and his numerous articles on Mach. Bradley's (1971) volume, *Mach's Philosophy of Science*, is helpful, as is Cohen and Seeger's (1970) volume on Mach in the Boston Studies in the Philosophy of Science.

losophy of science departed from that of Wilhelm Wundt. The influence of Mach's philosophy of science on the development of behaviorism, particularly B. F. Skinner's work, was cogently argued by Smith (1986, 1992, 1995, 1996; see also Chiesa, 1992; Marr, 1985), and the influence of Mach through Jacques Loeb was outlined by Pauly (1987).[3]

In this chapter, I focus on the substitution of function for cause. Although this principle may seem to be a relatively specific feature of Mach's work, I argue that this shift was fundamental to his conception of science, in that it represented an attempt to eliminate metaphysics from physics. Moreover, this position was taken up by leading American psychologists in defining their central task. The emergence of the language of independent and dependent variables and the elevation of experiment to psychology's supreme method was intimately tied to this aspect of Mach's philosophy of science.

The shift from cause to function meant much more than a shift in the epistemological position of leading academics. This change represents a specific embodiment of a technological model for scientific explanation (Smith, 1992). It set the stage and provided a justificatory rhetoric for psychologists to give practical recommendations to industry, the military, and society as a whole. To shift from cause to function is to alter the relationship of scientific inquiry to practical affairs.[4] I examine how the use of functions was embedded within Mach's "economical" principles of scientific activity, his views of technology, and the vision of social progress he shared with engineer Josef Popper-Lynkeus (1838–1921). The emphasis on functions meshed well with late-19th- and early-20th-century notions of social reform based on science. The traditional conception of the search for causes required a potentially endless examination of how causes produce their effects through fundamental natures, essences, and hidden mechanisms. But this search is rendered unnecessary if scientific explanation consists only of functional relations. By specifying what actions will produce change, functions thus guide and encourage the immediate, technological application of scientific knowledge for personal and social improvement.

THE DISCOURSE OF CAUSALITY

To understand what Mach accomplished with this shift, it is necessary to locate his discussions of *cause* within the 2,400-year-old discourse on

---

[3]For additional discussions of Mach's influence in psychology, see, for example, Arens (1985), Day (1998), Holton (1993), MacKenzie (1976), and Tibbetts (1975). For a discussion of the relationship between Mach's views and the development of Gestalt psychology, see Ash (1995).

[4]Analysis of this problem must be undertaken with caution: A number of "functionalisms" emerge in late-19th-century psychology. Although they bear some affinity, the substitution of function for cause is not coextensive with the general concern with the functioning of the organism and with treating the mind as adaptive or functional in the Darwinian sense.

this subject. Although the meaning of the term underwent continuous transformation, there is also a striking continuity in the discourse; issues and categories introduced by Aristotle reappear continuously.[5] Moreover, it is necessary to understand how the status and elimination of causality from science, a persistent issue for philosophers of science, was essential to Mach's program for the elimination of metaphysics.

Despite mistranslations, misunderstandings, and misuses, the Aristotelian division of "four causes" had a profound influence on Western thought (Winston, 1985). The passage in Book II, chapter 3 of *Physics* is most commonly used in discussions of Aristotle on cause:

> In one sense then, (1) that out of which a thing comes to be and which persists, is called 'cause,' e.g. the bronze of the statue, the silver of the bowl, and the genera of which the bronze and the silver are species. In another sense (2) the form or the archetype, i.e. the statement of the essence, and its genera are called 'causes' (e.g. of the octave the relation of 2:1, and generally number), and the parts in the definition. Again (3) the primary source of the change or coming to rest; e.g. the man who gave advice is a cause, the father is cause of the child, and generally what makes of what is made and what causes change of what is changed. Again (4) in the sense of end or 'that for the sake of which' a thing is done, e.g. health is the cause of walking about. . . . This then perhaps exhausts the number of ways in which the term 'cause' is used. (Aristotle, as cited in McKeon, 1947, pp. 122–123)

These few sentences define (1) material, (2) formal, (3) efficient, and (4) final cause, although these names were imposed by later writers. The analysis is more complex than this passage suggests; Aristotle classified the "mode" of causation along several dimensions (e.g., potential vs. actual) and discussed the status of chance and spontaneity as causes (*Physics*, Book II.3, II.4). Formal, efficient, and final cause often coincide, and the same thing may serve as one kind of cause in one case and as another kind of cause in a different case (see Charlton, 1970).

There exists an enormous body of scholarly debate regarding the four causes, ranging from ancient writers to St. Thomas Aquinas to contemporary philosophers (see Gotthelf, 1976; Hocutt, 1974; Sorabji, 1980). There is consensus that cause is not the best translation of the word *aitia* and that this unfortunate translation has created substantial misunderstanding (Hocutt, 1974; Vlastos, 1969). *Aitia* literally means "answer" and is connected with the idea of "blame" or "accountability" (Charlton, 1970; Randall, 1960). To say that the bronze causes the statue makes little sense to us. Aristotle was seeking explanation, particularly explanation derived by syllogistic reasoning. Sorabji (1980), Randall (1960), and others have

---

[5]The most useful general sources on causality are Bunge (1959) and Wallace (1972). For more recent discussions, see Salmon (1998) and Sosa and Tooley (1993).

noted that only efficient cause in any way resembles a cause in the contemporary sense, and even this resemblance is deceptive.[6] Thus, the four causes should not be thought of as causes in the modern sense, but must be understood as the four "reasons why" that are necessary for understanding.

In scholastic thought, Artistotle's view of causality was preserved and elaborated, and the concepts of formal and final cause were harnessed for support of Christian theology. Although many of Aristotle's original conceptions were lost or distorted, Medieval and Renaissance writers framed their explanation of natural phenomena in terms of Aristotle's four categories of cause. Even during the 1600s, Harvey's work on circulation reflected an Aristotelian framework of explanation (see Wallace, 1972, Vol. I). But it is with Harvey's contemporary, Francis Bacon, that there is a clear attempt to reconstruct the Aristotelian conception of causes. Contrary to presentist conceptions of Bacon, he continued to be "Aristotelian" in many important ways (Urbach, 1987). His use of Aristotle's four causes was not quite the same as in Aristotle, although the categories are preserved. Bacon moved toward dividing natural philosophy into "physic" (i.e., science) and "metaphysic" and thereby limiting the kinds of explanation appropriate for science. Bacon assigned the material and efficient causes to physic and the formal and final causes to metaphysic. In *The Advancement of Learning* and later in *De Dignitate et Augmentis Scientiarum* Bacon (1623/1860) argued,

> for the handling of final causes in physics has driven away and overthrown the diligent inquiry of physical causes, and made men to stay upon these specious and shadowy causes, without actively pressing the inquiry of those which are really and truly physical; to the great arrest and prejudice of science. For this I find done, not only by Plato, who ever anchors on that shore, but also by Aristotle, Galen, and others who also very frequently strike upon these shallows. For to introduce such causes as these, . . . "that the leaves of trees are for protecting the fruit from the sun and wind;" or "that the clouds are formed above for watering the earth" . . . is a proper inquiry in Metaphysic, but in Physic it is impertinent. (p. 363)
>
> For the inquisition of Final Causes is barren, and like a virgin consecrated to God produces nothing. (p. 365)[7]

These writings, often taken out of context, came to be part of the common notion that Aristotle was a barrier to scientific progress. This charge was often repeated in modern times and has even appeared in psychology (e.g.,

---

[6]Bunge (1959) argued that "as has been usual since the beginnings of modern science," the term *cause* should be restricted to mean "efficient cause" only (p. 33).

[7]I have quoted from the English translation of *De Dignitate et Augmentis Scientiarum* (Bacon, 1623/1860), which contained expanded sections of the original 1605 *Advancement of Learning*. I believe the English translation of *De Dignitate et Augmentis Scientiarum* is clearer in meaning for the modern ear than is the original passage in *The Advancement of Learning*.

Brainerd, 1979). What is important is that this is the first clear attempt to separate metaphysics from science and instead join science to practical matters under the rubric of "production of effects." Whatever the limitations of Bacon's influence and the well-known shortcomings of his methods (e.g., see Blake, Ducasse, & Madden, 1960), his program for the reform of the Aristotelian system altered the discourse on causality.

The widespread interest in Hume's (1739/1927) conception of causality must also be considered an important attempt to redefine the role of metaphysics. Hume's famous critique of "necessary connection" in cause and effect and his phenomenalistic treatment of causality as mere perception of regularity seems to foreshadow Mach's ideas in an important way. Both involve curtailment of metaphysics in science. But it is clear that Mach did not read Hume until after his own ideas on cause and function had been formed (Blackmore, 1972).

In his *Popular Scientific Lectures*, Mach (1894/1943) spoke derisively of Aristotle as unable to "learn from facts." He argued that natural science was enmeshed in Aristotelian concepts for 2,000 years, and the rise of natural science was only possible when it had thrown off the "fetters" of Aristotelian thought (pp. 348–349). However, he was not Baconian and noted the foolishness of Bacon's methods for enumerating facts through his tables of instances. As Bacon's critics argued, this method was never used by any successful scientist. Nevertheless, Mach clearly continued the project of the elimination of metaphysics, and his work shares other Baconian features (Smith, 1995). While John Stuart Mill and others came to treat cause as identified with efficient cause only, Mach went even further and removed all traces of metaphysical necessity from the relationship.

MACH INTRODUCES FUNCTION

In 1872, Mach published an account of his epistemological stance, which he had previously described in sensationalist terms as "based on a study of the physiology of the senses" (1872/1911, p. 9). In this short book, *The History and Root of the Principle of Conservation of Energy*, Mach first introduced his new conception of causality in the context of his discussion of perpetual motion and its impossibility. He described "the law of causality," quoting from an 1850 work by Fechner: "Everywhere and at all times, if the same circumstances occur again, the same consequence occurs again; if the same circumstances do not occur again, the same consequence does not" (p. 60). Mach went on to describe how it was unnecessary to introduce, as Fechner and others did, any notions of "space" and "time" into the discussion of causality, and he justified this elimination of superfluous concepts on the grounds of "economy," as he would continue to do. The law of causality was then reduced to the idea that every phenomenon is a function of other phenomena. . . . *Thus the law of causality is sufficiently characterized by saying that it is the presupposition of the mutual dependence of phenomena.* Certain idle questions, for example, whether the cause precedes or is simultaneous with the effect, then vanish by themselves. (p. 61, emphasis in original)

Mach noted that "for the investigator of nature there is nothing else to find out but the dependence of phenomena on one another" (p. 63). Thus functional relations, to be expressed mathematically, now constitute the only form of scientific explanation. The introduction of any other explanatory entity, such as "force," which was not tied to phenomena experienced as sensations, would be unacceptably metaphysical. Much later, philosopher Hugo Dingler noted the relationship between metaphysics and causality and wrote to Mach in 1913,

for if there is no immanent causality of things, then the last justification for every kind of metaphysical and externally unexplainable powers, which are irresponsible and make things inconceivable in principle, falls. In other words, the last refuge of metaphysics collapses. (1992, p. 104)

For Mach, the importance of functions was embedded within his emphasis on sensations and his general position of "epistemological phenomenalism" (Blackmore, 1972), in which only sensations are "real." Mach's emphasis on sensations shared some features of the epistemology of Bishop Berkeley, as Mach recognized. By sticking to a purely descriptive concept of functional relations in mathematical form, the equations would express only the relationship between sensations and would introduce no more complex elements than necessary.

Fechner's (1860/1966) *Elements of Psychophysics* provided an early model for the descriptive use of mathematical functions in the context of psychological phenomena. Mach attributed his interest in functional explanations to both Fechner and Herbart, and his personal contact with Fechner was particularly important to him. But Mach knew that Fechner's ontology differed from his and that Fechner's aims were not quite toward the elimination of the metaphysical. Nor is it clear that Fechner meant his law to be "causal" or to substitute for cause in the way that Mach intended. The *Naturphilosophie* in some of Fechner's work would also have been problematic for Mach. Although Mach came to criticize Fechner's psychophysics and his dual aspect psychophysical parallelism, he never doubted the value of psychophysics and the importance of psychology for physics.

Mach was hardly the first to develop a program for the removal of metaphysics from science.[8] Nor was he the last, given that Henri Poincaré

---

[8]See Tolman, chapter 9, this volume, for an additional discussion of the relationship between metaphysics and science, particularly scientific psychology.

and Karl Pearson, who was heavily influenced by Mach, were both concerned with expunging metaphysical entities. It might be thought that Mach was merely following the Comtean lead. That is, Mach's position seems to be entirely consistent with Comte's "positive stage," in which the search for abstract entities would be given up in favor of the search for "invariable relations of succession and resemblance" (Wallace, 1972, Vol. 2, p. 88). Mach himself noted the affinity of his aims with those of Comte. But there are important differences in the role that each assigned to psychology, and Comte's emphasis on the social aspects of mind has no clear counterpart in Mach (see Thompson, 1975). Beyond that, it is difficult to imagine that Mach could support the grand vision of Comte or his three stages as a natural law. Both Mach and Comte may be considered "positivists" in the general sense, although Mach steadfastly denied that he was a positivist.

Mach repeated and elaborated his statement on causality in most of his subsequent books, including the one that B. F. Skinner drew on, the 1883 *Science of Mechanics* (Smith, 1986). In the preface, Mach stated that part of his aim was to get rid of "metaphysical obscurities," by which he meant both removing superfluous concepts and placing the concepts of mechanics in historical context, as he had done earlier with the conservation of energy. For Mach, these two aspects were tied, in that demonstrating the historically contingent nature of scientific concepts would assist in the elimination of metaphysics.

In his famous *The Analysis of Sensations and the Relation of the Physical to the Psychical*, first published in 1886 and translated into English in 1893, Mach discussed the problem of causality in detail. The title of the first chapter tells all: "Introductory Remarks: 'Antimetaphysical.'" He repeated the theme that "all that is valuable to us is the discovery of *functional relations*, and that what we want to know is merely the dependence of experiences on one another" (p. 35, emphasis in original). These functional relations are descriptive and do not imply any inner powers or essences. In chapter 5, he addressed the Aristotelian tendency to attribute biological phenomena to final causes and commented favorably on the work of Jacques Loeb, whose studies of tropisms represented for Mach a proper causal analysis of a biological phenomenon.[9] That Mach would bring up the issue of final cause illustrates how the Aristotelian categories remained an important issue, even for a physicist. He sensed that evolution provided a solution to the problem of teleology, although he did not elaborate on this insight. His discussion of causality and teleology argued for a symbiotic, mutually beneficial relationship between biology and physics.

Mach (1905/1976) discussed the issue of cause and function again in

---

[9]Mach viewed his own position as "antimechanistic" and would have rejected some of the purely mechanistic features in Loeb's work.

Knowledge and Error and also did so several times in his *Popular Scientific Lectures* (1894/1943) given to general and nonprofessional audiences from the 1870s on.

> We call cause an event to which another (the effect) is constantly tied. . . . In the more highly developed natural sciences the concepts of cause and effect are constantly becoming rarer and more restricted in their use. . . . As soon as we can characterise the elements of events by means of measurable quantities . . . the mutual dependence of elements is much more completely and precisely represented by the concept of a function than by those of cause and effect. (1905/1976, p. 205)

In *Knowledge and Error*, Mach also began to emphasize the role of experiment more explicitly than in previous works:

> Experiment can be described as the autonomous search for new reactions or their interconnections. (p. 148)
> By arbitrarily varying a certain group of elements or a single one, other elements will vary too or perhaps remain unchanged. The basic method of experiment is the method of variation. (p. 149)
>
> Positive examination is made much easier if we first eliminate everything that has no influence on the elements whose dependence on others are to be tested, and thus restrict the relevant area. . . . Great experiments have always simplified their arrangements in such a way that only the factor in question remained in evidence while all other influences become negligible. (p. 151)

Although Mach did not explicitly connect the search for functions with this concept of experiment, it was clear to his readership that the mathematical use of "function" implied statements of the form $y = f(x)$, which in turn implied the concepts of independent and dependent variables.[10]

In emphasizing the role of experiment in the discovery of functional relations, Mach's ideas were part of and helped create a changing discourse on the division of "observation" and "experiment." The word *experiment* is derived from the Latin *experiri*, which means simply to try or test. In pre-Renaissance use, the meaning of experiment was not clearly separate from that of experience. Subsequently, the word was used in diverse ways to describe a variety of procedures, such as diagnosis or dissection (Hacking, 1975). Bacon, whom Hacking (1983) dubbed the "first philosopher of experimental science" (p. 246), outlined numerous varieties and subvarieties of experimentation, although many of his instances would not count as experiments by the standards of contemporary psychologists. The modern distinction between experimentation and observation can be found most clearly in John Frederick William Herschel's (1830/1987) widely read work,

---

[10]For an additional discussion of the mathematical aspects of Mach's use of function, see Menger (1970).

A *Preliminary Discourse on the Study of Natural Philosophy*, in which he contrasted "noticing facts as they occur" with "putting in action causes and agents over which we have control, and purposely varying their combinations" (p. 76). John Stuart Mill (1843/1974) repeated this distinction but, like Herschel, hedged on whether experiment and observation differ in degree rather than kind. Nevertheless, Mill was clear that only with "active" experimentation (i.e., manipulation) could the causes of a phenomenon be determined.[11]

William Stanley Jevons (1874/1958) also sought to clarify the relationships among observation, experiment, and cause:

> When we merely note and record the phenomena which occur around us in the ordinary course of nature we are said *to observe*. When we change the course of nature by the intervention of our muscular powers, and thus produce unusual combinations and conditions of phenomena we are said *to experiment*. . . . Experiment is thus observation *plus* alteration of conditions. (p. 400)
>
> One of the most requisite precautions in experimentation is to vary only one circumstance at a time, and to maintain all other circumstances rigidly unchanged. (p. 422)
>
> Almost every series of quantitative experiments is directed to obtain the relation between the different values of one quantity which is varied at will, and another quantity which is thereby caused to vary. We may conveniently distinguish these as respectively the *variable* and the *variant*. (p. 440, emphasis in original)

Jevons's "variable" and "variant" are clearly equivalent to the later use of independent and dependent variables, and the general position is consistent with but not derived from Mach. Although Mach was probably not influenced by Jevons, he respected Jevons's philosophy of science and recommended his work to his students. Clearly there was a general trend from the 1870s on to identify the program of all science as the manipulation of variables.

Mach's view that functional relations were the only kind of scientific explanation was fully consistent with the views of philosopher Richard Avenarius. In *The Analysis of Sensations*, Mach described their agreement in detail. But Avenarius was much more difficult to understand than Mach, and although he was certainly influential among early German psychologists, the Avenarius version of causality and functional relations was probably not influential for North American psychology.[12] Moreover, Mach as

---

[11]Wundt (1902) also distinguished between *observation* and *experiment*, but the meaning of these terms in relation to causality was quite different than for Mill and Mach. For a general discussion of scientific method in Galileo, Bacon, Newton, Herschel, Mill, and others, see Blake et al. (1960).

[12]I have been unable to identify any English translations of Avenarius. Although American psychologists of the turn of the century usually read German, lack of translations would certainly have restricted his impact.

a physicist was a much more appealing authority for those psychologists eager to ally themselves with natural science and to distance themselves from the problems of idealism and philosophy in general.

The frequency with which Mach took up the issue of "cause into function" indicates that this theme was not some minor aspect of Mach's work, whose importance is now exaggerated by our presentist eyes. The issue was central to his philosophy of science, and it was to Mach that so many turned for a philosophy of science. Ironically, Mach denied that he was a philosopher or that his analysis of science was philosophical.

MACH'S PERVASIVE INFLUENCE

Mach's *Analysis of Sensations* was widely admired in late-19th- and early-20th-century academic circles and went through seven editions. Boring (1950) described it as Mach's most influential work. Karl Pearson greatly admired the book, and Mach's influence can be readily discerned in Pearson's highly influential *The Grammar of Science*. Pearson (1892/1937) reproduced the famous "self-inspection of the ego" drawing from *Analysis of Sensations* and the entire discussion is suffused with Mach's ideas: "sensations as the ultimate source of the materials of knowledge" (p. 60). Like Mach, Pearson rejected such concepts as "force" when used as a cause, describing *force* as "unknown and possibly unknowable" (p. 103). *Causes* were defined as "the successive stages of a routine of experience" (p. 113). His discussion drew at times on ideas of Hume and Mill, but his conception was fully consistent with Mach's emphasis on description as explanation. "First Causes" and other metaphysical concepts were clearly outside of science. Scientific laws were to be seen as a "brief statement or formula," which summarizes "the relationship between a group of facts" (p. 72). The differences in Pearson's treatment of science from that of Mach, including his more severe "scientism" are beyond the scope of this chapter. It is important to note that Pearson's position did not involve an emphasis on manipulation of variables, which became a critical feature of 20th-century psychology. Nevertheless, the consistent themes in Mach and Pearson illustrate the general importance of a shifting conception of causality. For the Galton–Pearson study of individual differences, legitimate scientific explanation could be obtained through the reduction of such difference to variables and the discovery of their correlations (see Danziger, 1997; Dzinas & Danziger, 1997). In Pearson's view, correlation could replace the problematic conception of causality.[13]

Mach's conception of science also greatly influenced E. B. Titchener. In his introductory textbook, Titchener (1911) noted that he would have

---

[13]I am indebted to Ray Fancher for alerting me to this aspect of Pearson's thought.

reproduced Mach's drawing of the self-inspection of the ego but by omitting it, he hoped "to extend the circle of Mach's readers" (p. 547). Titchener (1922) even took the trouble to publish a summary of Mach's 1863 lectures on psychophysics, which were unavailable in English, in the *American Journal of Psychology*. In his description of the lectures, Titchener characterized Mach's view as allowing that psychology could become an exact science in the same way as physics. According to Titchener, Mach quoted Quetelet on the idea that experiments "yielded varied outcomes because of chance" but that chance is subject to law, and the "intellectual elements of our social life, the psychological processes, are no less uniform than the rest" (p. 214). Thus, Mach could be used as an important authority on the legitimacy of psychology as a science. Beyond Titchener's general admiration, it is clear from Danziger's (1979) analysis that Titchener's philosophy of science was fully allied with that of Mach and in conflict with Wundt's position.

Titchener was also influenced by Avenarius and used his distinction between "independent" physical experiences occurring in the nervous system and "dependent" psychological experiences."[14] This use of *independent* and *dependent* is clearly not the same use as the *independent* and *dependent* *variables* (*x* and *y*) of a mathematical function, in which the terms are interchangeable. However, Boring (1950) suggested that the Avenarius formulation was important for Titchener's general use of the term *dependent* to apply to experience that "depended" on the experiencing individual. In this sense it is a rather easy, if misleading, linguistic leap to speak of psychological events as dependent variables. Moreover, it was in the context of his presentation of Titchener's project, *The Physical Dimensions of Consciousness*, that Boring (1933) introduced the first clear statement of the modern definition of *experiment*:

> The experimental method, upon which all science rests, is, logically considered, a method of the induction of a generalized correlation by means of controlled concomitant variations. In the simplest experiment there are always at least two terms, an independent variable and a dependent variable. The experimenter varies *a* and notes how *b* changes, or he removes *a* and sees if *b* disappears. He repeats until he is satisfied that he has the generalization that *b* depends upon *a*. The independent variable, *a*, can now properly be spoken of as a *cause* of the dependent variable, *b*. An observed correlation of this sort is causal in Hume's sense of *cause* . . . at a very simple level we may establish by experiment functional dependencies of the form $y = f(x)$, which states the law whereby *y* changes when *x* is varied. (pp. 8–9, emphasis in original)

Thus Boring, Titchener's devoted student, promoted the Machian concep-

---

[14] This characterization of Avenarius is based on Boring (1950) and should be interpreted with caution.

tion of function and cause. One year later, Woodworth (1934) introduced the same formulation in his introductory textbook and developed it further in his 1938 *Experimental Psychology* (see Winston, 1988, 1990).[15]

Danziger (1979) showed how Mach's philosophy of science and his use of function for explanation was distinct from Wundt's voluntarism and his concept of "psychic causality." Titchener and Boring took up the Machian position rather than Wundtian position, and this choice was related to the well-known distortions in the historiography of Wundt. For Danziger, this critical disjuncture separated Wundt and Dilthey,[16] who maintained that *Geisteswissenschaft* was essentially a different kind of inquiry than *Naturwissenschaft*, from Ebbinghaus, Külpe, and Titchener who made no such distinction, at least for psychology. Identifying functional relations as *the* exclusive form of explanation is a critical aspect of this split. The future direction of psychology was best summarized by Ebbinghaus (1885/ 1913) in the opening remarks of his book on memory, in which he defined *scientific method*:

> This method, indeed, has been so exclusively used and so fully worked out by the natural sciences that, as a rule, it is defined as something peculiar to them, as *the* method of natural science . . . its logical nature makes it generally applicable to all spheres of existence and phenomena. . . . We all know of what this method consists: an attempt is made to keep constant the mass of conditions which have proven themselves causally connected with a certain result; one of these conditions is isolated from the rest and varied in a way that can be numerically described; then the accompanying change on the side of the effect is ascertained by measurement or computation. (p. 7, emphasis in original)

Although Mach's philosophy of science achieved broad support, his reliance on sensations as the basic reality did not please everyone, and it was possible to accept his emphasis on functions without commitment to his epistemological phenomenalism. For example, Vladmir Ilyich Lenin found the growing influence of Mach's views among Russian intelligentsia to be a threat to proper understanding of the world (see Kern, 1983). In his *Materialism and Empirio-Criticism*, Lenin (1908/1927) argued that the Mach–Avenarius position on knowledge was a dangerous "solipsism."[17] Not all psychologists were approving of Mach's sensationistic position. Carl

---

[15]So pervasive is this way of speaking that it is difficult for psychologists to imagine any other. Experiments in particle physics typically do not look for the way in which the manipulated variable functions as a cause (see Franklin, 1990, for examples). That is, the experimental arrangements are for testing a precise theoretical prediction about the behavior of the particles, and the manipulation is secondary to these aims. For additional discussions of experiment, see Franklin (1986) and Gooding, Pinch, and Schaffer (1989).

[16]See Teo, chapter 10, this volume, for a discussion of Dilthey's ideas.

[17]An irony regarding positivism and Marxism is that in contemporary discussion, positivists are often associated with epistemological realism and Marxists with relativism, when at the time of Mach and Lenin, Mach was considered the relativist, and Lenin argued for a kind of realism.

Stumpf and Theodor Lipps were early critics, and Stumpf argued that Mach's sensationistic monism "dissolves into nothing." Oswald Külpe also attacked Mach, but not until 1902; up to that time he was clearly in agreement with Mach on systematic issues. Külpe considered the Würzburg research on imageless thought to provide a clear refutation of the primacy of sensations. But these disagreements do not mean that Külpe and Mach disagreed on the fundamental nature of science, and these criticisms did not diminish Mach's general influence as a philosopher of science.

SCIENCE, ECONOMY, AND SOCIAL IMPROVEMENT

The importance that Mach attached to functional as opposed to causal explanation was not only embedded in his emphasis on sensations but also was tied to his notions of "economy" in science. Mach's outlook was Darwinian but not Spencerian. Human beings had overriding biological needs and had to economize their efforts to survive and prosper. Scientific research for mere pleasure or curiosity could not be afforded. Instead, the most abstract understanding of the world, expressed as mathematical functions, would provide the most economy of effort. Mach's position went far beyond any simple notion of parsimony. Good scientific activity required economy of thought in order to make use of the knowledge gathered by other scientists; economy of energy expenditure, work, and time; economical methods of inquiry; use of mathematical formulae for an economical description of phenomena; the use of abbreviation, schematization, and abstraction for greater economy of thought and effort; and the removal of unnecessary distinctions, such as "appearance" and "reality" (see Blackmore, 1972, pp. 173–174). According to Bradley (1971), Mach's economic standpoint required that the fewest number of laws and "judgments" be used in scientific accounts. Like Mach's view of functional relations, his analysis of economy was introduced in his 1872 *History and Root of the Principle of the Conservation of Energy* and elaborated in all of his other major works.

To make science a search for functions rather than causes is central to the economical aspects of science that were so important to Mach. The use of functions for explanation would, in this view, eliminate wasteful inquiry into hidden powers and essences. Having found the correct equation, whether it is Weber's law, Fechner's law, or S. S. Stevens's power function in psychophysics, we do not need to inquire why the world is this way, for that is a question of metaphysics. We can move to the next scientific problem and the next solution to help us survive as biological beings, and "orient" ourselves, to use Mach's term.

The issue of cause and function would be only a matter of philosophy and scientific practice were it not that this view is part of a much broader question. Seen in context of the theory of scientific economy, the substitution of function for cause implies an enhanced relationship between science and technology. Mach hoped to bring about a different relationship between scientific knowledge and practical affairs. Most of Mach's scientific work had clear practical implications or was directly practical. His photographic studies of ballistics and shock waves were of enough value to attract the support of the Austrian Navy and the assistance of Krupp in providing a cannon range. This work led eventually to the eponymous Mach number, not formally given until 1928, and to a technical device for measuring shock waves, the Mach–Zehnder Interferometer (see Cohen & Seeger, 1970). For Mach, the way in which such work was described, that is, in terms of functions, encourages and facilitates a scientific strategy that is eminently practical. Finding ways to produce effects without concern over their metaphysical status is a means of "getting on with it" so that effects can be put to use, thereby fulfilling Mach's requirement of economy of effort.

Moreover, if manipulation of variables via experiment is required to determine functional relationships, as Mach emphasized in *Knowledge and Error* (see above), then the Machian approach clearly overlaps with the Baconian, interventionist model of science that Smith (1992) aptly termed the "technological ideal," in contrast to a purely theoretical approach to science. Mach's emphasis on abstract representations through mathematical formula may appear to be a defense of purely theoretical science, but it is not. Mach believed that abstract, mathematical formulae would be the most economical and useful means of representing knowledge. He elaborated on the utility of science by describing how its results served the general process of evolution in his 1883 address as newly installed rector of the University of Prague (Mach 1894/1943). Mach did not propose that science would produce a Baconian "New Atlantis," and he did not offer a sweeping vision of a society transformed by science. Nevertheless, he rejected the distinction between science and technology and argued for a new role of technical education.

In the 1880s, Mach became part of the *Gymnasium* reform movement in Germany. Mach and others hoped the traditional *Gymnasium* emphasis on Greek and Latin could be shifted toward a more practical and science-oriented approach. This movement, led by Friedrich Paulsen, argued for a greater role for the more technically oriented secondary schools, the *Realgymnasium* and the *Realschule*. Graduates of these schools should have equal rights of entry into the universities, Mach argued.[18] In general, Mach's view of education was consistent with his view that all human activity should satisfy biological needs in the most economical way possible.

---

[18]See McClelland (1980) and Ringer (1969) for discussion of the relationship between the secondary schools and the German universities.

He opposed the regimentation of the *Gymnasium* and its supremacy.[19] His philosophy of education was informed by his view of the technical, biological value of science, although he did not oppose the teaching of classical subjects. Mach was deeply concerned with education throughout his career and wrote textbooks that were widely used in secondary schools. He viewed his own teaching as an example of the principle of economy through the reduction of phenomena to functional relations (e.g., see Mach, 1872/1911, p. 88).

Mach's close friendship with the engineer Josef Popper-Lynkeus was instrumental in the development of his educational philosophy as well as his broader social philosophy. This friendship began in Vienna in 1862, where Mach was *Privatdozent* after receiving his degree and before obtaining a position at Graz. The two men immediately took to each other. Popper, who used the pseudonym Lynkeus, helmsman of Jason's ship *Argonaut*, was from a poor Jewish family in Bohemia. He attended religious school, then a technical school in Prague, and then went to the Imperial *Polytechnikum* in Vienna. His brilliance was recognized by his teachers, who proposed him for an assistant professorship at the *Polytechnikum* when he was 18. He was denied the position because of his Jewish background, in accord with the existing regulations in 1856 (Wachtel, 1955, p. 3). He worked at menial jobs, attended classes in physics at the university, and achieved some, financial stability through his clever and highly useful inventions. Popper-Lynkeus also wrote extensively on social issues. By the 1870s, he proposed a plan for a guaranteed annual wage and government labor service for the unemployed (see Wachtel, 1955). In addition, Popper-Lynkeus wrote on physics, mathematics, aeronautics, machine technology, Voltaire, anti-Semitism, Tolstoy, Goethe, human rights, and individualism.[20] According to Blackmore (1972), Popper-Lynkeus extended Mach's interest in social reform, Voltaire, and the Enlightenment.

However, Popper-Lynkeus did not view the goals of technology only in terms of Mach's "economic" principles. In his biography of Jacques Loeb, Pauly (1987) summarized Popper-Lynkeus's view:

> He did not consider material improvement to be the major significance of technology. For him, technology expressed a fundamental element of the human spirit, and could be justified on the same grounds as fine art: its ability to stimulate "aesthetic sensations." The inventor, he said, was motivated by artistic fervor, and the greatest products of technology, such as undersea telegraph cables and recent developments in aeronautics were important not for the utility but for purely "aesthetic reasons." Popper-Lynkeus himself devoted much of his time in the

---

[19]Mach had unpleasant experiences in his *Gymnasium* education and in general did not do well in this environment.
[20]Popper-Lynkeus is also known for his theory of dreams, which Freud (1942) later noted was a remarkable precursor to his own.

1880s and 1890s to possibilities of lighter-than-air flight, although he saw little utility in such work; the development of aeronautics was a "definite form of Idealism," and as such justified itself. (p. 44)

Although Popper-Lynkeus was more idealistic in this regard than Mach, they shared the "engineering impulse" of the 19th century. But they did not apply this formula to social engineering via increased social regulation. Mach had a love of freedom and a fear of the state that prevented him from supporting such visions of social reform. He ridiculed the idea that the state or the group was more important than the individual, and he opposed authoritarian regimes and the use of force in any form. Popper-Lynkeus (1910/1995) went further in his forceful tract, *The Individual and the Value of Human Life*. He opposed utilitarianism and argued that the murder of one individual could never be justified for the general good, the benefit of the state, progress, or any reason. Mach and Popper-Lynkeus could not and did not support other approaches to science and society that emerged at the turn of the century, such as Ernst Haeckel's romanticized Monist League and the application of science for the good of the social organism (see Gasman, 1971; Weindling, 1989). Although Mach's philosophy of science emphasized experimental control and the determination of variables that produced change, his social philosophy allowed innovation but did not argue for the scientific control of humanity.

The technological model for science with its emphasis on functional relations was bound to be of great appeal in the period of industrial development during which Mach enjoyed his greatest influence. Although the last quarter of the 19th century was characterized by economic slowing during the depression of 1873–1895, the period after 1905 saw the further concentration of industrial might into huge cartels with enormous power. In a number of countries, particularly England, this second industrial revolution led to concerns over national efficiency. Weiss (1987) argued that these concerns with the ability to compete against the industries of other nations were also an important issue in Germany. As Danziger (1997) noted, concern over industrial efficiency was intertwined with concern over efficiency in education, viewed as essential for maximizing economic output.

Mach's notions of economy and the antimetaphysical search for functional relations could readily be conceived as supporting the search for greater industrial and educational efficiency. The analysis of functional relations was fully consistent with the growing importance of Taylor's (1911/1967) scientific management, which explicitly emphasized the variables that determined efficiency. The work of Ernst Meumann and others on "experimental pedagogy" invoked Machian concepts of economy in learning (Danziger, chap. 3, this volume). By the early 1900s, educational researchers in Germany, England, and the United States took up the search for the most effective educational techniques through experimental manipulation of classroom conditions.

Although he was neither a pragmatist in the sense of Charles S. Peirce nor a progressive in the sense of John Dewey, Mach's view of functional relations, science, and technology fit well with the climate of American pragmatism and progressivism of the early 20th century. Given the belief of many American progressives in the value of science for transforming society, it is tempting to assume that Mach's technological views played an important role in the development of social science at the University of Chicago and elsewhere.[21] However, such an assumption is unwarranted, and the complex interrelationship of pragmatism, progressivism, the social gospel, Christianity, and the use of science for social reform is beyond the scope of this chapter (see Kloppenberg, 1986; Noble, 1958). In the early 20th century, there were many versions of how science might bring about social change, and not all were focused on experimental intervention (see Shore, 1987). Nevertheless, in the recently industrialized culture of the United States, where Hugo Münsterberg's (1913) *Psychology and Industrial Efficiency* was a best-seller, metaphysical speculation could be seen as a barrier to social and economic progress. In contrast, Mach's marriage of science and technology would provide the most economic strategy in every sense. Unlike the *Geisteswissenschaft*, which provided only *Verstehen*, the discovery of functions allowed specification of the sources of change and could therefore justify interventions to produce more efficient workers and a stable social order.

In the United States, Mach's substitution of function for cause was promoted most clearly by biologist Jacques Loeb, who wrote worshipfully to Mach that "Your ideas are scientifically and ethically the basis upon which I stand and upon which I think the natural scientist has to stand" (quoted in Blackmore, 1972, p. 130). On the role of functions in explanation, Loeb (1912/1964) could not have been more Machian when he declared that "All 'explanation' consists solely in the presentation of a phenomenon as an unequivocal function of the variables by which it is determined" (p. 26). Loeb's emphasis on functional relations was essential to his view of biology and his preference for experimentation over naturalistic observation (Pauly, 1981). As carefully detailed by Pauly (1987) and Smith (1986, 1995), Loeb had an important influence on American psychology through both J. B. Watson and B. F. Skinner. Mach was not a behaviorist, but his philosophy of science was adaptable as a discursive resource for supporting behaviorism. Seen in Machian terms, behavior requires no further explanation than identification of the variables that produce it.

---

[21]Some sociologists, particularly Franklin Giddings at Columbia and William Thomas at Chicago, were influenced by the work of Mach and Loeb, according to Ross (1991).

Watson was greatly influenced by his work with Loeb at the University of Chicago (see Buckley, 1989; Watson, 1936). He elevated the notion of control to a premier value in psychology, and Pauly (1987) argued that the Watsonian promise of a technology of behavior through manipulation and control lies clearly in the Mach–Loeb tradition. Moreover, Watson argued against introspection by drawing on the notion that the behaviorist "shuts his eyes" to metaphysical problems (Watson, 1920). Not particularly sophisticated in philosophy,[22] Watson used a Machian conception of natural science, but without the mathematics, to justify laying aside the philosophical issues that tied the nascent discipline of psychology to its roots.

The use of Mach's approach to functional relations is more clearly represented in the work of B. F. Skinner. Like Watson, Skinner was influenced by Loeb. He read Loeb's work as an undergraduate and in graduate school worked under Loeb's follower, physiologist William Crozier. Skinner read and admired Mach's work and the influence was profound, according to Day (1998). In an interview with Holton (1993), Skinner reported that "I was totally influenced by Mach via George Sarton's course, and quickly bought Mach's books, *Science of Mechanics* and *Knowledge and Error*" (pp. 15–16). By the 1930s, Skinner had developed a philosophy of science that was entirely Machian.[23] Smith (1986, 1995) analyzed in detail how Skinner's elimination of mentalistic constructs, his disavowal of theories, his analyses of language and history, and his emphasis on adaptation were all Machian in outlook (see also Marr, 1985).

The affinity of Skinner's philosophy to that of Mach is particularly clear on the issue of causality and functions. In *Science and Human Behavior*, Skinner (1953) wrote,

> the terms "cause" and "effect" are no longer widely used in science. . . . The terms which replace them, however, refer to the same factual core. A "cause" becomes a "change in an independent variable" and an "effect" a "change in a dependent variable." The new terms do not suggest *how* a cause causes its effect: they merely assert that different events tend to occur together in a certain order. (p. 23, emphasis in original)
>
> The external variables of which behavior is a function provide for what may be called a causal or functional analysis. (p. 35, emphasis in original)

This aspect of Skinner's philosophy has remained a critical feature of all experimental behavior analysis research. However, one important feature of Mach's philosophy of science was missing from Skinner's work after 1931. Although his early research involved some mathematical represen-

---

[22] Watson (1936) wrote in his autobiography, "God knows I took enough philosophy to know something about it. But it wouldn't take hold" (p. 274). This quote may also be interpreted as evidence of Watson's disdain for philosophy rather than a lack of sophistication.

[23] Smith (1996) argued that Skinner's philosophy was also substantially Baconian, especially in regard to social improvement.

tations (Coleman, 1987), Skinner subsequently did not require that the functional relations be expressed in mathematical form.

CONCLUSION

Mach's shift of the scientific enterprise from the examination of causes to the use of functional relations represented a critical moment in the long history of causality as a linguistic and cultural artifact. Early-20th-century psychologists could now use the writings of a noted physicist to distance themselves from troublesome questions about the nature of human beings and how they should be investigated. Such questions could be put aside as metaphysical problems. A methodological emphasis on the manipulation of independent variables flowed naturally from this shift, and the adoption of this position undergirded a methodological hegemony of experimentation that lasted through most of the century (see MacMartin & Winston, 2000).

Although Skinner's work may represent the purest form of Machian philosophy of science in American psychology, Mach's influence on the formation of scientific psychology was certainly more general by the 1930s. For E. C. Tolman and others, functions and variables were united with the emerging concept of operationism for the analysis of behavior (see Green, 1992). With the support of powerful psychologists like Tolman, Titchener, Boring, and Woodworth, the Machian language of functional relationships could be used in textbooks and in the discussion of experimental findings to shape psychologists' view of explanation. A Machian philosophy of science encouraged the vision of psychology as a technological and practical enterprise.[24]

However, Mach's philosophy of science was not tied to a scientistic philosophy of personal and social improvement. Although psychologists of later decades may have enlisted Mach's philosophy of science in the service of controlling behavior, this was not the vision of Mach or of Popper-Lynkeus. Instead, they balanced their engineering ideal of science against what Blackmore called Mach's "half-individualism" and "half-socialism" in their political philosophy. Mach's substitution of function for cause may have resonated with notions of social control, but his concern was with simple concepts of justice, redistribution of wealth, adult education, and reducing excessive state and ecclesiastic power. It is unlikely that he would have supported the invocation of his philosophy of science for the social science interventions of the mid-20th century or the extension of experimentation by psychologists to nearly all aspects of human life.

---

[24]See Mills (1998) for a useful discussion of the relationship between behaviorism and progressivism.

REFERENCES

Arens, K. (1985). Mach's "psychology of investigation." *Journal of the History of the Behavioral Sciences, 21*, 151–168.

Ash, M. (1995). *Gestalt psychology in German culture, 1890–1967: Holism and the quest for objectivity.* New York: Cambridge University Press.

Bacon, F. (1860). Of the dignity and advancement of learning. In J. Spedding, R. L. Ellis, & D. D. Heath (Eds.), *The works of Francis Bacon. Vol. IV: Translations of the philosophical works* (pp. 275–495). London: Longman. (Original work published 1623)

Blackmore, J. T. (1972). *Ernst Mach: His work, life and influence.* Los Angeles: University of California Press.

Blackmore, J. T. (Ed.). (1992). *Ernst Mach—A deeper look.* Dordrecht, The Netherlands: Kluwer.

Blake, R. M., Ducasse, C. J., & Madden, E. H. (1960). *Theories of scientific method.* Seattle: University of Washington Press.

Boring, E. G. (1933). *The physical dimensions of consciousness.* New York: Century.

Boring, E. G. (1950). *History of experimental psychology* (2nd ed.). New York: Appleton-Century-Crofts.

Bradley, J. (1971). *Mach's philosophy of science.* London: Athlone Press.

Brainerd, J. (1979). Further replies on invariant sequences, explanation, and other stage criteria. *Behavioral & Brain Sciences, 2*, 149–154.

Buckley, K. W. (1989). *Mechanical man: John Broadus Watson and the beginnings of behaviorism.* New York: Guilford Press.

Bunge, M. (1959). *Causality: The place of the causal principle in modern science.* Cambridge, MA: Harvard University Press.

Charlton, W. (Trans.). (1970). *Aristotle's physics, Books I & II.* Oxford, England: Clarendon Press.

Chiesa, M. (1992). Radical behaviorism and scientific frameworks: From mechanistic to relational accounts. *American Psychologist. 47*, 1287–1299.

Cohen, R. S., & Seeger, R. J. (Eds.). (1970). *Ernst Mach: Physicist and philosopher* (Boston Studies in the Philosophy of Science, Vol. VI). Dordrecht, The Netherlands: D. Reidel.

Coleman, S. R. (1987). Quantitative order in B. F. Skinner's early research program, 1928–1931. *Behavior Analyst, 10*, 47–65.

Danziger, K. (1979). The positivist repudiation of Wundt. *Journal of the History of the Behavioral Sciences, 15*, 205–230.

Danziger, K. (1990). *Constructing the subject: Historical origins of psychological research.* New York: Cambridge University Press.

Danziger, K. (1997). *Naming the mind: How psychology found its language.* Thousand Oaks, CA: Sage.

Day, W. (1998). The historical antecedents of modern behaviorism. In R. W.

Rieber & K. Salzinger (Eds.), *Psychology: Theoretical–historical perspectives* (2nd ed., pp. 301–354). Washington, DC: American Psychological Association.

Dingler, H. (1992). Letter to Ernst Mach, June 24, 1913. In J. Blackmore (Ed.), *Ernst Mach—A deeper look* (p. 104). Dordrecht, The Netherlands: Kluwer.

Dzinas, K., & Danziger, K. (1997). How psychology got its variables. *Canadian Psychology, 38,* 43–48.

Ebbinghaus, H. (1913). *Memory: A contribution to experimental psychology* (H. A. Ruger & C. E. Bussenius, Trans.). New York: Teachers College. (Original work published 1885)

Fechner, G. (1966). *Elements of psychophysics* (Vol. 1; E. G. Boring & D. H. Howes, Eds.; H. E. Adler, Trans.). New York: Holt, Rinehart & Winston. (Original work published 1860)

Franklin, A. (1986). *The neglect of experiment.* New York: Cambridge University Press.

Franklin, A. (1990). *Experiment, right or wrong.* Cambridge, England: Cambridge University Press.

Freud, S. (1942). My contact with Josef Popper-Lynkeus (1932). *International Journal of Psycho-Analysis, 23,* 85–87.

Gasman, D. (1971). *The scientific origins of National Socialism: Social Darwinism in Ernst Haeckel and the German Monist League.* London: MacDonald.

Gooding, D., Pinch, T., & Schaffer, S. (Eds.). (1989). *The uses of experiment: Studies in the natural sciences.* New York: Cambridge University Press.

Gotthelf, A. (1976). Aristotle's conception of final causality. *Review of Metaphysics, 30,* 226–254.

Green, C. (1992). Of immortal mythological beasts: Operationism in psychology. *Theory and Psychology, 2,* 287–316.

Hacking, I. (1975). *The emergence of probability.* New York: Cambridge University Press.

Hacking, I. (1983). *Representing and intervening.* New York: Cambridge University Press.

Hanfling, O. (1981). *Logical positivism.* New York: Columbia University Press.

Herschel, J. F. W. (1987). *A preliminary discourse on the study of natural philosophy* (facsimile ed.). Chicago: University of Chicago Press. (Original work published 1830)

Hocutt, M. (1974). Aristotle's four becauses. *Philosophy, 49,* 385–399.

Holton, G. (1993). *Science and anti-science.* Cambridge, MA: Harvard University Press.

Hume, D. (1927). An enquiry concerning human understanding. In C. W. Hendel, Jr. (Ed.), *Hume: Selections* (pp. 107–252). New York: Scribner's. (Original work published 1739)

Jevons, W. S. (1958). *The principles of science: A treatise on logic and scientific method.* New York: Dover. (Original work published 1874)

Kern, S. (1983). *The culture of time and space*. Cambridge, MA: Harvard University Press.

Kloppenberg, J. T. (1986). *Uncertain victory: Social democracy and progressivism in European and American thought, 1870–1920*. New York: Oxford University Press.

Lenin, V. I. (1927). *Materialism and empirio-criticism: Critical comments on a reactionary philosophy*. New York: International Publishers. (Original work published 1908)

Loeb, J. (1964). *The mechanistic conception of life* (D. Fleming, Ed.). Cambridge, MA: Harvard University Press. (Original work published 1912)

Mach, E. (1911). *The history and root of the principle of conservation of energy* (P. E. Jourdain, Trans.). Chicago: Open Court. (Original work published 1872)

Mach, E. (1943). *Popular scientific lectures* (T. J. McCormack, Trans.). La Salle, IL: Open Court. (Original work published 1894)

Mach, E. (1959). *The analysis of sensations and the relation of the physical to the psychical* (C. M. Williams, Trans.). New York: Dover. (Original work published 1886)

Mach, E. (1976). *Knowledge and error: Sketches on the psychology of enquiry* (T. J. McCormack & P. Filches, Trans.). Dordrecht, The Netherlands: D. Reidel. (Original work published 1905)

MacKenzie, B. (1976). Darwinism and positivism as methodological influences on the development of psychology. *Journal of the History of the Behavioral Sciences, 12*, 330–337.

MacMartin, C., & Winston, A. S. (2000). The rhetoric of experimental social psychology, 1930–1960: From caution to enthusiasm. *Journal of the History of the Behavioral Sciences, 36*, 349–364.

Marr, M. J. (1985). 'Tis the gift to be simple': A retrospective appreciation of Mach's *The Science of Mechanics. Journal of the Experimental Analysis of Behavior, 44*, 129–138.

McClelland, C. E. (1980). *State, society, and university in Germany, 1700–1914*. New York: Cambridge University Press.

McKeon, R. (Ed. & Trans.). (1947). *Introduction to Aristotle*. New York: Random House.

Menger, K. (1970). Mathematical implications of Mach's ideas: Positivistic geometry, the clarification of functional connections. In R. S. Cohen & R. J. Seeger (Eds.), *Ernst Mach: Physicist and philosopher* (Boston Studies in the Philosophy of Science, Vol. VI, pp. 107–125). Dordrecht, The Netherlands: D. Reidel.

Mill, J. S. (1974). *A system of logic ratiocinative and inductive*. Toronto, Ontario, Canada: University of Toronto Press. (Original work published 1843)

Mills, J. A. (1998). *Control: A history of behavioral psychology*. New York: New York University Press.

Münsterberg, H. (1913). *Psychology and industrial efficiency*. Boston: Houghton-Mifflin.

Noble, D. (1958). *The paradox of progressive thought*. Minneapolis: University of Minnesota Press.

Pauly, P. J. (1981). The Loeb–Jennings debate and the science of animal behavior. *Journal of the History of the Behavioral Sciences, 17*, 504–581.

Pauly, P. J. (1987). *Controlling life: Jacques Loeb and the engineering ideal in biology*. New York: Oxford University Press.

Pearson, K. (1937). *The grammar of science*. London: J. M. Dent. (Original work published 1892)

Popper-Lynkeus, J. (1995). *The individual and the value of human life* (A. K. Kelley, Trans.). Lanham, MD: Rowman & Littlefield. (Original work published 1910)

Randall, J. H. (1960). *Aristotle*. New York: Columbia University Press.

Ringer, F. (1969). *The decline of the German mandarins: The German academic community, 1890–1933*. Cambridge, MA: Harvard University Press.

Ross, D. (1991). *The origins of American social science*. New York: Cambridge University Press.

Salmon, W. (1998). *Causality and explanation*. New York: Oxford University Press.

Shore, M. (1987). *The science of social redemption: McGill, the Chicago school, and the origins of social science in Canada*. Toronto, Ontario, Canada: University of Toronto Press.

Skinner, B. F. (1953). *Science and human behavior*. New York: Free Press.

Smith, L. D. (1986). *Behaviorism and logical positivism: A reassessment of the alliance*. Palo Alto, CA: Stanford University Press.

Smith, L. D. (1992). On prediction and control: B. F. Skinner and the technological ideal of science. *American Psychologist, 47*, 216–223.

Smith, L. D. (1995). Inquiry nearer the source: Bacon, Mach, and *The Behavior of Organisms*. In J. T. Todd & E. K. Morris (Eds.), *Modern perspectives on B. F. Skinner and contemporary behaviorism* (pp. 39–50). Westport, CT: Greenwood Press.

Smith, L. D. (1996). Knowledge as power: The Baconian roots of Skinner's social meliorism. In. L. D. Smith & W. R. Woodward (Eds.), *B. F. Skinner and behaviorism in American culture* (pp. 56–82). Bethlehem, PA: Lehigh University Press.

Sorabji, R. (1980). *Necessity, cause and blame*. Ithaca, NY: Cornell University Press.

Sosa, E., & Tooley, M. (Eds.). (1993). *Causation*. New York: Oxford University Press.

Taylor, F. W. (1967). *The principles of scientific management*. New York: Norton. (Original work published 1911)

Thompson, K. (Ed.). (1975). *August Comte: The foundation of sociology*. New York: Wiley.

Tibbetts, P. (1975). The doctrine of "pure experience": The evolution of a concept from Mach to James to Tolman. *Journal of the History of the Behavioral Sciences, 11*, 55–66.

Titchener, E. B. (1911). *A text-book of psychology*. New York: Macmillan.

Titchener, E. B. (1922). Mach's "Lectures on Psychophysics." *American Journal of Psychology, 33*, 213–222.

Urbach, P. (1987). *Francis Bacon's philosophy of science*. London: Open Court.

Vlastos, G. (1969). Reasons and causes in the *Phaedo*. *Philosophical Review, 78*, 291–325.

Wachtel, H. (1955). *Security for all and free enterprise: A summary of the social philosophy of Josef Popper-Lynkeus*. New York: Philosophical Library.

Wallace, W. A. (1972). *Causality and scientific explanation* (2 vols.) Ann Arbor: University of Michigan Press.

Watson, J. B. (1920). Is thinking merely the action of language mechanisms? *British Journal of Psychology, 11*, 87–104.

Watson, J. B. (1936). John Broadus Watson. In C. Murchison (Ed.), *A history of psychology in autobiography* (Vol. 3, pp. 272–281).Worcester, MA: Clark University Press.

Weindling, P. (1989). *Health, race, and German politics between national unification and Nazism, 1870–1945*. New York: Cambridge University Press.

Weiss, S. F. (1987). *Race hygiene and national efficiency: The eugenics of Wilhelm Schallmayer*. Berkeley: University of California Press.

Winston, A. S. (1985). The use and misuse of Aristotle's four causes in psychology. In S. Bem & H. Rappard (Eds.), *Studies in the history of psychology and the social sciences: Vol. 4* (Proceedings of the 1985 Conference of CHEIRON, European Society for the History of the Behavioral and Social Sciences, pp. 90–103). Leiden, Germany: Psycholigishe Instituut van de Rijkuniversiteit Leiden.

Winston, A. S. (1988). Cause and experiment in introductory psychology: An analysis of R. S. Woodworth's textbooks. *Teaching of Psychology, 15*, 79–83.

Winston, A. S. (1990). R. S. Woodworth and the "Columbia Bible": How the psychological experiment was redefined. *American Journal of Psychology, 103*, 391–401.

Winston, A. S., & Blais, D. J. (1996). What counts as an experiment: A transdisciplinary analysis of textbooks, 1930–1970. *American Journal of Psychology, 109*, 599–616.

Woodworth, R. S. (1934). *Psychology* (3rd ed.). New York: Holt.

Woodworth, R. S. (1938). *Experimental psychology*. New York: Holt.

Wundt, W. (1902). *Outlines of psychology* (4th ed., C. H. Judd, Trans.). Leipzig, Germany: Engelmann.

7

CHARLES BABBAGE, THE ANALYTICAL ENGINE, AND THE POSSIBILITY OF A 19TH-CENTURY COGNITIVE SCIENCE

CHRISTOPHER D. GREEN

Charles Babbage (1791–1871) is widely known today as the inventor of several machines that were mechanical precursors of the modern electronic digital computer. He frequently receives mention in introductory computer science texts and is often called the "inventor of the computer" or the "first computer scientist." Alongside such celebratory blurbs about Babbage, one can often find brief accounts of Ada Byron Lovelace (1815–1852), who is known primarily for having published a series of notes about one of Babbage's machines—the Analytical Engine. In recent years, both figures have expanded their range from computer science textbooks to cognitive science textbooks as well. Both are typically described as having foreshadowed the foundational article of faith of cognitive science—that human brains are, in essence, biological computers and that human thought is nothing more than the running of a program on such a computer.

In this chapter I evaluate the claim that Babbage and Lovelace were cognitive scientists "ahead of their time." In the first half I describe the historical events leading up to Babbage's invention of the Analytical Engine and the publication of Lovelace's notes about it. In the second half I turn to an examination of the contents of her notes, as well as the often-forgotten article to which they were appended and to the writings of Babbage himself, in order to discover to what degree any of them had in mind what is commonly attributed to them by the cognitive scientists of today.

THE INVENTION OF THE ANALYTICAL ENGINE

The September 1843 issue of Richard Taylor's *Scientific Memoirs*—an English journal that specialized in communicating Continental European scientific activities to the British scientific community—contained an anonymous translation of an article by an unknown Italian military engineer, Luigi Frederico Menabrea (1809–1896). The article had originally been published a year before in French in the Swiss journal *Bibliothèque Universelle de Genève*. Menabrea would later go on to become a general in Garibaldi's army and eventually foreign minister and premier of the newly unified Italian state, but in the early 1840s that was all still years away. A little ironically, the article was about a machine then being constructed in London by an Englishman, Charles Babbage, called the "Analytical Engine."

The article was based on a series of lectures that Babbage had given about his invention in Turin, Italy, in 1840 at the invitation of the prominent Italian scientist Baron Giovanni Plana (1781–1864). The machine was not yet built—indeed it would never be built—but Babbage had come equipped with reams of drawings, diagrams, and other documents hoping to generate excitement about his new project on the Continent that he had found himself utterly unable to generate in his native land. Babbage's expectation seems to have been that the highly respected Baron Plana himself would write an article about the lectures, thereby giving Babbage and his new engine a stamp of legitimacy that even the nationalistic English would have to recognize, but this was not to be. Plana—then older than 60, 10 years Babbage's senior—begged off the job, pleading ill health, and gave it to his younger colleague, Menabrea, who was then about 30, 20 years Babbage's junior.

The article was an enthusiastic endorsement of the Analytical Engine and its prospective powers. It began, however, with a strong warning to the reader not to confuse it with Babbage's earlier, better-known project, the "Difference Engine." The warning was well placed. Everyone who mattered in England knew of the fiasco surrounding the attempt to build that machine, and it was important, if Babbage was to earn back the confidence of the scientific community and ultimately of the British government, that the two be distinguished from each other.

Babbage's reputation as a man of science to be watched was established early; when as a student at Cambridge he and two of his friends—John Herschel (1792–1871), son of the discoverer of Uranus (1781) William Herschel (1738–1822), and George Peacock (1791–1858), who would later become Dean of Ely—formed the Cambridge Analytical Society in 1812. The primary mission of the society was to replace the calculus notation entrusted to the British mathematical community by Isaac Newton (1642–1727) just over a century before with the notation developed by G. W. F. Leibniz (1646–1716). The upholding of the Newtonian notation was a matter of some national pride for the British, for the nasty priority dispute between Newton's and Leibniz's partisans over the discovery of calculus still echoed in the very traditional halls of Cambridge. Unfortunately for the British, Newton's notation was difficult to manipulate algebraically, and they were now some 50 years behind the mathematical developments of their Continental colleagues, who had, of course, used Leibniz's notation from the first. Babbage, Herschel, and Peacock aimed to put a stop to what they called the "dot-age" of Cambridge (a satirical reference to the dots used to indicate derivatives in the Newtonian notation) and replace it with the "pure d-ism" of Leibniz (who used the letter d to indicate the same).[1]

In 1816 the friends published a translation of a Continental textbook on calculus, Sylvestre-François Lacroix's *Traité du Calcul Différentiel et du Calcul Intégral* (1810), and with the help of William Whewell (1794–1866) —who, although an ally, never seems to have been an actual member of the Analytical Society—managed to change the notation used in the Cambridge math exams. By the 1820s, in the wake of a slew of new papers demonstrating the power of the Leibnizian notation, the revolution was complete. For his efforts, Babbage was made a fellow of the Royal Society at the age of only 24.

His "revolutionary fervor" was not spent, however. Frustrated with the stodgy and aristocratic Royal Society, Babbage, Herschel, and several other "entrepreneur–scientists" (see Ashworth, 1994; Fancher, chap. 1, this volume) formed the rival Astronomical Society in 1820. Sir Joseph Banks (1743–1820), then president of the Royal Society for more than 40 years, opposed them as he opposed the establishment of most scientific societies dedicated to special topics within science. He would die within the year,

---

[1] Cambridge mathematician Robert Woodhouse had earlier used the Continental notation in his *Principles of Analytical Calculation* (1803), in which he attempted to reformulate Lagrange's (1797) approach to the foundations of calculus (see Dubbey, 1978, chap. 2), but his work had little impact on the practices of English mathematicians of the day. Indeed, Woodhouse moderated four mathematics examinations at Cambridge between 1804 and 1808, using the old Newtonian fluxionary notation in each (Dubbey, 1978, p. 37).

however, and the nascent Astronomical Society had access to old William Herschel's giant 40-foot reflector telescope, so there was no stopping the upstart group. The Astronomical Society began life by attacking the Royal Society-endorsed Board of Longitude, which was then making up a set of new astronomical tables. Although the Astronomical Society won the debate (the board, headed by physicist Thomas Young, folded in 1828), they managed to alienate many in the Royal Society, and Babbage's career as an irritant to the establishment, as well as his reputation as a bit of a crank, was under way.

While busy discovering the errors in the Board of Longitude's tables (and just about everyone else's), Babbage hit on the idea of developing a machine that would calculate and print the required numbers automatically, so that there could be no mistakes either in computation or copying. The machine he designed implemented a then-common mathematical technique for calculating polynomials, from which the values of a wide array of other functions could be approximated. The technique was called the "method of differences," and thus the machine was dubbed the "Difference Engine."[2] He built a small working model in 1822, for which he won the Astronomical Society's Gold Medal for 1823. He applied for assistance to the Royal Society, the presidency of which had been assumed by Humphrey Davy (1778–1829), to build a full-scale version of the engine. Davies Gilbert, the Royal Society's treasurer, lobbied the government on Babbage's behalf. Tory Robert Peel, then home secretary, likened the machine to the Trojan horse and refused to support it. The Duke of Wellington, however, recognized its potential and requested the chancellor of the exchequer to supply £1000 for its construction in 1823 (Hyman, 1982, p. 52).

The money was long in coming but was eventually received. Babbage found that the machine was more expensive to build than he had expected, so he asked for and received more money from the government, and then more, and still more. By 1833, a decade later, he had received more than £17,000 and still no working machine had been completed (but for a new scale model that he kept in his house as a showpiece), so the government, exasperated, finally suspended the project (officially withdrawing their support in 1842). Peel is reported to have quipped that, if ever completed, the engine should first be set to calculating how much money went into its construction.

The difficulties had not been entirely Babbage's fault. The engine had

---

[2] A point often glossed over is that the revolution Babbage instigated in mathematical notation was grounded in a Lagrangian approach to the foundations of calculus, under which "evanescent" quantities, such as Newton's "fluxions," Leibniz's "infinitesimals," and D'Alembert's "limits," were replaced by the less controversial polynomial approximations of continuous functions made possible by Taylor's Theorem—precisely what the Difference Engine used for its computations. Thus, Babbage's first calculating machine and his earlier work on calculus were closely connected conceptually.

turned out to be far more difficult to engineer than he had expected. He had toured the factories of England, researching the means to make its construction more efficient. Then, in 1827, his wife of 13 years died suddenly, as did his father and one of his children. In his grief he toured Europe through much of the next year. Never one to stop working completely, however, he devoted much of his travel to studying Continental means of industry and manufacture. While in Europe he was awarded the Lucasian Chair in mathematics at Cambridge, Newton's old position.

The early 1830s were a time of great political upheaval in England. The first of the Great Reform Bills was passed in 1832, transferring the bulk of the vote from the outlying boroughs to the urban industrial centers and enfranchising nearly a quarter of a million middle-class citizens. Babbage, a banker's son, was naturally on the side of reform, chairing the election committee of reform advocate William Cavendish in Cambridge in 1829 and 1831 and standing for Parliament (unsuccessfully) himself in north London (Finsbury) in 1832 and 1834. He saw himself as attempting to engineer similar "liberalizing" reforms within science as well. In 1830 he published *Reflections on the Decline in Science in England*, an overt attack on the Royal Society and in particular on its new president Davies Gilbert, the very man who had lobbied the government on behalf of the Difference Engine a decade before (see, e.g., Patterson, 1983, pp. 55–68).

In 1832, Babbage published *On the Economy of Machinery and Manufactures*. The relation of this book to his work on the Difference Engine is made clear in the fist sentence:

> The present volume may be considered as one of the consequences that have resulted from the calculating engine, the construction of which I have been so long superintending. Having been induced, during the last ten years, to visit a considerable number of workshops and factories, both in England and on the Continent, for the purpose of endeavouring to make myself acquainted with the various resources of mechanical art, I was insensibly led to apply to them those principles of generalization to which my other pursuits had naturally given rise. (p. 1)

That would not be the end of his discussion of the engine either. In chapter 20 he described, in very approving terms, the system set up by Marie De Prony (1755–1839) in Revolutionary France for the calculation and publication of new logarithmic and trigonometric tables. Faced with this monumental task, De Prony had applied Adam Smith's (1723–1790) analysis of the division of labor (*Wealth of Nations*, 1776, chap. 1) to what was a mental task rather than to traditional manual labor. He established three divisions of laborers: the first section was to consist of the best mathematicians in the land, who would seek out or develop the easiest methods of calculating the functions desired; the second section, consisting of six or eight junior mathematicians, would take the formulas developed by the first section and plug in the actual numbers required; the third section, made up of 60 or 80 people who could only add and subtract, would do the actual computations and return the results to the second section for checking. This procedure, Babbage famously concluded,

> enables us to purchase and apply to each process precisely the quantity of skill and knowledge which is required for it: we avoid employing any part of the time of a man who can get eight or ten shillings a day by his skill in tempering needles, in turning a wheel, which can be done for sixpence a day. (p. 201)

The middle third of the same chapter consists of Babbage's description of his Difference Engine and hinted that alone it could replace the whole third division of laborers in De Prony's system. He closed with a brief comparison to the way in which labor is divided in a mine, leaving no doubt of his intentions—even when the "raw materials" and "finished products" are mental the same industrial principles apply as would in a factory. It is notable as well that throughout the chapter the emphasis is on efficiency and economy; the nature of mental processes themselves is never at issue. Babbage seems to have assiduously and subtly dodged the question of the nature of the mind throughout his career.

On the Economy of Machinery and Manufactures was probably the most important work of Babbage's career. Its publication was instrumental in his being asked to run for Parliament in 1832. It was read by Karl Marx in 1847, the year before the publication of the *Communist Manifesto* (1848), and Marx cited it in both *The Poverty of Philosophy* (1847) and in *Das Kapital* (1867). It was also quoted extensively in John Stuart Mill's *Principles of Political Economy* (1848).

In the following year, 1833, Babbage first met Ada Byron, the only legitimate child of the poet Lord Byron, who had died fighting for the freedom of Greece nine years earlier. Ada had never known her father. He had left Lady Byron when Ada was only a month old and had left England forever five months later. Nevertheless, her father's shadow preceded her wherever she went, and in 1833, at age 17, she was enjoying her first London season. Among other things, Babbage was well known for his Saturday soirées, and Lady Byron and her daughter were invited, along with much of London Society. Babbage's scale model Difference Engine was displayed along with other mechanical devices of a more entertaining nature.

Lady Byron recorded that in mid-June 1833 they went to see what she called the "*thinking* machine (for so it seems)" at Babbage's house (cited in Stein, 1985, p. 42). This is particularly interesting because Babbage seems to have always carefully avoided saying that his machine could actually think. What Lady Byron's remark shows, though, is that the idea was "in the air" even if Babbage had not put it there or even wanted it there. Lady Byron also recorded that Babbage demonstrated the machine calculating squares and cubes for his guests and then showed how it could count up to 10,000 by ones, but without any apparent change in its operation, suddenly start increasing the gap between numbers by one at each count: 10,002, 10,005, 10,009, etc. He would later use a similar example in his *Ninth Bridgewater Treatise* (1837) to argue, *contra* Hume and others, that miracles could be "programmed" into the mechanism of nature (i.e., that they need not be truly "supernatural"—except in as much as God had "programmed" the mechanism in the first place).

Another of Babbage's guests, Sophia Frend, recorded in her memoirs,

> I well remember accompanying [Ada Byron] to see Mr. Babbage's wonderful analytical engine. While other visitors gazed at the working of this beautiful instrument with the sort of expression, and I dare say the sort of feeling, that some savages are said to have shown in first seeing a looking-glass or hearing a gun. . . . Miss Byron, young as she was, understood its working, and saw the great beauty of the invention. She had read the Differential Calculus to some extent. (cited Stein, 1985, p. 41)

This passage is often trotted out to demonstrate Ada Byron's precocity, but it is not to be trusted. It was written nearly 50 years after the events took place, and given that Babbage had not yet even conceived of the Analytical Engine, much less built one, it is clear that she is mistaken about some of the details. Moreover, Ada had not yet begun to study calculus and would not until 1840.

Sophia Frend was, however, one these "nexus people" who, although not eminent in her own right, had strong connections to virtually all the major players in this story. She was a lifelong friend of Lady Byron's and the daughter of mathematician William Frend, who had tutored Lady Byron in basic mathematics when she was just young Annabella Milbanke (the tutoring that had led Lord Byron to refer to her endearingly as his "Princess of Parallelograms" when courting her and, not so endearingly, as the "Mathematical Medea" when leaving her). William Frend had later been hired by Lady Byron herself to teach Ada mathematics for a time as well, but he had not taught her any calculus. His mathematical views were quite old-fashioned. He had not been a participant in the revolution wrought by Babbage and his Cambridge colleagues. Sophia Frend would soon marry one of the prime inheritors of the new mathematical landscape, however—Augustus De Morgan (1806–1871), the man more responsible than anyone but perhaps George Boole (1815–1864) for developing the abstract algebra that is the conceptual foundation not only of modern mathematics and logic but also of modern computational theory. What is more, De Morgan, between 1840 and 1842, taught Ada calculus.

Ada Byron was a regular guest in Babbage's home, often accompanied by Mary Somerville (1780–1872), a family friend and the most accomplished British woman scientist of her day. Somerville was so highly respected by the Royal Society for her 1831 translation of Laplace's *Méchanique Céleste* and for her own book *On the Connexion of the Physical Sciences* (1835) that a bust of her was placed in the Royal Society's entrance hall. The members never let her officially join the society, however, because of her sex. In any case, there is no indication of any intellectual collaboration between Ada Byron and Babbage at this time. Babbage was just on the verge of conceiving of the Analytical Engine, and Ada Byron's life was about to become very busy indeed.

In 1835 Ada Byron married William King, an old school chum of Somerville's son, Woronzow Greig. In 1836 she had her first child, a son. In 1837 she had her second child, a daughter. During the first half of 1838 she was struck down with a serious illness, possibly cholera. In the summer of 1838, her husband was raised to Earl of Lovelace by the newly crowned Queen Victoria and she to Countess of Lovelace. In 1839, she had her third and final child, a second son. Only then, in the fall of 1839, looking to return to the mathematical studies of her youth (and strongly encouraged to do so by her mother and husband, who both thought it would suppress her supposed "Byronic tendencies"), did she write to Babbage, asking if he knew someone who might be able to teach her calculus. Ignoring the implicit invitation, he said he did not but that he would keep an eye out. Finally, in June 1840, De Morgan, who had since married Sophia Frend and who was just then in the process of publishing his own calculus textbook in serial form, agreed to tutor her by correspondence.

At the time De Morgan was also a leading figure in a mathematical revolution of perhaps even greater magnitude than that led by Babbage, Herschel, and Peacock more than two decades before. He, along with Peacock, Whewell, and a few others, were putting forward the argument that algebra, far from being merely a technique for manipulating mathematical expressions, is a discipline of its own concerned with formal relations among symbols in general and not necessarily mathematical at all. The issues were quite intricate (see, e.g., Fisch, 1994; Richards, 1987, 1991, 1992), but John Passmore captured the gist of the debate extraordinarily clearly when he wrote the following:

They denied, in the first place, that in such an algebraic law as

$$a + b = b + a$$

a and *b* need stand for quantities. Anything whatever could be substituted for *a* and *b*, they said, provided only that it satisfy this law. And to the contention that only quantities could satisfy it, since only quantities are addible, they replied that the plus sign need not stand for addition: it could signify any relation of such a kind that when it is substituted for the plus sign this law still holds. To take De Morgan's example, the plus sign could mean "tied to," since if *a is tied to b*, then also *b is tied to a*. Thus $a + b$ is still equal to $b + a$. (Passmore, 1957, p. 122, emphasis in original)

During the middle and late 1830s, Babbage began developing a design for a new machine he called the Analytical Engine. Unlike the Difference Engine, which could only calculate functions reducible to the method of differences, the Analytical Engine would be able to calculate any function whatsoever. Indeed, he often claimed that ultimately it would be able to carry out symbolic algebra, then considered to be one of the highest forms of rational thought known. To accomplish this extraordinary task, Babbage adapted the technology developed by Joseph-Marie Jacquard (1752–1834) in his famous automated loom of 1801: He would lash cards together end-to-end and punch holes in them that could be "read" by a number of moveable pins in the machine. The holes would "encode," as we would now say, information about which operations to use over which symbols. Given a sophisticated enough control system for the cards, one would be able to repeat the same set of cards an indeterminate number of times (now called "looping," but he called it "backing" the cards), and one would be able to decide which cards to execute on the basis of intermediate results obtained during the computational process (now known as "conditional branching"). Both processes are central to modern computing theory.

Babbage attempted to obtain support for his new project but found it impossible to do so. Few understood the potential of the new invention. Of those who did, even fewer thought that it would be practicable to build a machine so complex. Fewer still believed that Babbage was the man to finish the project, given the fiasco with the still-unfinished Difference Engine, even if the machine were buildable in principle. Babbage began on his own nevertheless. He hired draftsmen and engineers and converted his own coach house to a workshop so he could oversee the work more closely than he had with the Difference Engine. Then, in 1840, Babbage received the invitation from Plana to lecture on the new engine in Turin. He jumped at the chance to earn the endorsement of so prominent an European scientist. After returning to England in November 1840, Babbage spent a good deal of 1841 corresponding with Menabrea about the article he would write based on Babbage's lectures, prompting the young Italian to entirely rewrite his article at one point (Hyman, 1982, p. 190). In short, Babbage's hand was not far from the article written under Menabrea's name. Babbage's involvement was well-known at the time as well. So closely was his connection with the Menabrea paper thought to be that more than a decade later, William Parsons, Earl of Rosse (1855), described it in his 1854 presidential address to the Royal Society as explaining Babbage's views.[3]

In January 1842 Menabrea wrote to Babbage that the final version of the article was ready to go to the *Bibliothèque Universelle* and, as mentioned above, it appeared in October of that year. Being written in French and in a Swiss journal, however, the paper was not destined to have much impact on the English scientific community nor on the government on which Babbage depended.

In February 1843, Charles Wheatstone—coinventor of the telegraph and a friend of both Babbage and the Lovelaces—suggested to Ada that she produce an English translation of Menabrea's article for Taylor's *Scientific Memoirs*. According to Babbage, when Ada presented him with the completed translation, the preparation of which he had not been previously aware, he asked why she had not written, instead, an original article of her own. She is said to have replied that the idea had never occurred to her. He reported that he then suggested that she write some notes explicating parts that Menabrea had left vague or that had been since superseded by new developments. He and Ada worked closely on the notes throughout the spring and summer of 1843. Dozens of letters and drafts flew back and forth between Ada and Babbage, and personal meetings were frequent. The question of how much of them, in the final analysis, is original to Ada and how much is really Babbage's ideas communicated through her is a subject of continuing controversy. The notes, more than twice as long as the article to which they were appended, were completed by August 1843 and were published the following month. Although the translation was anonymous (as was common for both male and female translators of the day), each note was followed by the initials "A. A. L." Their authorship, however, was an open secret in the London scientific community.

WAS THE ANALYTICAL ENGINE THOUGHT TO BE COGNITIVE?

Ada Lovelace's translation of and notes to Menabrea's article did not have the impact that Babbage must have hoped they would. Although Lovelace was a bright person, she was not a serious scientist or mathematician. She had never before published a scientific article, nor did she publish another in the remaining nine years of her tragically short life. There can be little doubt that Babbage's main goal in working with Lovelace was to have a public show of support from a member of the nobility who might have some influence on the government. There was talk at the

---

[3]Indeed, the French translator of the speech for the journal *Cosmos,* rendered the passage such that Babbage himself had written it under the pseudonym of "Menabrea." Menabrea (1855/ 1989) himself felt compelled to respond insisting that he was, in fact, the true author.

time, apparently begun by Wheatstone, of having Lovelace tutor Prince Albert in the sciences. What better influence over governmental science policy could there have been? It came to nothing, however.

The article, although received well in its day, was soon forgotten, as was Babbage, for the most part. It was not until modern computers began to be developed that his work was really "rediscovered." Howard Aiken, designer of the Harvard Mark I computer in the 1940s, repeatedly paid homage to Babbage and claimed to have been the one to finally fulfill "Babbage's Dream," as he often put it, but it is reasonably certain that he knew little of Babbage's actual designs, nor did the architecture of the Mark I owe anything to that of the Analytical Engine (indeed, the Mark I was not capable of conditional branching and thus was really a giant calculator rather than a true computer). It was simply a way of lending historical legitimacy to the Mark I project (Cohen, 1988). He seems to have not even been aware of the Lovelace translation and notes until well after the project was complete. There is a brief mention of Lovelace in Douglas Hartree's (1949) *Calculating Instruments and Machines*, but it was Alan Turing's classic article "Computing Machinery and Intelligence" (1950) that put her back in the public mind, claiming that she had been the first to object that computers can never be truly original, but can only do what people program them to do. Soon thereafter, Bertram Vivian Bowden used her image in the frontispiece of his edited volume *Faster Than Thought; A Symposium on Digital Computing Machines* (1953), as well as presenting the first modern account of Lovelace's work and reprinting her full translation and notes for the first time in almost 70 years. He seems to have inspired the now-common claim that she was the first computer programmer (although he did not quite make it himself), an honor that almost certainly should fall to Babbage.

Since then, Lovelace and Babbage have been frequently made to play the role of "trailblazers" in books and articles not only about computer science but in those about cognitive science as well (e.g., Gardner, 1985; Garnham, 1987; Haugeland, 1985; Hofstadter, 1979; Pylyshyn, 1984). The question is, then, whether this status is really justified. Were either Babbage or Lovelace of the opinion that the Analytical Engine really would have been able to think—like humans think—if it had been completed? In this half of the chapter I try to show that Babbage seems to have been wary of answering this question straightforwardly throughout his life. Lovelace sometimes wrote as if she believed it to be true but at other times made what appear to be forthright denials of the possibility. Given that Babbage had so much influence over her writing, it is interesting to speculate about why he allowed her to occasionally stray over this line if he was unwilling to do so himself. One reason he restrained himself may have been, or so I argue, that for him to have done so would have made him appear to endorse mechanistic materialism. To this his religious convictions would seem to have been opposed, and it would likely have been tantamount to professional suicide in early Victorian England (see, e.g., Winter, 1997). First I examine the Menabrea–Lovelace article for indications of the kind of cognitive theory, if any, that is contained therein. Then I survey Babbage's comments on the topic and offer an interpretation.

Menabrea (1842/1843) opened his article by claiming that the tasks of mathematics may be divided into two parts, "one of which may be called the mechanical, . . . while the other demanding the intervention of reason, belongs more specially to the domain of the understanding" (p. 669). Machinery, he went on almost analytically, may be used to execute the mechanical portion of mathematics. After a brief mention of Pascal's mechanical adding machine, Menabrea then reviewed the portion of Babbage's *Economy of Machinery* in which De Prony's scheme for producing mathematical tables was discussed and stated outright that the third section of workers could be replaced by the Difference Engine (which he described in terms very much like those in Babbage's earlier treatise). Here, Lovelace inserted her first note. She first took pains to deny that the Analytical Engine has any relation whatever to the Difference Engine—a claim that Babbage needed to make stick if he were to have people take seriously his pleas for support for the new project. She went on to describe the difference between them:

> In studying the action of the Analytical Engine, we find that the peculiar and independent nature of the considerations which in all mathematical analysis belong to *operations*, as distinguished from *the objects operated upon* and from the *results* of the operations performed upon those objects, is very strikingly defined and separated. . . .
>
> It may be desirable to explain that by the word *operation*, we mean *any process which alters the mutual relation of two or more things*, be this relation of what kind it may. . . . In abstract mathematics, of course operations alter those particular relations which are involved in the consideration of number and space. . . . But the science of operations . . . is a science of itself and has its own abstract truth and value; just as logic has its own particular truth and value, independently of the subjects to which we apply its reasonings and processes. (cited in Menabrea, 1842/1843, pp. 692–693, emphasis in original)

Here we have a fairly standard formulation of the new formal approach to algebra then being pioneered by Lovelace's calculus teacher De Morgan. One would expect that Lovelace learned this orientation toward algebra from De Morgan himself, but there is little discussion of such theoretical issues in the letters between them dating from the time he was teaching her calculus. One of the books De Morgan assigned her to read, however, was Peacock's *Treatise on Algebra* (1830) in which the revolutionary distinction was first made between *arithmetical algebra*—the traditional manipulation of numerical expressions via symbols—and *symbolic algebra*—a new general discipline of abstract symbol manipulation, of which the arithmetical form was but a single application. Even more interestingly, Babbage himself had written a manuscript in 1821 entitled *The Philosophy of Analysis*, which anticipated many of the algebraic ideas put forward by Peacock almost a decade later. Why Babbage never published this manuscript remains unknown—he seems to have become distracted by other projects such as the building of the Difference Engine—but it is known that Peacock, a core member of Babbage's Analytical Society at Cambridge, read the manuscript in May 1822 and found it to be "of very great interest" (see Dubbey, 1978, chap. 5, esp. pp. 95–107).[4]

Returning to consideration of Ada Lovelace's Note A, she went on to exemplify her claims about abstract algebra with what has become one of her most quoted claims:

> Supposing, for instance, that the fundamental relations of pitched sounds in the science of harmony and of musical composition were susceptible of such expression and adaptations, the engine might compose elaborate and scientific pieces of music of any degree of complexity or extent. The Analytical Engine is an *embodying of the science of operations*. (cited in Menabrea, 1842/1843, p. 694, emphasis in original)

Today this passage is often mistaken for the claim that the engine would be "intelligent" enough to compose music, but that is not really its thrust at all. The aim is to drive a wedge between abstract algebra—the "science of operations"—and mathematics; to show that the operations can operate over symbols representing objects other than numbers, such as musical notes (however, see Anderson, chap. 8, this volume, on the use of musical metaphors with respect to the mind during this era).

After describing the differences between the two engines even more fully, Ada Lovelace then made a claim that might seem to virtually commit her, and perhaps Babbage, to mechanistic materialism with respect to the mind (at almost the very moment that Hermann Helmholtz, Ernst Brücke, Emile du Bois-Reymond, and Rudolf Virchow were declaring themselves to be mechanists in Berlin):

> In enabling mechanism to combine together *general* symbols in successions of unlimited variety and extent, a uniting link is established between the operations of matter and the abstract mental process of the *most abstract* branch of mathematical science. . . . We are not aware of its being on record that anything partaking in the nature of what is so well designated the *Analytical* Engine has been hitherto proposed, or even thought of, as a practical possibility, any more than the idea

---

[4]Becher (1980) argued that the algebraical innovations of both Babbage and Peacock were prefigured in the work of Robert Woodhouse (1803), with which they were both familiar. Woodhouse preceded Babbage as Lucasian Professor of Mathematics at Cambridge (Newton's old chair) and died in 1827, less than three years before the publication of Peacock's *Algebra*.

of a thinking or of a reasoning machine. (cited in Menabrea, 1842/
1843, p. 697, emphasis in original)

Notice how she seemed to claim outright that the Analytical Engine serves
as a "uniting link" between mind and matter but then at the end of the
passage seemed to back away, saying that no one else had yet proposed a
machine like the Analytical Engine *any more than* they had proposed a
thinking machine: Thus an apparently literal claim is reduced to a mere
analogy. The last third of Note A is devoted almost exclusively to defend-
ing Babbage's actions with respect to the still-unbuilt Difference Engine
over the previous decade.

Returning to Menabrea's original text, having just stated that the
Difference Engine could replace De Prony's third section of workers—those
who actually carry out the calculations—he went on then to virtually
claim—although he is not completely explicit—that the new Analytical
Engine could replace the second section as well—those who plug the numbers into the formulas produced by the expert mathematicians in the first
section. He was careful to point out, however, that the machine "must
exclude all methods of trial and guess-work, and can only admit the direct
process of calculation." This is necessarily the case, he went on to say,
because "*the machine is not a thinking being,* but simply an automaton which
acts according to the laws imposed upon it" (p. 675, emphasis added). This
would seem to close the matter definitively, but Lovelace added a footnote
to this passage, saying that "this must not be understood in too unqualified
a manner. The engine is capable, under certain circumstances, of *feeling*
about to discover which of two or more possible contingencies has occurred" (cited in Menabrea, 1842/1843, p. 675, emphasis added). What
exactly she meant by this is not entirely clear, but she appears to be referring to the engine's conditional branching ability. Why she took this to
manifest itself as a "feeling" is anyone's guess, although Babbage's occa-
sional picturesque references to this power as "foresight" may be the cause.

So already we can see a tension between two ways of viewing the
machine. On the one hand, according to Lovelace, it "unites" matter and
mentality. She could not quite bring herself to call it a "thinking machine,"
but she was willing to say that it "feels" in some sense. On the other hand,
according to Menabrea, it is definitely not a "thinking being"; just an
automaton. Under other circumstances one might regard this simply as a
difference of opinion, but because both of these writers had one and the
same mentor—Charles Babbage—a more interesting dynamic may be at
play.

Menabrea said nothing more about the possible relation between the
operation of the Analytical Engine and that of the human mind in the
rest of his article, but Lovelace included one more major speculation in
her notes—the passage Turing would call over a century later the "Lovelace Objection" to artificial intelligence:

It is desirable to guard against the possibility of exaggerated ideas that might arise as to the powers of the Analytical Engine. In considering any new subject, there is frequently a tendency, first, to *overrate* what we find to be already interesting or remarkable; and, secondly, by a sort of natural reaction, to *undervalue* the true state of the case, when we do discover that our notions have surpassed those that were really tenable.

The Analytical Engine has no pretensions whatever to *originate* anything. It can do whatever we *know how to order it* to perform. It can *follow* analysis; but it has no power of *anticipating* any analytical relations or truths. (cited in Menabrea, 1842/1843, p. 722, emphasis in original)[5]

If there were ever a question of Ada Lovelace's believing that the machine would actually be able to think, this passage would seem to scotch it—certainly Turing thought so—but in combination with her earlier statements about it unifying mind and matter and its being able to feel, it is hard to know exactly what opinion to attribute to her or to her mentor Babbage.

Babbage's own comments on the topic were usually very careful. He almost invariably referred to the machine's activities as being able to "replace" or "substitute for" mental activities or as being "analogous" to mental activities but only very rarely as being able to carry them out itself. For instance, in his autobiography (Babbage, 1864/1994), in the midst of a discussion of his problems with mechanizing the process of "carrying" from one column of numbers to another in addition problems, he said, "the mechanical means I employed to make these carriages bears some slight analogy to the operation of the faculty of memory" (p. 46).[6] With this deflationary statement in place, he said later on the same page that "it occurred to me that it might be possible to teach mechanism to accomplish another mental process, namely—to foresee" (p. 46). He then went on to explain what we would call "conditional branching."

What are we to think of Babbage's "true" beliefs on the matter? Was the first comment about memory a mere "foot in the door" that would allow him to slide to the stronger claim about foresight, or is the claim about foresight to be regarded as a mere "shorthand" for his real position,

---

[5]It is interesting to compare these words to some written by Babbage about the Analytical Engine two years earlier, in 1841: "It cannot invent. It must derive from human intellect those laws which it puts in force in the developments it performs. It cannot, in fact, do anything more than perform with absolute precision and in much shorter time those series of operations which the hand of man might itself much more imperfectly accomplish" (cited in Collier, 1990, p. 178, from Vol. VII of the papers deposited by H. M. Buxton at the Museum of the History of Science, Oxford).

[6]Note the relation here to the concepts of memory used in later decades by Wilhelm Wundt and Hermann Ebbinghaus, described by Danziger (chap. 3, this volume). Ebbinghaus might have been happy to call this "actual memory," whereas Wundt would likely have scoffed at the idea.

given just above it, that the activities of the machine are only "slightly analogous" to mental activities? In an 1837 paper entitled "On the Mathematical Powers of the Calculating Engine" (that went unpublished until 1973), Babbage wrote the following in a footnote:

> In substituting mechanism for the performance of operations hitherto executed by intellectual labour it is continually necessary to speak of contrivances by which certain alterations in parts of the machine enable it to execute or refrain from executing particular functions. The *analogy* between these acts and the operations of mind almost forced upon me the *figurative* employment of the same terms. They were found at once convenient and expressive and I prefer continuing their use rather than substituting lengthened circumlocutions. [emphasis added]
>
> For instance, the expression "the engine *knows*, etc." means that one out of many possible results of its calculations has happened and that a certain change in its arrangement has taken place by which it is compelled to carry on the next computation in a certain appointed way. (1989, Vol. 3, p. 31)

An even more interesting passage occurs in the posthumous biography of Babbage written, at his direction, by his longtime friend Harry Wilmot Buxton (not published until 1988). It begins as though a profound claim concerning the intelligence of the engine is about to be defended:

> It is manifest that the language of algebra is more simple and precise than the symbols of language expressed by sound, and it would seem therefore within the range of our intelligence to be able to reduce our thoughts in most cases into the form of mathematical language, and thus adapt the subject of our enquiry to the operations of the Analytical Engine. (p. 155)

Buxton went on, however, to make a rather vague claim about Babbage's aspirations in this regard—"Mr. Babbage entertained no doubt of the possibility of extending the powers of the Analytical Engine, far beyond the domain of abstract analysis" (p. 155)—and then he immediately shifted to a very long quotation from Hobbes in which it was claimed that reasoning is nothing more than calculation. Buxton then suggested that the Analytical Engine could have established Hobbes's claim if only it had been equipped with letters of the alphabet and the plus and minus signs in addition to numerals. Having gotten this far, however, he closed with the admission that "as Mr. Babbage himself has not recorded his views upon the subject, it might be deemed presumptuous to indulge in speculations or enter into details which he did not deem necessary" (p. 156). So it would appear that even Babbage's closest friends were not of the opinion that he believed his machines to be literally intelligent.

CONCLUSION

In this chapter I have attempted to establish that, contrary to what is often found in textbooks, Babbage did not believe the Analytical Engine to have been a contribution to what we would now call "cognitive science." Why might Babbage have refrained from taking such a step? Such speculation was rampant about him: Lady Byron had called even the lowly Difference Engine a "thinking machine"; Buxton certainly entertained the idea that human reasoning might be nothing more than what the Analytical Engine was intended to do; even Ada Lovelace intermittently raised the possibility. What held Babbage back?

Two things come to mind. The first is that in Regency and early Victorian England, declaring oneself to be a mechanist materialist with respect to the mind would have been professionally foolish in the extreme. Allison Winter (1997) has written a fascinating chapter on the philosophical traps of this sort that the physiologist William Benjamin Carpenter— who, incidentally, briefly served as tutor to the Lovelace's children—had to avoid in launching his career during the 1830s and 1840s; dangers that, for instance, John Eliotson, the famed mesmerist, had failed to negotiate effectively, leading to his resignation from University College in 1838.

Tempting as it might be, one should not conclude that Babbage somehow "secretly" believed the Analytical Engine to be truly intelligent but would not say so publicly for fear of the censure of his community. Babbage, although liberal, appears to have been a sincerely religious man, as were his closest colleagues: Whewell was a minister, Peacock was ordained and turned explicitly to questions of theology in the 1830s, and even Herschel's work has been described as evincing an attitude of "steadfast piety" (Richards, 1992, p. 55; also, contrast this with the attitude, described in Fancher, chap. 1, this volume, of the English scientists who reached intellectual maturity in the wake of Darwin's *Origin of Species*). When Whewell's Bridgewater treatise was published in 1833, the first in a series of works commissioned explicitly to defend the thesis (primarily against Hume) that God's hand can be discovered in the organization of the natural world, Babbage felt compelled to write a book-length response, his so-called *Ninth Bridgewater Treatise* (1837). Significantly, Babbage's objection to Whewell was not that he defended "natural theology," as it was then called, but rather that Whewell had argued that nothing of the divine could be found in the "deductive" sciences but only in "inductive" forms of knowledge. Babbage was incensed, not only because this excluded the truths of mathematics from the realm of "divine truths"—a position Babbage was keen to defend—but also because the intent of Whewell's remarks was to devalue the work of recent Continental scientists (e.g., Leonhard Euler, Pierre-Simon Laplace, Joseph-Louis Lagrange). Babbage thought these to be the very examples to which the English should look to improve their science. Whewell, however, favored the work of much earlier "divinely inspired" (in Whewell's opinion) scientists such as Copernicus, Johannes Kepler, and more importantly—because more British—Robert Boyle and Newton (Richards, 1992, pp. 60–61). Although Babbage argued that miracles might be the result of a "divine mechanism" the underlying principles of which humans can only partially comprehend, his suggestion was not that God Himself is such a mechanism; it was, by contrast, that only a divine intelligence could craft a mechanism so intricate as that found in nature.

To conclude then, Babbage does not seem to have regarded the Analytical Engine as a kind of intelligence or even as revealing anything of particular significance about the nature of human activity. Attributions of such opinions to him by modern cognitive scientists and their intellectual kin are primarily anachronistic. His primary interests in his engines were industrial and economic. He saw them as bringing the very same principles of division of labor to the realm of mental work that he supported in the realm of manufacture. Indeed, one might argue that the powers of his engines served to distinguish precisely between those aspects of the human mind that were thought to be merely mechanical and those that were regarded as being truly original, creative, rational, and ultimately divine in character.

REFERENCES

Ashworth, W. J. (1994). The calculating eye: Baily, Herschel, Babbage and the business of astronomy. *British Journal of the History of Science, 27,* 409–441.

Babbage, C. (1832). *On the economy of machinery and manufactures.* London: C. Knight.

Babbage, C. (1837). *Ninth Bridgewater treatise.* London: J. Murray.

Babbage, C. (1989). On the mathematical powers of the calculating engine. In M. Campbell-Kelly (Ed.), *The works of Charles Babbage* (Vol. 3, pp. 15–61). New York: New York University Press.

Babbage, C. (1994). *Passages from the life of a philosopher.* New Brunswick, NJ: Rutgers University Press. (Original work published 1864)

Becher, H. W. (1980). Woodhouse, Babbage, Peacock, and modern algebra. *Historia Mathematica, 7,* 389–400.

Bowden, B. V. (Ed.). (1953). *Faster than thought: A symposium on digital computing machines.* New York: Pitman.

Buxton, H. W. (1988). *Memoir of the life and labours of the late Charles Babbage Esq., F.R.S.* Cambridge, MA: MIT Press.

Cohen, I. B. (1988). Babbage and Aiken, with notes on Henry Babbage's gift to Harvard, and to other institutions, a portion of his father's Difference Engine. *Annals of the History of Computing, 10,* 171–193.

Collier, B. (1990). *The little engines that could've: The calculating machines of Charles Babbage*. New York: Garland.

Dubbey, J. M. (1978). *The mathematical work of Charles Babbage*. Cambridge, England: Cambridge University Press.

Fisch, M. (1994). "The emergency which has arrived": The problematic history of nineteenth-century British algebra—A programmatic outline. *British Journal of the History of Science, 27*, 247–276.

Gardner, H. (1985). *The mind's new science*. New York: Basic Books.

Garnham, A. (1987). *Artificial intelligence: An introduction*. London: Routledge & Kegan Paul.

Hartree, D. R. (1949). *Calculating instruments and machines*. Urbana: University of Illinois Press.

Haugeland, J. (1985). *Artificial intelligence: The very idea*. Cambridge, MA: MIT Press.

Hofstadter, D. R. (1979). *Gödel, Escher, Bach: An eternal golden braid*. New York: Random House.

Hyman, A. (1982). *Charles Babbage: Pioneer of the computer*. Oxford, England: Oxford University Press.

Lacroix, S.-F. (1810). *Traité du calcul differentiel et du calcul intégral*. Paris, France: Courcier.

Lagrange, J. L. (1797). *Théorie des fonctions analytique* [Theory of analytic functions]. Paris, France: Imprimerie de la Republique.

Menabrea, L. F. (1842). Notions sur la machine analytique de M. Charles Babbage [Thoughts on the Analytical Engine of Mr. Charles Babbage]. *Bibliothèque Universelle de Genève, 41*, 352–376.

Menabrea, L. F. (1843). Sketch of the Analytical Engine invented by Charles Babbage Esq. (A. A. Lovelace, Trans.). *Scientific Memoirs, 3*, 666–731. (Original work published 1842)

Menabrea, L. F. (1989). Letter to the Editor of *Cosmos*. In Martin Campbell-Kelly (Ed.), *The works of Charles Babbage* (Vol. 3, pp. 171–174). New York: New York University Press. (Original work published 1855)

Passmore, J. (1957). *A hundred years of philosophy*. London: Duckworth.

Patterson, E. C. (1983). *Mary Somerville and the cultivation of science, 1815–1840*. The Hague, The Netherlands: Martinus Nijhoff.

Peacock, G. (1830). *A treatise on algebra*. Cambridge, England: Cambridge University Press.

Pylyshyn, Z. W. (1984). *Computation and cognition: Toward a foundation for cognitive science*. Cambridge, MA: MIT Press.

Richards, J. L. (1987). Augustus De Morgan, the history of mathematics, and the foundations of algebra. *Isis, 78*, 7–30.

Richards, J. L. (1991). Rigour and clarity: Foundations of mathematics in France and England, 1800–1840. *Science in Context, 4*, 297–319.

Richards, J. L. (1992). God, truth, and mathematics in nineteenth century England. In M. J. Nye, J. L. Richards, & R. Stuewer (Eds.), *The invention of physical sciences: Intersections of mathematics, theology and natural philosophy since the seventeenth century* (pp. 51–78). Dordrecht, The Netherlands: Kluwer.

Rosse, W. P., Earl of. (1855). Address of the president. *Proceedings of the Royal Society, 7,* 248–263.

Stein, D. (1985). *Ada: A life and a legacy.* Cambridge, MA: MIT Press.

Turing, A. M. (1950). Computing machinery and intelligence. *Mind, 59,* 433–460.

Winter, A. (1997). The construction of orthodoxies and heterodoxies in early Victorian England. In B. Lightman (Ed.), *Victorian science in context* (pp. 24–50). Chicago: University of Chicago Press.

Woodhouse, R. (1803). *Principles of analytical calculation.* Cambridge, England: Cambridge University Press.

8

INSTINCTS AND INSTRUMENTS

KATHARINE ANDERSON

The Great Exhibition of the Industry of the Nations in London in 1851, the first in an international series of such pageants, paid tribute to a record of industrial, commercial, and scientific progress that, for contemporaries, defined the age. There, throngs of visitors could witness many marvels, including the precision instruments of a new generation of scientific investigators. Passing alongside the self-recording barometers and delicate thermometers, and down the aisle from the electric telegraphic equipment, a visitor to the Crystal Palace (as the exhibition hall was called) encountered an unusual exhibit: the Atmospheric, Electromagnetic Telegraph, conducted by Animal Instinct, or the Tempest Prognosticator for short. An elaborately ornamented tabletop device (Figure 8.1), the prognosticator consisted of pint-sized glass bottles arranged in a circle, each containing a leech that, when disturbed by atmospheric conditions, crawled into the top of a bottle and triggered a signal. Its inventor was a medical gentleman from Whitby, Yorkshire, named, appropriately enough, George Merryweather (1793–1870). As Merryweather pointed out, the device could be linked easily to a central telegraph network. His account of the invention triumphantly invited the reader to consider that with his "Whitby pygmy Temples" (Browne, 1949, p. 134), he "could cause a little

Figure 8.1. The Atmospheric, Electromagnetic Telegraph, conducted by animal instinct, called the Tempest Prognosticator (Merryweather, 1851).

Leech, governed by its instinct, to ring Saint Paul's great bell in London as a signal for an approaching storm" (Merryweather, 1851, p. 48).

Eccentric as it was, the Tempest Prognosticator nevertheless displayed some of the representative issues involved in 19th-century sciences of the mind. The object embodied widely shared assumptions about both the nature of instruments and animal sensibilities. It engaged with long-standing debates about the mechanical operations of the mind, the role of the senses in thought, and the nature of the boundaries that sustained reason, will, and intellect as the province of the human mind. Brought before the public in that setting of industrial triumph and in the company of precision instruments and electrical novelties, however, the prognosticator also suggests how these debates on the nature of the mind shifted during the technological and scientific developments of the Victorian era. The plausibility and appeal of the Leech Prognosticator was based on several related ideas, all important to the formation of psychological thought during the rest of the century. These included an understanding of the mechanical operations of sensibility in general, an understanding of the precision and infallibility of instinctive behavior, and the importance of instruments to modern civilization.

The goal then of the following discussion is to indicate how animal instinct, the motive force of Merryweather's machine, figured in debates about the mind. Crucial here was the ambiguous relative position of instinct and reason. The complex instinctive behavior of some "lower" forms of life modeled a key attribute and value of scientific and technological civilization. In their enviable and natural precision, they prefigured and even surpassed the heights scaled by rational man. An instrument such as the Tempest Prognosticator, however, enrolled this physiological accuracy in the service of human society, restoring the triumph of reason and machines.

Similarly nuanced judgments of the relationship of mechanical activity and thought processes have become familiar in the history of psychology in some settings, such as the development of psychophysics or the rise of the laboratories of experimental psychologists toward the end of the century. My account in this chapter proposes that attention move beyond these situations toward a broader cultural context in which both scientific investigators and popularizers assumed that natural bodies and machines were intimately connected. Contemporary understandings of bodies and machines co-evolved, so that elaborating on one reflected experiences and accounts of the other. To acknowledge these developments, historians of psychology need to attend to particular encounters among machines, instruments, and minds rather than simply assuming the general influence of Cartesian ideas. The chapter also argues, as will be clear from some of the less canonical writers exploited here, that such contextualized histories can emerge from popular writings, where commonplaces can be explored and mined (Cooter & Pumfrey, 1994; Lightman, 1997).

INSTRUMENT AND ANALOGIES

In 19th-century Britain, several factors sharpened traditionally controversial points about the mind. As in earlier periods, mental operations offered a minefield studded with explosive political and religious charges. Difficult issues included the distinction between humans and other animals, the existence and significance of free will, and the reach of materialist explanations of physiology. But such issues took their shape under new circumstances. First, the rapid development of physiology from the 1830s and 1840s, especially associated with the German school emerging from the laboratory of Johannes Müller (1801–1858), bared the physical structures of the nervous systems of all living things. These studies explicitly demonstrated, for instance, that the nervous structure of the leech and other mollusca was a kind of lowest common denominator, related point by point to that of more complex forms of life (e.g., Müller, 1838, p. 594; Richard, 1973; Wigglesworth, 1973). Second, technological changes transformed the understanding of mechanical processes in British culture. Although machinery did not lose altogether its grubby associations with trade, the power and precision of industrial manufacture gave it a new prestige, something that Charles Babbage (1792–1871) was among the first to recognize and express (see Green, chap. 7, this volume). Third, the social and political upheaval associated with industrialization heightened concern with the natural basis of social order. Physiological models of sensibility, which outlined the sphere of reflexive behavior, and the influence of the will and reason over that sphere provided a means of conceptualizing proper social behavior and defining individual responsibility.

Finally, by the 1860s and 1870s, ambitious leaders of scientific culture in Britain pursued materialist philosophies more aggressively. No crude materialists, these men fully acknowledged that, in exploring mental processes, science was working at the limits of its powers of explanation. The "causal connections" between "molecular motion and states of consciousness" remained obscure (Tyndall, 1874/1898b, p. 356). Yet this perspective (an increasingly influential one, as Fancher's study of Francis Galton's circle shows; see chap. 1, this volume) insisted that only a rigorously materialist line of inquiry would lead to enlightenment. Retreating to concepts of soul, spirit, or free will was scientifically intolerable.

In the context of the developments sketched above, automatic behavior offered an important approach to the study of the mind. Defining the nature and limits of automatic behavior outlined the gradations of mental processes, from reflex to reason (Young, 1970/1990). Moreover, a focus on automatic operations provided striking analogies with instruments and machines, whose capacities could perhaps help define those of the mind. Modern physiological methods had intimately connected technologies and organic function. Experimenters relied on new instrumental methods of exploration, with important consequences for the guiding assumptions and questions of their research. Physical sensibility could be thought of as fundamentally mechanical because an experimental subject's limb movement, blood flow, and so forth could be viewed, measured, and inscribed by machines (Coleman, 1977). Mental physiology was subject to the same conception, but with the difference that the extent or limits of its automatism or mechanical nature remained more philosophically charged. On the one hand, then, investigations of automatic responses turned to human subjects, exploring mesmeric phenomena, aphasia, intermittent amnesia, and so on (see, e.g., Winter, 1998, and the exchange between Huxley, 1874/1893b, and Carpenter, 1876/1891). On the other hand, automatic behavior and all it implied for the conception of the mind was studied through the sensibility of (nonhuman) animals and especially through instinct.

To explore these ideas about instinct and thus treat the prognosticator as more than a simple curiosity, I begin by acknowledging the significance of the term *instrument*. Historians of science have become increasingly interested in analysis of instruments as part of the recovery of the practice and materiality of science (Golinski, 1998a, pp. 131–161; Hankins & Silverman, 1995; Hankins & Van Helden, 1994; Warner, 1990). These studies emphasized the tight connections among instruments, audiences, and texts. As summarized by Hankins and Van Helden, instruments fill several key purposes. Designed for display and persuasion, they are tools used to build the authority of scientists in front of various audiences, from colleagues to patrons. As powerfully material versions of arguments and ideas, moreover, instruments readily assume importance within popular culture, becoming metaphors, illustrations of theory, and the embodiment of proper scientific work. Most significantly for the purposes of this chapter, Hankins and Van Helden pointed to the slipperiness of instruments when used to study living organisms. The boundary between the organism and the instrument is easily blurred (p. 5). This slipperiness should be kept in mind because it invades contemporary discussions of instincts. Instruments that are used to study the mind tend to become models that represent the mind, whereas the language of instrumentality recalls both material techniques or objects and the model of the mind. Consider, for instance, the famous definition of materialism as "the doctrine of bodily instruments" (Tyndall, 1874/1898a) or the musical analogy used by the physiologist William Carpenter (1802–1875):

> While the Human organism may be likened to a keyed instrument, from which any music it is capable of producing may be called-forth as the will of the performer, we may compare a Bee or an other Insect to a barrel-organ, which plays with the greatest exactness a certain number of tunes. (1876/1891, p. 61)

In the sciences of the mind, then, *instrument* and *instrumentality* were complex words. They evoked the distinction between volitional workings of the mind and automatic workings of the mind or, to place the distinction in increasingly crude terms, between intelligence and instinct, and between animals and humans.

Looking at the rhetorical history of the word *instrument* in physiological discussions suggests how constantly writers explored these boundaries. By the 19th century, a long and honorable tradition promoted the com-

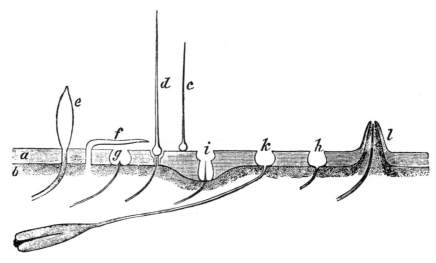

Figure 8.2. The sense organs of insects from Lubbock (1888/1899, p. 56), a work written for a wide readership. Lubbock, an independently wealthy researcher and a member of the London scientific elite, was well known to Victorians for his experimental work on the smell and sight of bees and other insects (for his work, see Clark, 1997).

parison of organs of sense to scientific as well as musical instruments. In a well-known passage of the *Origin of Species*, for instance, Charles Darwin's (1809–1882) description of the eye deliberately evoked a sensitive, regulated instrument. Darwin noted the "inimitable contrivances" of the eye, the "adjustments of focus," and the "correction of spherical and chromatic aberration" that made the eye such a remarkable organ (1859/1985, p. 217). This comparison worked symmetrically. In the recent work by Hankins and Silverman (1994), *Instruments and the Imagination*, the authors described the efforts of Charles Wheatstone (1802–1875) in the 1840s to replicate the physiology of the eye in the design of his stereoscope (pp. 148–177).[1] When comparing organs and instruments, the line between analogy and identity was a thin one and easily crossed: Rather than the eye "recalling" an instrument, or an instrument imitating the eye, the eye may become an instrument and the instrument an eye. Writing toward the end of the century, English entomologist John Lubbock (1834–1914) showed how readily the transition from analogy to identity occurred when he described the antennae of insects (Figure 8.2). The structure K, in the labeled diagram accompanying Lubbock's text, is simply a "flask-like or-

---

[1] Wheatstone himself epitomized the connections between musical instruments, physiology of the sense organs, and modern scientific apparatus. A professor of natural philosophy at King's College London, he was the son of a musical instrument manufacturer and had entertained London audiences early in his career with a lyre whose strings were set invisibly in action by sympathetic resonance with a distant pianoforte—a scenario with some parallels to Merryweather's instrument.

gan," just as structure I is a "champagne-cork-like organ." Lubbock's text drew on work of an earlier observer who noted a "small pit leading to a long delicate tube which . . . dilates into an elongated sac having its end inverted." Lubbock, however, proceeded to refer to the "curious flasks," (losing both the more qualified language of the diagram and the earlier language of sacs and tubes) and ended with the suggestion that the remarkable organs "serve as microscopic stethoscopes" for the ants and certain bees that possessed them (1888/1899, pp. 56–57, 115). The unfolding language shows how a more detailed understanding of insect organs of sensation was conceptualized by analogy to scientific instruments—the microscope and the stethoscope—tools that Lubbock's own generation of scientists familiarly used to penetrate their subjects.

Similar analogies and identities operated in accounts of the nervous system as a whole. One important instrumental analogy, as the quotation above from Carpenter suggests, was musical. The mechanical replication of a human voice using musical instruments was a lively 18th-century tradition on the Continent and in Britain (Hankins & Silverman, 1995, pp. 178–198). As articulate speech was seen as a key attribute of a rational mind, however, more comprehensive comparisons emerged readily. The representative expression came from George Cheyne (1671–1743), an influential medical writer who provided advice for the sound body and mind for generations of readers from the 1740s on.

> The Human Body is a Machine of an infinite Number and Variety of different Channels and Pipes, filled with various and different Liquors and Fluids . . . the Intelligent Principle, or *Soul*, resides somewhere in the Brain, where all the Nerves, or Instruments of Sensation terminate, like a *Musician* in a finely fram'd and well-tun'd Organ-Case; . . . these Nerves are like *Keys*, which, being struck on or touch'd, convey the sound and Harmony to this sentient Principle or *Musician*. (Cheyne, 1735/1990, pp. 4–5, italics in original)

In the 19th century, evocations of musical instruments remained powerful and commonplace. James Hinton (1822–1875), for instance, as a young London physician in 1851, told his fiancée authoritatively that "the brain bears just the same relation to the spirit that your piano does to you" (cited in Hopkins, 1892, p. 72). William George Ward (1867), the intellectual leader of conservative Catholicism in Great Britain, included an elaborate metaphor on the piano and the activating spirit of body and mind in his attack on materialist ideas. As Ward's reaction suggested, by this date, musical instruments became associated with an anti-materialist position on the mind (cf. Carpenter, 1876/1891, p. 61, 1888/1970; Huxley, 1897, pp. 132–133). Increasingly, another, explicitly modern instrument was invoked instead to explain the mind: the electric telegraph, invented in 1837. The exchange of words by electrical impulse, coupled to an older tradition of mechanical and instrumental references, became the dominant Victorian model for the mind.

A few examples show the extent of the analogy and its characteristic forms. Carpenter published an extended comparison of the nervous system with the telegraph in his *Principles of Mental Physiology* (1876/1891). Both, he noted, require an originating action and a conductor. The production of the electrical current by chemical reaction in telegraphy is like the reaction that takes place between the blood and the central nerve cells or peripheral nerve fibers (p. 38). The "axis cylinders" of neighboring nerve fibers are protected with insulator, "just as are the numerous wires . . . which are bound up together in the aerial cable of the District Telegraph" (p. 35). Carpenter's reliance on telegraphy was shared by Hermann Helmholtz (1821–1894) as he developed his theories of the mechanics of vision and hearing in the 1850s and early 1860s. Helmholtz had close contacts with the telegraphic engineering community and used their equipment to develop his experimental apparatus. Timothy Lenoir (1994) showed that Helmholtz thought of the nervous system as a telegraph in the direct, literal sense that Lubbock also found natural in his thinking about insect sensibility. For Helmholtz, "telegraphy was not simply a useful model for representing and thinking about vision and hearing," Lenoir noted; "the eye was a photometer; the ear a tuning fork interrupter with attached resonators" (p. 187). In a work first published in German in 1863 and published later in English as *On the Sensations of Tone as a Physiological Basis for the Theory of Music* (1885), Helmholtz discussed the analogy at length in a passage that emphasized modern technological sophistication.

> Nerves have been often and not unsuitably compared to telegraph wires. Such a wire conducts one kind of electric current and no other; it may be stronger, it may be weaker, it may move in either direction; it has no other qualitative differences. Nevertheless, according to the different kinds of apparatus with which we provide its terminations, we can send telegraphic dispatches, ring bells, explode mines, decompose water, move magnets, magnetise iron, develop light, and so on. So with the nerves. The condition of excitement . . . is everywhere the same, but . . . it produces motion, secretions of glands, increase and decrease of the quantity of the blood, of redness and warmth of individual organs, and also sensations of light, of hearing, and so forth. (cited in Lenoir, 1994, p. 207)

As with Darwin's and Wheatstone's characterizations of vision noted above, the analogy between the mind and telegraph was symmetrical. The intellectual and organic model for the telegraph confirmed the significance of this novel technology. In 1858, during the first heady success of a trans-Atlantic line, a London newspaper rhapsodized about the powers of the telegraph, calling it a "ministering spirit . . . the intellectual and moral power which is the prime mover of all other powers." The telegraph "extends indefinitely the dominion of the mind" and we can "anticipate . . . a complete network of electric filaments [which] will overspread every civilized land in the world, and converge to great ganglionic cables" stretching across all the oceans. The telegraph, moreover, epitomized the culture of the modern age, becoming a model for the scientific intercourse that would guide progress and lead to social order. "How immensely must this increase the facilities of the experimentalist," suggested the writer. With the "philosophers" and their telegraphic "data" leading the way, the new technology will "furnish to the great body of our race, a sensitive apparatus . . . which will keep men conscious of their mutual dependency" and the importance of social and political harmony ("The Electric Telegraph," 1858, p. 5).

Yet if the mind was an instrument, whose sophistication could be modeled by the technological capacities of modern man, the extent to which it was exclusively materialist remained undefined. The reference to its "ministering spirit" gave telegraphy itself an ambiguous extramaterial quality. The study of instinct directed itself to resolving this point.

ANIMAL INSTINCT AND PRECISION: THE GEOMETER BEE

Instinct afforded a particularly important pivot in the debates over the mind because of two traditional associations or qualities. By definition an animal function, it marked the boundary between animals and man. Human reason and free will were canonically a substitute for the instinct of animals. As one writer reassuringly explained, "[instincts] are only proofs that man is the noblest creature since they are the results of a power which deprives the animal to a very large extent both of will and judgement" (Garratt, 1856, p. 27). Perhaps more significant still in the 19th century, instinct was by definition precise in its operation, an example of a reflexlike response, infallible and exact. As the *Encyclopaedia Britannica* entry on instinct explained, "perfection and uniformity are seen in the products of instinctive toil, imperfection and variety are the consequences of human labour having the process and the result always within the sphere of its cognition" ("Instinct," 1856, p. 391). Studies of instinct indicated that complex actions carrying all the appearance of intelligence could be considered innate, essentially indistinguishable from automatic physical operations like digestion. Accordingly, instinct demonstrated the power of a materialist explanation of mental operations.

As Thomas Huxley (1825–1895), an eminent physiologist and a leading light of British scientific life, put it in his 1874 lecture "On the Hypothesis that Animals Are Automata," *instinct* means "actions [which] are the result of . . . physical organisation." By using the word, he went on, humans indicate the belief that animals are machines. The lower animals may have sensations, emotions, and ideas, but these are set in motion by "the special apparatus" of the nervous system (1874/1893b, p. 241). Carpenter, who disagreed profoundly with Huxley's materialism, nevertheless agreed that much behavior in humans as well as in animals can be considered physiologically in the mechanical category of reflexes and instincts. "So far as any Animal is dominated by instinct, it is a creature of necessity; performing its instrumental part in the economy of Nature . . . an automaton executing that limited series of actions for which its Mechanism fits it" (Carpenter, 1876/1891, pp. 100–101). Although Carpenter strenuously maintained the distinguishing role of intelligence and will in the human mind, he readily acknowledged that it was not a constant or necessary aspect of human behavior. Humans could be as automatic as machines, as instinctive as animals—statements that in this context were entirely equivalent. He noted the example of telegraph "transmitters" (a reference to human clerical staff), "who work the instruments without conscious thought . . . just as unconsciously and automatically as Wheatstone's transmitter [the machine] does" (pp. xviii–xx). The study of animal instinct thus became pivotal to conceptions of the mind and materialism, as a flourishing literature on the subject testified (Chadbourne, 1872; Garratt, 1856; "Instinct," 1856; Sebright, 1836).[2]

Nevertheless such investigations did not build a clear distinction between volition and reflex, intelligence and instinct, that could resolve the different perspectives of a Carpenter or a Huxley. Rather, they disturbingly emphasized that animal sensibilities could be so acute and complex as to foster the appearance of intelligence. Indeed, the common definition of instinct hinged on this verisimilitude.

To explore this point further, I turn to a particular case of animal instinct, the bees, which was the first and best example of instinctive behavior for nearly all writers on the subject, whether writing for a popular or specialized audience. From Seneca onward, bees exerted a powerful hold on the human imagination as industrious social insects, operating in complex and coordinated communities that offered a ready model for human society (Moss, 1996; Raylor, 1992). By the late 18th century, remarkable investigations into bee behavior, especially those of blind Swiss naturalist François Huber (1750–1814), had given further evidence for this fascination. (Variations of the glass hives that Huber had developed, which allowed direct observation of the insects' industry and talents, were a favorite attraction at the 1851 exhibition—in even the most literal sense, then, we can see they were part of the context for Merryweather's invention.) Bees offered the most specific and remarkable account of the appearance of intelligence. Throughout the 19th century, naturalists and scientific pop-

---

[2]Modern accounts of instincts, in contrast, tend to examine the role of ideas about instincts as a part of evolutionary debates (e.g., Radick, 2000; Richards, 1978, 1981).

ularizers as well the many writers on animal sagacity in general reiterated their talents (Edwardes, 1908/1916; Wakefield, 1803/1816). William Kirby's 1802 monograph on the bee was the definitive British account, summarizing the researches of the 18th century. Kirby later included a long discussion of the bee in his natural theological work, *On the Power, Wisdom and Goodness of God as Manifested in the Creations of the Animals and in Their History, Habits and Instincts* (1835).

The most popular account of the bees, however, judging from its ubiquitous citation elsewhere, seems to be that of Henry Brougham (1778–1868), the prominent liberal who wrote widely on political and educational reform (1839; for an example of his influence, see Lardner, 1856). Besides embodying the virtue of modern industry, Brougham's bee demonstrated the acute sensibilities of the lower animals and the complexities of instinctive behavior. Victorian accounts, drawing on Huber, emphasized their precision in technological terms. The bee flew straight to an established source of pollen, "her route . . . as straight as the flight of a bullet from a gun" (Lardner, 1856, p. 87; cf. Huber, 1821, p. 255), or as if guided by "a rudder and compass" operated by "the most consummate navigator" (Lardner, 1856, p. 82).

But the most remarkable feature of the bee was its hive. Here bees were proved to be not only extraordinary architects and engineers but powerful mathematicians, raising all the associations of deliberate and high intelligence that mathematical reasoning implied. The perfection of the structure had been exposed in the 18th century, with investigations of the Paris academician René Antoine Ferchault de Reamur (1683–1757) into the efficiency of the structure. Reamur had asked a colleague, Johann Samuel Koenig (1712–1757), to derive a shape of hexagonal cells that used the least material and conserved the greatest space (Figure 8.3). Koenig's theoretical solution, reached, as Lardner emphasized, with "the assistance of the infinitesimal calculus" (1856, p. 31), agreed with the best observational measurements—indeed, the latter, ever more carefully carried out, exposed an error in Koenig's original computations. The calculating abilities of bees, therefore, compelled comparison to the "highest resources to which analytical science had then obtained" (p. 31). As still another account of the bee's "intelligence" put it,

> it would take a senior wrangler at Cambridge ten hours a day, for three years together to know enough mathematics for the calculation of these problems, with which not only every queen bee, but every undergraduate grubs [sic] is acquainted the moment it is born. (Garratt, 1856, pp. 198–199)

Bees were therefore ideal geometers; that they cooperated together to build their cell walls and could modify them under experimentally produced constraints only enhanced the appearance of purposeful intelligence.

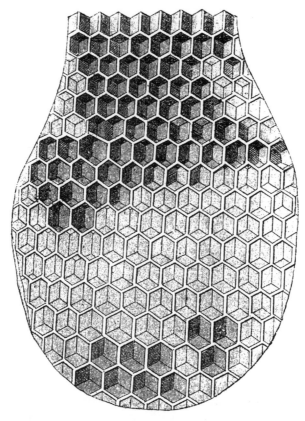

Figure 8.3. "The nice symmetry of these small cells/Where on each angle GENUINE Science dwells," from Lardner (1856, p. 56; for the poetic celebration, see Evans, 1806, Vol. 3, p. 28).

To what extent these abilities were innate became a point of importance for discussions of mental abilities in general. Interestingly, Darwin himself paralleled the complexity of organs/devices like the eye, noted earlier, with the complexity of the bee hive—"as wonderful in the mind as certain adaptations in the body—the eye for instance"—and concluded that if his theory explains one "it may explain the other" (quoted in Richards, 1981, pp. 211–212). This, of course, was precisely the conclusion of earlier naturalists who by contrast drew natural theological lessons from the study of animal instinct. Huber, Kirby, and Brougham all emphasized that the bee derived its superior abilities from an external providence. But, well before Darwin's interpretation of the subject, a materialist interpretation was equally plausible. The pious Brougham, for instance, wrote his account partly in response to this interpretation and included an extended attack on the speculation that hive building was innate in the sense of replicating some bodily shape of the bees themselves. In this argument, the body of the bee was itself a sort of template. In Brougham's view, the characterization of bee as "natural tool" underplayed the complexity of the bee's abilities and therefore reinforced a purely mechanical explanation. He insisted on a providential explanation. "Even if we suppose that her limbs," he argued, "would turn out to be instruments did we thoroughly understand them, she still, without being taught, has the power of working by means of them to a model exactly as men by experience learn to do" (Brougham, 1839, pp. 282–283; see Wood, 1877).

The stress on these remarkable abilities and the explicit comparison to humans were characteristic of discussions of instinct. There was also a striking tone of envy in the comparison. The intense appreciation of instinctive abilities pointed to the instability of the hierarchy of intelligence and sensibility. Both naturalists and physiologists framed sensibility on the one hand and intelligence and will on the other in an inverse relationship —the more sensible, the less intelligent, the more intelligent, the less sensible. Animal life, women, the rough and uneducated, rural populations, and other races of man were all more sensible than the urban European male (Cox, 1990; Figlio, 1975; Rodgers, 1986; Romanes, 1882; Rousseau, 1976). For instance, poet and novelist Thomas Hardy (1840–1928) provided an example of this well-established hierarchy in a vivid hybrid image of instrument, insect, and man, when he characterized the agricultural worker as "in person a sort of flesh-barometer, with feelers always directed to the sky and wind around him" (1886/1985, p. 257). A compelling racial example has been analyzed in Winter's (1998, pp. 187–212) recent work on mesmerism. Describing experimental mesmeric surgery in Calcutta in 1846, Winter indicated that for contemporaries, Indians made ideal mesmeric subjects (i.e., subjects in which volitional mental powers had been suspended) because they were more culturally primitive, closer to the natural order (p. 201). In contrast, according to one surgeon, "Western man has so far deserted Nature that in return she has renounced us as unnatural children and left us to our self-sufficiency and artificial resources" (p. 202). These words forcefully recalled the handicaps of a rational existence, marking a persistent gray undertone to comparisons of human and animal sensations in many different contexts. "In our social life . . . there are all sorts of concerns that prevent us from hearing the voice of nature, and which render us deaf and blind in the presence of the most evident signs," a meteorologist wrote. Although animals can "with certainty" predict changes in the weather from their sensations, man must "rely on those instruments which his intellect has devised, and which are, so to speak, substitutes for the instinct of the former" (Steinmetz, 1867, pp. 5–6). If instruments displayed human intelligence, then, they remained a substitute for an inadequate set of senses—or, more accurately perhaps, a set of senses made inadequate by the conditions of human social existence.

These examples indicate the ambivalent position that instincts and instruments came to hold in 19th-century discussions of the mind. On the one hand, mechanical precision was the identifying feature of the instinctive operations of the mind and therefore of its humbler and nonrational aspects. On the other hand, such precision was increasingly valued in the 19th century as the most admirable feature of rational thought, being, as the celebrated astronomer John Herschel (1792–1871) expressed it, "the very soul of science" (1830/1987, p. 122; cf. Wise, 1995). The precision of instruments managed the potential fallacies of human senses. Because, as Herschel commented in his influential *Preliminary Discourse on the Study of Natural Philosophy,*

> none of our senses . . . gives us direct information for the exact comparison of quantity, . . . in this emergency we are obliged to have recourse to instrumental aids, that is, to contrivances which shall substitute for the vague impressions of sense the precise one of number, and reduce all measurement to counting. (pp. 124–125)

If precision was the defining feature of modern science, it seemed to follow that automatic operations were more precise, and therefore more scientific, than the operations of intelligence. When scientific man was faced not with unreliable human senses, but their opposite, the relentless constancy and accuracy of animal senses, instruments again offered a solution. The substitute for natural automatism (such as the bees possessed) then was not simply reason, long study and experience, but artificial automatism, the mechanisms of scientific and technological man. In this context, the use of the term *instrument* to explain the mental operations involved in automatic behavior acknowledged its complexity but satisfactorily reinforced its mechanical and "unintelligent" nature by evoking the tools and values of modern science. Perhaps telegraphy superseded the piano as the dominant model for the mind because it more effectively addressed the tension between animal and human abilities. Its dramatic modernity provided a solution to the feelings of inferiority called up by the superior accuracy and complexity of instinctive behavior.

THE LEECH AS A PRECISION INSTRUMENT

These ideas provide the context for a better understanding for the plausibility of the Tempest Prognosticator as practical device. They also suggest how the device operated as a socially and politically significant model of mental operations. Manmade instruments that incorporated animal instincts combined the best of both worlds, using human scientific and technological ingenuity to harness the superior powers of lower forms of life. But they also dwelt on aspects of sympathy and judgment involved in their operation. Merryweather simultaneously characterized the Leeches (his "little comrades") as a precise and certain machine and as sensitive beings with feelings and even judgment. Merryweather referred to their "most remarkable sympathy" for the state of the air then noted that he arranged the bottles of the leeches in a circle "in order that the Leeches might see one another and not endure the affliction of solitary confinement." In other words, for Merryweather, the physiological and social sensibilities of the creatures were inseparable. He also purposely chose the number of leeches, 12, to represent what he called "a jury of philosophical Counsellors" (1851, pp. 45–46). The description of leeches as jury attributed powers of rational decision in collective sense to their operation. The arrangement of leeches then naturally modeled a sophisticated form of social bonds and directed those bonds to benevolent and orderly ends: the prediction of weather and exchange of human intercourse. The scientific jury, the elaborate ornament of Merryweather's device, his suggestion to link its dome to that of St. Paul's, and its exhibition at the international fair were all significant. These features confirmed the grandeur of Merryweather's conception of the instrument: modern, secular, philosophical, and benevolent.

An object like that invented by Merryweather materially represented the category of instruments and instrumentality that had emerged as a model conception in the sciences of the mind. It showed in action the conventional understanding of instinct and its role in the debates over the nature of mental processes. The Tempest Prognosticator incorporated the superior precision of lower forms of thought by literally turning instinct into a telegraphic process. It sought to incorporate for human use the superior sensibilities of lower forms of life, and in doing so, modeled an ideally precise way in which sensibility could lead to proper judgment, mechanizing the business of reason. By hooking animal instinct up to the electric telegraph, the Tempest Prognosticator embodied the argument that will and reason could control instinctive behavior and that this was the defining power of the superior human mind.

PRECISION AND THE LIMITS OF INSTRUMENTS

Yet it is worth emphasizing that the casual optimism of Merryweather's device was not so characteristic of these debates. As seen in several comments cited earlier, many treatments of instinct were more ambivalent or defensive or polemical. In conclusion, it seems worth exploring contemporary arguments that focused on the limits of instruments rather than simply assuming their ability to encapsulate and replicate sensibility, as Merryweather did. This juxtaposition of the sensitivity of the organism and insensitivity of our means of observing it meant strikingly different things to different observers. The flourishing contradictions in such accounts of the relationship between instrument and mind were more typical than Merryweather's confidence in technological progress and reason.

Both Thomas Henry Huxley and John Lubbock, leading physiologists, referred to the limits of scientific instruments as they sought to establish the complexity of the nervous system and its entirely mechanical operation past the current limits of what is visible. In his essay "On the Border Territory Between the Animal and Vegetable Kingdom" (1874/1893a), Huxley described a *nerve* as "nothing but a linear tract of specially modified protoplasm between two points of an organism—one of which is able to affect the other by the means of the communication so established." He argued that hence "even the simplest living being may possess a nervous system," in a clear denial of any significant border between humans and other forms of life. A reference to the microscope immediately thereafter called the reader's attention to another kind of boundary, a technological one, between animals and instrument-making humans. Here, too, there was no reassurance. Huxley suggested that current research into the structure of the nervous systems have indicated

> that the nerve fibres ... are simply the visible aggregations of vastly more attenuated filaments, the diameter of which dwindles down to the limits of our present microscopic vision, greatly as these have been extended by modern improvements of the microscope. (p. 165)

For Huxley, then, recognition of the complexity of nervous structures was linked to an acknowledgment of the inadequacy of human perception, even when assisted by instruments. Both comments established in different ways the common heritage of life and eroded the distinction between humans and other animals. Ultimately, this gave an equivocal account quite distinct from Merryweather's grand appropriation of the powers of the leech.

Writing some years later, Lubbock (1888/1899) echoed Huxley's comment. But he took it further by removing the positivist implication that human abilities to penetrate these structures will continue to increase with the improvements of the microscope. Rather Lubbock concluded that microscopes have reached the limit of their usefulness for exploring the minute structures of the nervous system of insects; microscopes already reach beyond the point at which the properties of light begin to interfere with and obscure vision. Lubbock reached the same conclusion as Huxley had: that the complexity of these systems defies our ability to fully distinguish between the sensibilities of living beings. Certainly, Lubbock argued, our very real limitations mean that we cannot impose our judgment about any hierarchy of sensations.

> The smallest sphere of organic matter which could be clearly defined with our most powerful microscopes may be, in reality, very complex;

> . . . there may be an almost infinite number of structural characters in organic tissues which we can at present foresee no mode of examining. (p. 191)

Lubbock went on from this point to draw an unexpected and eloquent conclusion about the range of human senses and those of insects. "We cannot measure the infinite by our own narrow limitations," he insisted, and speculated on "fifty other senses," as variable as our own. "To [insects], it [the world] may be full of music which we cannot hear, of colour which we cannot see, of sensation we cannot conceive" (p. 192).

Huxley and Lubbock thus claimed that even with the most sophisticated aids, humans cannot fully penetrate the workings of nature. The argument undermined the technological distinction between humans and animals, and of course the instability of this distinction was the more compelling because of the erosion of any biological one. However, the picture of the limits of human instruments and sensibilities was remarkably ambiguous. Even as it supported openly materialist explanations, as in Huxley's case, it simultaneously opened the doors to a wider range of explanations of mental powers, potentially implying that subtler forces may operate beyond our grasp. Such a suggestion lent itself to those who sought strenuously to resist materialist doctrines. Lubbock's picture of the world beyond our "narrow limitations," for instance, mirrored remarks made by Carpenter in the long preface on automatism in the fourth edition of his *Principles*, in which he went head to head with Huxley over the implications of automatic behavior. There Carpenter noted that the "Automatist," as he called his materialist opponents, could not dismiss uncertainty as a stage in our knowledge, to be overcome as we grasp the complexity of "antecedent conditions." In other words, when facing uncertainty, the Automatist has no right to assume the absence of an "'unconditioned' or self-originating element." To speak of the "instrumentality" of the mind, as Carpenter repeatedly did in his work, was to recall this vital qualification: the mind was an instrument, a fundamentally passive object activated ultimately by another agency, and not "self-originating" (1876/1891, pp. xxviii–xxx).

CONCLUSION

In characterizing the mind as an instrument, Victorians sustained a constant reference to the authority of modern science and technology that helped them to navigate the tricky waters of materialism. However different their interpretations of the nature of the mind, Huxley and Carpenter indicated how sensibility was linked in an intimate relationship to ideas about instruments, which represented simultaneously models of mental processes, the means of observing the mind, and a vital remaining symbol of the distinction between animals and humans. Instinct, that crucial boundary between animals and humans, played an important role in debates about the mind, providing examples of complex, purposeful behavior, like hive building in the bees, that was nevertheless by definition unintelligent and demonstrably innate. The automatic character of instinct assumed new meaning in the 19th century as it undermined the technological evidence of the superior rationality of humankind. Animals were simply better instruments, more precise and more efficient. Merryweather's Tempest Prognosticator, with its circle of super-sensible leeches, sought to harness this superior efficiency in a new kind of barometer that coupled the range of the leeches' atmospheric sensation with the range of the electric telegraph. His device showed the appeal and the implications of linking mental processes and instruments.

One generalization of the connections made in this chapter then leads to the importance of analogies and models in scientific work. In this context it is noteworthy that Green (chap. 7, this volume) argues by contrast that Charles Babbage and Ada Lovelace strictly limited the mental analogies they proposed for their calculating engines in order to resist the intellectual and social contamination of overtly materialist ideas. Clearly students of the mind accommodated themselves to the promise and risk of analogy differently in different circumstance, but we can also speculate that it was more difficult to limit such analogies in the second half of the century. In the 1838 translation of his work, *Elements of Physiology*, Johannes Müller explicitly cautioned readers against comparing nerves and electricity. "To speak of an electric current in the nerves," he insisted, was "quite as symbolical an expression as if we compared the action of the nervous principle to light or magnetism" (p. 640). But following the spectacular discoveries in physical sciences that unified all three phenomena, it may be that Müller's caution rang hollow. Carpenter, for instance, an individual who certainly shared Babbage's concerns about the social and political implications of materialist doctrine, had no difficulty rejecting Müller's injunction. In any case, the power of analogy lies partly in its imprecision. As the discussion above indicates, considerable ambiguity remained in any description of the mind as instrument. Studies of instinct and animal sensibility shared the same ambivalence. They could lead to fully materialist conceptions of mechanical mental processes, or preserve a sense of passive automatism, that called for an external guiding spirit (cf. Castle, 1987; Golinski, 1998b; Schaffer, 1999).

Merryweather's Tempest Prognosticator is admittedly an oddity. Yet it embodied assumptions about instinct and machinery that were significant because they were ordinary rather than novel. The appearance of the prognosticator suggests that the instrument-driven psychology pursued in laboratories of the later 19th century emerged from familiar understandings about the precision of machines and the precision of some categories of mental operations that were in place well before the first research centers for experimental psychology appeared. The significance of instruments in psychology needs to be traced outward to the kind of industrial context that is so vividly embodied in the presence of the prognosticator at the Great Exhibition. Such connections have become part of the standard interpretation of the work of certain individuals like Babbage or Helmholtz, but because of their stature, it becomes tinged with the suggestion of extraordinary prescience or insight, rather than indicating a deeply ordinary set of assumptions which they brilliantly pursued.

REFERENCES

Brougham, H. (1839). Observations, demonstrations, and experiments upon the structure of the cells of bees. In *Dissertations on subjects of science connected with natural theology* (Vol. 1, pp. 218–336). London: Knight.

Browne, H. B. (1949). *The story of Whitby Museum*. Hull, England: A. Brown.

Carpenter, W. B. (1891). *Principles of mental physiology with their applications to the training and discipline of the mind, and the study of its morbid conditions* (4th ed.). New York: Appleton. (Original work published 1876)

Carpenter, W. B. (1970). *Nature and man: Essays scientific and philosophical*. Farnborough, England: Gregg International. (Original work published 1888)

Castle, T. (1987). The female thermometer. *Representations, 17*, 1–27.

Chadbourne, P. A. (1872). *Instinct: Its office in the animal kingdom and its relation to the higher powers in man*. New York: Putnam.

Cheyne, G. (1990). *The English malady*. London: Routledge. (Original work published 1735)

Clark, J. F. M. (1997). The ants were duly visited: Making sense of John Lubbock, scientific naturalism and the senses of social insects. *British Journal for the History of Science, 30*, 151–176.

Coleman, W. (1977). *Biology in the nineteenth century: Problems of form, function and transformation*. Cambridge, England: Cambridge University Press.

Cooter, R., & Pumfrey, S. (1994). Separate spheres and public places: Reflections on the history of science popularization and science in popular culture. *History of Science, 32*, 237–267.

Cox, S. (1990). Sensibility as argument. In S. M. Conger (Ed.), *Sensibility in transformation: Creative resistance to sentiment from the Augustans to the Romantics* (pp. 63–82). London: Associated University Presses.

Darwin, C. (1985). *Origin of species*. London: Penguin. (Original work published 1859)

Edwardes, T. (1916). *The lore of the honey bee* (7th ed.). London: Methuen. (Original work published 1908)

The electric telegraph. (1858, August 28). *The Illustrated News of the World and Drawing Room Portrait Gallery of Eminent Personages From Photographs*, p. 5.

Evans, J. (1806). *The bees: A poem in four books with notes moral political and philosophical*. Shrewsbury, England: Eddowes.

Figlio, K. (1975). Theories of perception and the physiology of mind in the late eighteenth century. *History of Science, 12*, 177–212.

Garratt, G. (1856). *Marvels and mysteries of instinct, or curiosities of animal life*. London: Longman.

Golinski, J. (1998a). *Making natural knowledge: Constructivism and the history of science*. Cambridge, UK: Cambridge University Press.

Golinski, J. (1998b, May). *Putting the weather in order: Narrative and discipline in eighteenth-century weather diaries*. Paper presented at the William Andrews Clark Memorial Library, University of California at Los Angeles. Retrieved on February 2, 2000, from the World Wide Web: http://www.unh.edu/history/golinski/paper3.htm

Hankins, T., & Silverman, R. (1994). *Instruments and the imagination*. Princeton, NJ: Princeton University Press.

Hankins, T., & Van Helden, A. (1994). Instruments in the history of science. *Osiris, 9*, 1–6.

Hardy, T. (1985). *Mayor of Casterbridge*. London: Penguin. (Original work published 1886)

Herschel, J. F. W. (1987). *A preliminary discourse on the study of natural philosophy*. Chicago: University of Chicago Press. (Original work published 1830)

Hopkins, E. (Ed.). (1892). *Life and letters of James Hinton* (7th ed.). London: Kegan Paul.

Huber, F. (1821). *New observations on the natural history of bees* (3rd ed.). Edinburg, Scotland: W & C Tait.

Huxley, T. H. (1897). *Hume with helps to the study of Berkeley*. London: Macmillan.

Huxley, T. H. (1893a). On the border territory between the animal and vegetable kingdom. In *Science and culture* (pp. 156–186). New York: Appleton. (Original work published 1874)

Huxley, T. H. (1893b). On the hypothesis that animals are automata and its history. In *Science and culture* (pp. 206–252). New York: Appleton. (Original work published 1874)

Instinct. (1856). In *Encyclopaedia Britannica* (8th ed., Vol. 12, pp. 391–392). London: Adam & Charles.

Kirby, W. (1835). *On the power, wisdom and goodness of God as manifested in the creation of the animals and in their history, habits and instincts*. London: W. Pickering.

Lardner, D. (1856). The bee. *Museum of Science and Art* (Vol. 10, pp. 1–112). London: Walton & Maberly.

Lenoir, T. (1994). Helmholtz and the materialities of communication. *Osiris, 9*, 185–207.

Lightman, B. (1997). 'The voices of nature': Popularizing Victorian science. In B. Lightman (Ed.), *Victorian science in context* (pp. 187–211). Chicago: University of Chicago Press.

Lubbock, J. (1899). *On the senses, instincts and intelligence of animals with special reference to insects.* London: K. Paul, Trench, Trubner. (Original work published 1888)

Merryweather, G. (1851). *An essay explanatory of the Tempest Progosticator in the building of the great exhibition for the works of industry of all nations.* London: Churchill.

Moss, A. (1996). *Printed common-place books and the structuring of Renaissance thought.* New York: Oxford University Press.

Müller, J. (1838). *Elements of physiology* (W. Baly, Trans.). London: Taylor & Walton.

Radick, G. (2000). Language, brain function, and human origins in the Victorian debates on evolution. *Studies in the History and Philosophy of the Biological and Biomedical Sciences, 31,* 55–75.

Raylor, T. (1992). Samuel Hartlib and the commonwealth of bees. In M. Leslie & T. Raylor (Eds.), *Culture and cultivation in early modern England* (pp. 91–129). Leicester, England: Leicester University Press.

Richard, G. (1973). The historical development of nineteenth and twentieth century studies on the behaviour of insects. In R. Smith, T. Mittler, & C. Smith (Eds.), *History of entomology* (pp. 477–502). Palo Alto, CA: Annual Reviews & Entomological Society of America.

Richards, R. (1978). *The evolution of behaviour: Theories of instinct in the nineteenth century, with an essay on animal instinct and intelligence before Darwin.* Unpublished doctoral dissertation, University of Chicago, Chicago.

Richards, R. (1981). Instinct and intelligence in British natural theology: Some contributions to Darwin's theory of the evolution of behaviour. *Journal of the History of Biology, 14,* 193–230.

Rodgers, J. (1986). Sensibility, sympathy, benevolence: Physiology and moral philosophy in *Tristram Shandy.* In L. J. Jordonova (Ed.), *Languages of nature: Critical essays on science and literature* (pp. 117–158). London: Free Association Books.

Romanes, G. J. (1882). *Animal intelligence.* London: K. Paul, Trench.

Rousseau, G. S. (1976). Nerves, spirits and fibres: Towards defining the origins of sensibility. *Blue Guitar, 2,* 125–153.

Schaffer, S. (1999). Enlightened automata. In W. Clark, J. Golinski, & S. Schaffer (Eds.), *Sciences in enlightened Europe* (pp. 126–165). Chicago: University of Chicago Press.

Sebright, Sir J. (1836). *Observations upon the instinct of animals.* London: Gossling & Egley.

Steinmetz, A. (1867). *Sunshine and showers: A compendium of popular meteorology.* London: Reeve.

Tyndall, J. (1898a). The Belfast address. In *Fragments of science: A series of detached* essays, addresses and reviews (Vol. 2, pp. 135–202). New York: Appleton. (Original work published 1874)

Tyndall, J. (1898b). Science and man. In Fragments of science: A series of detached essays, addresses and reviews (Vol. 2, pp. 335–372). New York: Appleton. (Original work published 1874)

Wakefield, P. (1816). Instinct displayed in a collection of well authenticated facts exemplifying the extraordinary sagacity of various species of the animal kingdom. Boston: Cummings & Hilliard. (Original work published 1803)

Ward, W. G. (1867). Science, prayer, free will and miracles. The Dublin Review, 8, 255–298. (Original published anonymously)

Warner, D. J. (1990). What is a scientific instrument? British Journal for the History of Science, 23, 83–93.

Wigglesworth, V. B. (1973). Insect physiology. In R. Smith, T. Mittler, & C. Smith (Eds.), History of entomology (pp. 203–228). Palo Alto, CA: Annual Reviews & Entomological Society of America.

Winter, A. (1998). Mesmerized: Powers of mind in Victorian Britain. Chicago: University of Chicago Press.

Wise, M. N. (Ed.). (1995). The values of precision. Princeton, NJ: Princeton University Press.

Wood, J. G. (1877). Nature's teachings: Human invention anticipated by nature. London: Daldy, Isbister.

Young, R. M. (1990). Mind, brain and adaptation in the nineteenth century: Cerebral localization and its biological context from Gall to Ferrier. Oxford, England: Oxford University Press. (Original work published 1970)

9

PHILOSOPHIC DOUBTS ABOUT PSYCHOLOGY AS A NATURAL SCIENCE

CHARLES W. TOLMAN

With Kant, complication both of thought and statement was an inborn infirmity, enhanced by the musty academicism of his Königsberg existence. With Hegel it was a raging fever. Terribly, therefore, do the sour grapes which these fathers of philosophy have eaten set our teeth on edge. (William James, 1890, p. 366)

Philosopher William James was very impatient with philosophy. What commanded his patience was natural science. Thus, when he wrote his *Principles of Psychology* (1890), his intention was not to write yet another philosophical psychology but to lay the foundation of what he considered to be a natural scientific psychology. In the preface he wrote, "I have kept close to the point of view of natural science throughout this book" (p. v). He believed that this point of view could be maintained by the principle that "psychology when she has ascertained the empirical correlation of the various sorts of thought or feeling with definite conditions of the brain, can go no farther—can go no farther, that is, as a natural science" (p. vi). If psychology tries to go farther, "she becomes metaphysical." Little, it appears, did he imagine that this principle would drive psychology in the

20th century into forms of anti-intellectualism bleaker even than he surely would have tolerated. But he set the tone for those misconstructions and lent them "philosophical" legitimacy.

It may be questioned whether James fully appreciated the "metaphysics" that he rejected. It is certain, however, that most of those who were inspired by or took encouragement from his anti-intellectualism did not. This lack of appreciation, born largely of ignorance, came, moreover, to infect nearly all of the academically influential psychologies of the 20th century. The psychological literature continues to contain disparaging comments and distorted caricatures of major nonempiricist philosophers and their philosophies. I focus here on the two philosophers most maligned in this process: Immanuel Kant (1724–1804) and Georg Wilhelm Friedrich Hegel (1770–1831). The latter is thought generally to be irrelevant to the advance of scientific psychology; the former is alleged to have been not only irrelevant but also an impediment to the progress of psychology.

KANT ON PSYCHOLOGY AS NATURAL SCIENCE

On the whole, Kant delayed rather than furthered the progress of psychology. (Walter B. Pillsbury, 1929, p. 117)

Pillsbury typified the post-Jamesian contempt for philosophy—especially for Kantian philosophy—that was becoming fashionable among the new "scientific" psychologists. In a particularly well-known expression of this fashion, American psychologist John Broadus Watson remarked, "God knows I took enough philosophy to know something about it. But it wouldn't take hold. I passed my exams but the spark was not there." He went on to say that he did get something from the "British School" of philosophers, "mainly out of David Hume, a little out of Locke, a bit out of Hartley, nothing out of Kant, and strange to say, least of all out of John Dewey" (1930/1961, p. 274). Watson said he never knew what Dewey was talking about and, at the time of writing in 1930, still did not. Watson was known for advising his students not to waste time on philosophy, a discipline that had to be left behind if psychology was serious about establishing itself as a separate field of scientific endeavor. In his biography of Watson, David Cohen (1979, p. 25) observed that Watson was "fascinated" by Hume, who "freed him intellectually," making an interesting comparison with Kant's claim that Hume aroused him from his "dogmatic slumbers" (Kant, 1783/1947, p. 7). Although Hume did not solve the question of philosophy's dogmatism—far from it, in Kant's view—he saw the problem that Kant devoted his life's work to overcome. By contrast, Hume's works do not appear to have alerted Watson to the problem. He openly embraced dogmatism (although not precisely Hume's), with the ostensible end of cutting his chains to philosophy. But then, Watson admitted that he had got nothing out of Kant.

Watson was far from unique in this. His expressed views epitomized, however crudely, the then-dominant position among American psychologists, who were busy purchasing recognition in universities run by businessmen who valued what was technical and utilitarian and understood the simple evidence of the senses. These were men of action who had no time for metaphysical speculation. Psychology, as we know, achieved its status in the American universities during the early part of the 20th century by courting the applied interests of business, education, and the military and by overtly distancing itself from philosophy. Psychology claimed instead the status of science, which was thought of, in positivistic fashion, as an enterprise naturalistic and distinct from—one might even say "devoid of"—philosophy.

As Danziger (1990) reminded us, Kant framed, however inadvertently, the possibility of psychology as a discipline separate from philosophy by his identification of a nonphilosophical object of investigation: the inner sense. John Locke and other mental philosophers had made the distinction between sensation and reflection, but they had not distinguished between awareness of mental states and deliberate observation of such states. It was Kant who, in the course of his attempt to transcend the apparent opposition between empiricism and rationalism, made this distinction. Kant accepted from empirical philosophy the notion of an inner sense, a world of private experience. He then asked whether the objects of such a sense could form the basis of a science, as do the objects of the outer senses. His answer was

> a decided no, because science, unlike everyday experience, involves a systematic ordering of sensory information in terms of a synthesis expressed in mathematical terms. The material provided by the inner sense was, however, resistant to mathematization, and so there could not be a science of mental life, or psychology. (Danziger, 1990, p. 19)

This distinction of Kant's entailed the differentiation between the domain of philosophy and that of a separate psychology. The Empiricists had not made that distinction, but in sharply differentiating

> between mental life as it is present to subjective self-awareness and the general principles in terms of which that life is organized, . . . Kant clearly separated the domains of philosophy and psychology and thereby raised the question of psychology as a nonphilosophical empirical discipline. (Danziger, 1990, p. 20)

But from the purely empirical nature of this discipline and its resistance to mathematization (because its phenomena took place in time only, not in space), "it followed that psychology would never be a true science." Moreover, to become a science, its special method of introspection would have to yield to mathematical treatment in the way that the visual data of astronomy, for example, yielded to mathematical treatment. But this would not happen, and so the subject had no future as a science. (Danziger, 1990, p. 21)

In his 1786 *Metaphysical Foundations of Natural Science*, Kant wrote that a "pure philosophy of nature," one that investigates only what constitutes the concept of nature, need not be mathematical, but any philosophy dealing with particular natural objects will only be a true science insofar as it is mathematical. He obviously had in mind Newtonian physics as a model. In contrast to physics, he cited chemistry as a discipline that, in his estimation, would never make the grade, because its principles were "merely empirical, allowing no representation a priori in its conception" (1786/1957, p. 15). All this, again, because its phenomena are incapable of being treated mathematically.

Psychology having the inner sense as subject matter was judged similarly, but the case against it was far more damaging than it was for chemistry. For one thing, whereas the object of chemistry was objective and open to analysis and experimentation, the object of the inner sense could be disassembled only in thought and its parts could not be put aside and then re-assembled at any time and in whatever way suited the observer. Still less, Kant maintained, could we deal with the inner sense objects of other cognizing subjects. Moreover, the very observation of the object necessarily altered and distorted the object (p. 16).

When it came to method, Kant noted in his 1798 *Anthropology* that observing oneself is different from merely noticing oneself. Observation is necessary but it could "easily lead to wild imaginings and insanity" (1798/1978, p. 15). It could lead to an exaggerated self-consciousness that interferes with ordinary life. The inner sense is subject to deceptions, which are hard to detect and can lead to fanaticism, visionariness, and mental illness. "The inclination to retire into oneself, together with its consequent delusions of the inner sense," he wrote, "can only be brought into order if man is returned to the external world, into the order of the things which present themselves to external senses" (p. 50).

Kant's objections were not limited to psychology's resistance to mathematization. Empirical psychology is also impoverished because it cannot yield any real knowledge beyond the empirical knowledge that the inner sense exists and has certain describable qualities. The comparison with chemistry is instructive here. Kant's reservation was that its object could only yield empirical knowledge. Without mathematics it could not produce the universal and necessary laws such as physics provides. Now we know that Kant's objection with respect to chemistry was historically overcome, already in Kant's time, by the theoretical and experimental work of Lavoisier and Dalton. It was particularly the atomic theory of Dalton that guaranteed the quantitative understanding of chemical change. But the empirical psychology of the inner sense has not experienced a similar redemption. It is evident that the inner sense will allow quantification only of its most superficial aspects and will remain largely restricted to immediate, descriptive empirical knowledge. The resulting psychology would not appear to have much prospect as a separate and self-sufficient discipline.

What was Kant's intention? Clearly, he felt that empirical psychology of the inner sense could never be a fully adequate natural science. What about exclusion from philosophy? In the *Critique of Pure Reason* he addressed the issue directly. "How," he wrote,

> are we to regard *empirical psychology*, which has always claimed its place in metaphysics, and from which in our times such great things have been expected for the advancement of metaphysics, the hope of succeeding by *a priori* methods having been abandoned[?] I answer that it belongs where the proper (empirical) doctrine of nature belongs, namely, by the side of *applied* philosophy, the *a priori* principles of which are contained in pure philosophy. . . . Empirical psychology is thus completely banished from the domain of metaphysics; it is indeed already completely excluded by the very idea of the latter science. In conformity, however, with scholastic usage we must allow it some sort of a place (although as an episode only) in metaphysics, and this from economical motives, because it is not yet so rich as to be able to form a subject of study by itself, and yet is too important to be entirely excluded and forced to settle elsewhere, in a neighborhood that might well prove much less congenial than that of metaphysics. (1781/1965, pp. 663–664, emphasis in original)

Thus, although he spoke of it as "completely banished from the domain of metaphysics," Kant did not cut empirical psychology off entirely from metaphysics, let alone philosophy, if only on economical grounds. In any event, the structural divisions of Kant's philosophy were sufficient in number and scope (e.g., metaphysics of nature, metaphysics of morals, logic, propaedeutic or criticism, and pragmatic or applied philosophy) to accommodate empirical or any other kind of psychology. Likewise, it is not evident that Kant banished empirical psychology entirely from the domain of natural science. Rather, he simply judged it to be an exceedingly poor candidate.

It is important to understand that empirical psychology does not exhaust the psychology in Kant's philosophizing. He accepted as part of his philosophy the rational psychology that was Cartesian in origin but more recently articulated by Christian Wolff. This was a doctrine of the soul that, in Kant's words, "professes to be a science built upon the single proposition 'I *think*'" (1781/1965, p. 329, emphasis in original). In contrast to empirical psychology, which was grounded in conscious experience, rational psychology was grounded in pure reason. Kant was also skeptical of this kind of psychology and presented a seemingly devastating critique of its paralogisms in his *Critique of Pure Reason*. But rational psychology was also not, as a result, excluded either from metaphysics or from philosophy in general.

Then there was Kant's own transcendental psychology of the a priori that underlay his transcendental logic and thus formed the foundation of his entire system. This was the aspect of Kant's philosophy that aroused Gottlob Frege, P. F. Strawson, and others to charge Kant with the crime of psychologism (see Kitcher, 1990). Without getting ourselves embroiled in this complex issue, it need only be noted that psychology is pervasive and indispensable in Kantian philosophy.

Yet another manifestation of psychology is found in Kant's pragmatic anthropology, the "applied philosophy" to which he imagined in the *Critique of Pure Reason* empirical psychology might be relegated. The psychology is immediately recognized from the major headings in his *Anthropology From a Pragmatic Point of View* of 1798. Part I of the work is "Anthropological Didactic" and is made up of three "books": "On the Cognitive Faculty," "On the Feeling of Pleasure and Displeasure," and "On the Faculty of Desire." Part II of the work is "Anthropological Characterization" and has to do with character or, as it would later be called, personality. It is this work that, in all of Kant's opus, epitomizes that which distinguishes his philosophy from rationalism and empiricism. Kant believed that all philosophy had to be grounded in and justified by actual conditions of human existence, in the ways in which ordinary people actually thought, felt, and acted. Everyday life was indispensable, both as the point of departure for all philosophizing and as the ground on which its truth would be tested. The *Anthropology* was Kant's attempt to map that ground (see van de Pitte, 1978). Its behavioral psychology would appear to have somewhat better chances as a natural science than the empirical psychology of the inner sense but, still, it could not be fully adequate to its subject matter as is the natural science of physics.

The epitaph on Kant's gravestone was taken from the concluding remarks of his *Critique of Practical Reason*, in which he wrote that there are two things that fill the soul with ever newer and growing wonder and awe: "The starry skies above and the moral law within" (1788/1990, p. 186). This reflects, significantly, the "architectonic" of his life's work:

> The legislation of human reason (philosophy) has two objects, nature and freedom, and therefore contains not only the law of nature, but also the moral law, presenting them at first in two distinct systems, but ultimately in one single philosophical system. The philosophy of nature dealt with all *that is*, the philosophy of morals with that which *ought to be*. (1781/1965, pp. 658–659, emphasis in original)

Correspondingly, there was a metaphysics of nature (e.g., 1786/1957) and a metaphysics of morals (e.g., 1785/1964), and there were two kinds of knowledge: *speculative, theoretical* knowledge and *practical, moral* knowledge. There was, moreover, nothing outside of what is and what ought to be. These categories are, and were intended by Kant to be, exhaustive of all that we are capable of thinking. The fully adequate psychology, like philosophy itself, would have to recognize its object as both nature and freedom. We are moved to think and act as we do out of considerations of both what is and what ought to be. Psychology would have to be a science that is both natural and moral.

If we look in Kant's work beyond the troublesome purely empirical and purely rational psychologies, we can see what such a psychology would be. Kant tells us that the metaphysics of morals is about "the principles which in *a priori* fashion determine and make necessary *all our actions*" (1781/1965, p. 659, emphasis in original). It is the metaphysics, in short, of practical reason, the reason according to which we govern our actions. We experience in ourselves the urgencies of wants, needs, desires, and passions, just as we experience the demands on us of the world and of our fellow human beings but, as human beings, we are not slaves to such urgencies and demands. The ability to think makes a difference. It creates a distance between us and that which, whether internal or external in origin, would otherwise naturally compel us, so that we are able to defer action and deliberate its best course.

Kant recognized in this a psychology of two sides. The first was the empirical, pragmatic one, the second that of reasons (a psychology of reasons as opposed to a rational psychology), which has contemporary philosophical counterparts in theories of intentional action. The relation between these two sides is an instance of the general antinomy of natural necessity and freedom.

The empirical, pragmatic psychology of appearances is, like all appearances, subject to the laws of nature. Thus,

> it follows that all the actions of men in the field of appearance are determined in conformity with the order of nature, by their empirical character and by the other causes which cooperate with that character; and if we could exhaustively investigate all the appearances of men's wills, there would not be found a single human action which we could not predict with certainty, and recognize as proceeding necessarily from its antecedent conditions. (1781/1965, p. 474)

This is a psychology obtained by "simply *observing* [persons], and in the manner of anthropology seeking to institute a physiological investigation into the motive causes of [their] actions" (p. 474, emphasis in original).

But there was, for Kant, a big difference between predicting and understanding. "Sometimes," he said,

> we find ... that the ideas of reason have in actual fact proved their causality in respect of the actions of men, as appearances; and that

these actions have taken place, not because they were determined by empirical causes, but because they were determined by grounds of reason. . . . Granted, then, that reason may be asserted to have causality in respect of appearance, its action can still be said to be free, even although its empirical character (as a mode of sense) is completely and necessarily free. (1781/1965, pp. 474–475)

We may be able to predict and control others on the ostensibly scientific belief that antecedent condition X causes action Y, but a full and correct understanding will only result from seeing that Y in fact occurs because subjects judge it the most sensible thing to do under condition X. A truly deliberate act can only be based on an evaluation of the soundness of reasons. The psychology of reasons (or psychology of intentional action) would be concerned with such a fuller understanding (see Beck, 1960, chap. 3) and it would be necessarily moral in character.

The problem of a natural scientific psychology thus appears to be that it cannot stand alone. Whether it regards its subject matter as the inner sense or observable behavior, it will never be able to fulfill the task of a true science, which is to reveal the universal and necessary laws that govern its object. Although a fully natural scientific physics may be positioned to do this for the physical world, a natural scientific psychology is doomed to failure from the outset. Only a psychology that is at once moral and natural has the capacity to rise above the merely empirical.

HEGEL ON THE PROSPECTS OF A SCIENTIFIC PSYCHOLOGY

Die spekulative Philosophie Hegel's erlag dem Ansturm der Erfahrungs-disziplinen und dieser vorsichtigen neuen Philosophie, und es begann eine langsame Restauration der philosophischen Wissenschaft.[1] (Oswald Külpe, 1895/1915, p. 38)

Külpe was confident that the older, metaphysically extravagant, idealist philosophies were dead and were in his time being replaced by the "more cautious new philosophy" of the "disciplines of experience." This more cautious philosophy was the same "positivist point of view" that William James advocated (1890, p. vi) and J. B. Watson and others practiced as a basis for psychology's imitation of physics as the model of natural science. Külpe proved right about the impending hegemony of positivist thinking in psychology in the 20th century, but his confidence in the result is now shared by an ever-decreasing minority. What were the ideas of Hegel that Külpe thought stood in the way of understanding the mind?

---

[1] "The speculative philosophy of Hegel succumbed to the onslaught of the disciplines of experience and their more cautious new philosophy, and there began a gradual recovery of the philosophical sciences."

Hegel was anything but sanguine about the prospects of at least two popular attempts to found scientific psychology in his own time: physiognomy and phrenology (see Sokal, chap. 2, this volume). Both doctrines are now commonly regarded as instances of pseudoscience, and psychologists today are likely to give nodding agreement to Hegel's judgments without, however, paying any attention to the details of his criticisms. Were these limited to the peculiarities of physiognomy and phrenology, or might they be generalized as a general critique of any attempt to found scientific psychology?

Before looking at Hegel's views on psychology, it is useful to sketch Hegel's general philosophical program. The task of philosophy for Hegel was literally to explain the universe. This meant revealing what was necessary and universal about all ideas, and this was done by showing how categories and concepts were deducible from more inclusive categories and concepts. Logic was thus foundational. He began with the single most inclusive category, Being, and proceeded to demonstrate how lesser categories proceeded from it. All categories were thus considered to be developmentally related, but this development was strictly logical, not necessarily temporal—although correspondence with temporal evolution was not ruled out. Methodologically then, Hegel would undertake the study of an aspect of the universe by showing how it was deduced logically from a more inclusive category.

Hegel's philosophy was an avowed idealism, deliberately founded on the classical Greek philosophies of Plato and Aristotle. What he shared with these philosophies, however, was not so much particular doctrines or understandings as an overall framework and approach to knowledge that gave priority to the idea. His idealism did not deny the independent material world; indeed, it vigorously affirmed it. He denied only that we could have any conception of the material world independent of our own thoughts about it. This is significantly different from Kant's doctrine of phenomena and noumena: Hegel declared that nothing was unknowable in principle. The possibilities of knowledge, although never fully realized, were in principle infinite.

In defining philosophy, Hegel contrasted it with ordinary, everyday ways of thinking, which he called "empirical." Philosophy concerned itself with the universal and necessary; the empirical concerned itself with particulars and appearances. The philosopher must explain memory; the man on the street is content to acknowledge that he has one. Empirical philosophy was thus for Hegel an oxymoron. In its quest for the universal and necessary, philosophy had to go beyond the world of appearances to the intelligible world of universals (the very reality of which empiricism denied). Good science, then, is philosophical, not merely empirical. Hegel tended to be vague about the distinction between science (*Wissenschaft*) and philosophy. He referred to logic, for instance, as "science" and to physics, psychology, ethics, and religion as "philosophical sciences." On the whole, philosophy and science together embraced all legitimate pursuits of real knowledge or truth (as opposed to that which is merely true). Everyday or nonphilosophic thought might deal with that which is true, but it does not deal with truth as such.

HEGEL'S PSYCHOLOGY

Among the sciences considered by Hegel in his *Enzyklopädie der philosophischen Wissenschaften* was a branch of study called *Psychologie*. This psychology is nested in a series of hierarchical triads (1830/1969, pp. 317–388), three of which are dealt with here. All of Hegel's triads reveal roughly the same progression of states. The thesis is entirely in itself. The subject takes itself as sole object and thus remains implicit, pure subject. This is then overcome in the antithesis by the subject's projection of itself outside itself, becoming for itself. The subject becomes explicit, lost in the object, and thus pure object. The synthesis is the resolution in which subject returns to itself without loss of object, affirming the reality of both subject and object, along with the internal, concrete relations between the two.

Hegel's first triad is the broad one on which his *Enzyklopädie* is organized: Logic, Nature, and Spirit (see Figure 9.1). Where Nature has Logic as its premise, Spirit has Nature as its premise. Spirit is the truth of Nature, a truth in which Nature itself disappears. This includes the disappearance of natural determinacy. With Spirit comes the development of freedom and self-determination. This takes place in three stages: Subjective Spirit, Objective Spirit, and Absolute Spirit. Subjective Spirit, preoccupied with itself, in itself, is focused on the particular and individual. One might imagine that it is busy with distinguishing itself from Nature. When that is accomplished, the task shifts to projecting onto the outer world itself, for itself, that which is distinct from Nature and universal to Spirit. This is the task of Objective Spirit, the principle manifestations of which are laws, morality, and social institutions. In the end Spirit returns to itself, fully conscious of itself in relation to that which it objectively creates. This new consciousness is then expressed in the highest of spiritual achievements: religion, art, and philosophy.

Hegel located Psychology within the dialectic of Subjective Spirit. In its progression from Nature to Objective Spirit (or society) it moves from something barely distinguishable from Nature to something that is able to use reason to grasp the character of its own and other universals. This movement entails, again, three stages: Soul, Consciousness, and Mind. It would not be totally unfaithful to Hegel to regard this entire process as psychological but, strictly speaking, Hegel identified each of these stages with a different science. Soul is the subject matter of anthropology; Con-

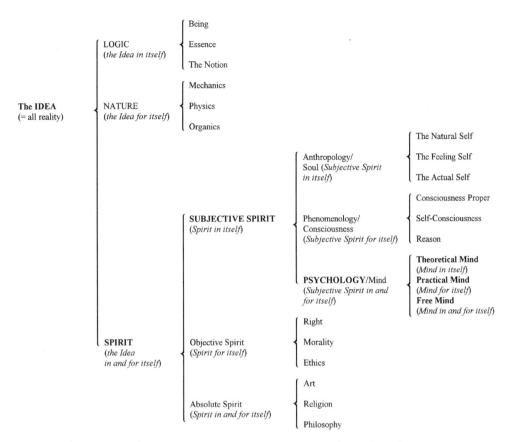

Figure 9.1. Relevant aspects of the Hegelian system (based on the *Enzyklopädie der Philosophischen Wissenschaften*; Hegel, 1830/1969).

sciousness, the subject matter of phenomenology; and Mind, the subject matter of psychology.

According to the now familiar dialectic, Soul is busy discovering itself. In the initial stage, which Hegel called "Natural Soul," there is a remaining oneness with Nature that is only gradually overcome through sensing of the Soul's own physical qualities and alterations. As the Soul becomes an object for itself it becomes Feeling Soul, characterized by feelings and the capacity for habit. Finally, the Soul distinguishes itself from its own content in a synthesis resulting in Actual Soul. This prepares the ground for the development of Consciousness, which proceeds through three stages: Sensuous Consciousness, Intellect, and, most important, the synthesis of Self-Consciousness, which includes development of appetite, desire, and the beginnings of reason.

Mind is the culmination of this process. The Soul is the Subjective Spirit in itself, that is, in a state of implicitness and undifferentiated unity. Consciousness is the putting forth of the Subjective Spirit, for itself, into otherness, opposition to itself in an object. Mind, the subject matter of psychology proper, is the grand synthesis of the Subjective Spirit. It is the return into itself of the Subjective Spirit, in and for itself, enriched by having gone forth in Consciousness.

The first stage in the dialectic of Mind is Theoretical Mind, in which occur the development of intuition, representation, and thinking; its development is implicit, concentrated on itself. The second stage is the Practical Mind, the going into otherness, now through action among other subjects in the objective world. Every aspect of Subjective Spirit that has up to this point developed is now applied to the problem of getting on consciously in the world. This requires a practical feeling for what is appropriate and what is inappropriate. It requires a recognition that the subject is no longer slave to impulses, but is capable of choosing among competing desires and impulses. Of course making the right choice and doing the right thing have a consequence. This is happiness. The lesson learned at this stage is that, while desires and choices have immediately to do with particulars, true satisfaction is not found in them. Satisfaction of one impulse simply leads to further impulses ad infinitum. The will, which is the developing characteristic of the Practical Mind, is led thus to seek satisfaction in universals. Real happiness is universal satisfaction.

The culmination of Mind, and thus also of Subjective Spirit, is the development of Free Mind. It puts itself forth into the world and contemplates itself there in objectivity. There it finds itself free, that is, not limited by anything but itself. It is now self-determining and infinite. This sets the stage for the next major projection into the objective world. In willing the universal, as universal, Free Mind wills itself, but in willing the universal, as individual, it wills that which transcends itself. This, as it turns out, is realizable only in concert with others. The stage is thus set for the development of Objective Spirit and the sociology and history that that implies.

At its highest level of development, therefore, the subject matter of psychology is the Free, Practical Mind, a willing mind that manifests itself in objective action, reflecting choices, and standards of the good. In short, it is a psychology of intentional action.

HEGEL'S CRITIQUE OF EMPIRICAL PSYCHOLOGY

Hegel's psychology was plainly philosophical. It was scientific only in the broad sense in which he used that label. Although it was empirical in both its grounding and its observable consequences, just as was Kant's, it was, again like Kant's, not an *empirical psychology* in the usual sense of the term. Hegel stated in no uncertain terms that an empirical psychology is constitutionally incapable of giving an adequate account of mind. In his argument in *The Phenomenology of Mind* (1807/1967, pp. 326–334), he anticipated two forms of empirical psychology: (a) an introspective form directed at the contents of mind and (b) a form that has all the earmarks of behaviorism, focusing on the organism's relation to its environment.

Empirical observation of one's own mind, or introspection, encounters thoughts. These are orderly and lend themselves to the easy formulation of Laws of Thought. But these laws are purely formal. They are empty abstractions and lack truth. That which is observed, said Hegel, has the manner of a content in itself.

> In the way in which this form or content, however, comes before observation *qua* observation, it gets the character of a content that is found, given, i.e. one which merely *is*. It becomes a passively existing basis of relations, a multitude of detached necessities, which as a definitely fixed content are to have truth just as they stand with their specific characteristic, and thus, in point of fact, are withdrawn from the form. (p. 330)

But this presumptive truth contradicts the actual truth which lies in the unity of content and form. Because they lack form, these contents are really just "vanishing moments in the unity of thought" (p. 330). Hegel said that the true form of thought is an active consciousness, but the connection between this activity and the observed content is lost in the mental attitude of observation.

But an empirical psychology is also to be found in the active practical reality of consciousness. This contains "the collection of laws in virtue of which the mind takes up different attitudes towards the different forms of its reality given and presented to it in a condition of otherness" (p. 331). The general thrust of this psychology is that the person is shaped by the otherness which it confronts in the world. But Hegel objected:

> On that account *what* is to have an influence on individuality, and what *sort* of influence it is to have—which, properly speaking, mean the same thing—depend entirely on individuality itself: to say that by such and such an influence this individuality has become this specifically determinate individuality means nothing else than saying it has been this all along. (p. 334, emphasis in original)
>
> If the external element is so constituted in and for itself as it appears in individuality, the latter would be comprehended from the nature of the former. We should have a double gallery of pictures, one of which would be the reflexion of the other: the one the gallery of external circumstance completely encompassing, circumscribing, and determining the individual, the other the same gallery translated into the form in which those circumstances are in the conscious individual. (pp. 334–335)

But this is entirely upside down. Owing to the freedom of the individuality, the world of the individual is only to be understood from the individual himself; and the influence of reality upon the individual, a reality which is represented as having a being all its own (*an und für sich*), receives through this individual absolutely the opposite significance— the individual either lets the stream of reality flowing in upon it have its way, or breaks off and diverts the current of its influence. In consequence of this, however, "psychological necessity" becomes an empty phrase, so empty that there is the absolute possibility that what is said to have this influence could equally well not have had it. (p. 335)

In short, this empirical "behaviorism" must assert that the individual is determined by the stimulus, while the testimony of our experience is that the effect of the stimulus depends entirely on what we make of it and what we decide to do about it.

Hegel noted that the idea of the individual being shaped by external circumstances leads to concerns about individual differences. To this he responded,

to describe how one man has more inclination for this, the other for that, how one has more intelligence than the other—all this is, however, something much more uninteresting than even to reckon up the species of insects, mosses, and so on. For these latter give observation the right to take them thus individually and disconnectedly (*begrifflos*), because they belong essentially to the sphere of fortuitous detailed particulars. To take conscious individuality, on the other hand, as a particular phenomenal entity, and treat it in so wooden a fashion, is self-contradictory, because the essential nature of individuality lies in the universal element of mind. (p. 333)

Hegel concluded that

individuality is what its world, in the sense of its own world, is. Individuality itself is the cycle of its own action, in which it has presented and established itself as reality, and is simply and solely a unity of what is given and what is constructed—a unity whose aspects do not fall apart, as in the idea of psychological law, into a world given *per se* and an individuality existing for itself. (p. 336, emphasis in original)

This is a matter of intelligibility that cannot be grasped empirically.

PHYSIOGNOMY, PHRENOLOGY, AND SO FORTH

The two widely popular attempts to establish a scientific psychology in Hegel's time did so by seeking laws that connected outer indicators with inner reality. *Physiognomy* sought these indicators in physical appearances, such as facial expression or handwriting. *Phrenology* sought them in peculiarities in the shape of the skull, assuming these to be closely related to the brain which, in turn, was assumed to be the organ of the mind.

Hegel granted a superficial plausibility to physiognomy: "We look at a man's face to see whether he is in earnest with what he says or does" (1807/1967, p. 345). The presumption of physiognomy as science, however, is that the connection between inner reality and outer expression is a necessary one. This Hegel contested: "It is . . . no doubt an expression, but at the same time only in the sense of a sign, so that to the content expressed the peculiar nature of that by which it is expressed is completely indifferent" (p. 345). There is, he says, no necessary unity between the two. The expression "is as much [reality's] countenance as its mask, which can be put off when it likes" (p. 346). At bottom, physiognomy is a confusion of the essential and the inessential. What is essential to mind is the self-determination to which no mere physical indicator can serve as index. It is the mind that determines the expression, not the expression that determines the mind. Hegel quoted Georg Christoph Lichtenberg: "If any one said, 'You act, certainly, like an honest man, but I see from your face you are forcing yourself to do so, and are a rogue at heart,'" the appropriate retort would be a "box on the ear" (p. 349).

Phrenology suffers a similar fate, without, however, being credited with even superficial plausibility. Hegel likened the thesis of phrenology to the belief that the taste of wine is determined by the form of the grape. Hegel remained dubious of any necessary relationship between the physical brain and the mind, but even if such could be proved, the case of phrenology would not be improved. "Furthermore," he said,

> even though the brain accepted the distinctions of the mind, and took them into itself as existential distinctions, and were a plurality of inner organs occupying each a different space, it would be left undecided whether a mental element would, according as it was originally stronger or weaker, either be bound to possess in the first case a more expanded brain-organ, or in the latter case a more contracted brain-organ, or just the other way about. (p. 357)

The basic problem with both of these pseudosciences is not that they miss the real physical indicators of mind. It is that they presume the existence of such indicators at all. To do so is to misapprehend the nature of mind, the most important aspect of which is its freedom from such indicators. This was, it will be recalled, the conclusion of his own psychology, that is, Free Mind.

But this freedom does express itself physically in meaningful and intelligible ways. "The true being of a man," he said, "is . . . his act; individuality is real in the deed" (p. 349).

> When it is a question of his being *qua* being, and the twofold being of bodily shape and act are pitted against one another, each claiming to be his true reality, the deed *alone* is to be affirmed as his genuine being—not his figure or shape, which would express what he "means"

to convey by his acts, or what any one might "conjecture" he merely could do. In the same way, on the other hand, when his performance and his inner possibility, capacity, or intention are opposed, the former *alone* is to be regarded as his true reality, even if he deceives himself on the point and, after he has turned from his action into himself, means to be something else in his "inner mind" than what he is in the act. (p. 350, emphasis in original)

It is not behaviorism that Hegel is advocating. On the one hand, the actor who is not deceiving himself may be deceiving others. There thus remains a fundamental ambiguity in action that reminds us that it is still something less than the mind itself. Moreover, Hegel would never suggest that we study action for its own sake, as Watson proposed for behaviorism. Action is represented by Hegel only as the most meaningful expression of Mind. As such it could serve as a legitimate subject matter for a psychology that has a clear understanding of just what the real context of action is.

CAUSES, REASONS, AND EXPLANATION

As mentioned at the outset, Hegel took the task of philosophy to be to explain the universe. He understood this to mean the deduction of the diverse categories of the universal. Now the methodology and subject matter of any science can be concisely summed up in the question of what its practitioners accept as constituting an explanation. Empirical psychology has typically followed the other special sciences like physics in adopting the causal explanation. The prominence of statistical correlation and preoccupation with experimental design in 20th-century psychology testifies amply to that. What was Hegel's attitude toward this kind of explanation?

Cause and effect were important categories in Hegel's logic. He acknowledged their role in scientific explanation, but he viewed that role as decidedly limited. As we already noted, knowledge of conditions can be useful in understanding particulars but, theoretically, it is universals that count, and the specification of causal conditions gives us no knowledge of these. Moreover, causation cannot explain even particulars. There may be practical value in knowing that B is invariably, or almost invariably, preceded by A. We know that when A occurs, B is to be expected. But there is nothing in this experience that allows us to deduce B from A. The two events are entirely different (if they were not, then there would be no question of causal explanation in the first place), and it is "impossible to see how one particular fact can produce an entirely different fact" (Stace, 1924/1955, p. 51).

The problem is made clearer if we put it into everyday terms. If I am puzzled about B and seek information that will dispel its mystery, would your saying A satisfy my need? Hardly! We must ask then: What kind of knowledge about a thing would enable us no longer to regard it as a mystery? Specification of a cause may be useful under certain circumstances, but it does not dispel puzzlement. What we want to know, according to Hegel, is how it is reasonable that such-and-such occurs or exists. What we need is knowledge from which we can deduce the occurrence or existence of B. We want to know why B must be the case.

In practice, "causal explanation," like "empirical philosophy," is an oxymoron. Causes may conceivably be elaborated so as to provide the needed deduction, but this is a theoretical elaboration of the sort that has been rare indeed in the history of so-called scientific empirical psychology as we have known it since the second half of the 19th century.

CONCLUSION

The outcome is, it appears, much the same as for Kant. We need to understand why people think, act, and feel as they do. The explanation will be found in reasons—partly in the reasons embodied in the individual's understandings and intentions, but mainly in the reasons embodied in Objective Spirit, that is, in social institutions. It is from these latter reasons that individuals draw the reasons of their personal intentions. What is needed, according to Hegel's account of the highest stage of individual Mind—namely, Free Mind—is an understanding of the reasons from which people deduce their own action. This would be a theory of intentions.

Kant and Hegel both insisted on psychologies that would be adequate to the distinct and unique nature of the human mind. It was this uniqueness that 19th-century science, especially evolutionary biology, but also physiology, was supposed to have eliminated. It was this empiricist naturalism that drove scientific psychology from its experimental beginnings to the various forms of mindless brain worship that overtook it in the late 20th century.

Were Kant and Hegel right in their pessimism about natural scientific psychology? History seems to provide an answer. What has scientific psychology got to show for itself? The faddish nature of experimental psychology in the 20th century is well-known. The same may be said of psychotherapy, except that in it more fads tend to run concurrently. There is overwhelming evidence of lack of agreement among clinical psychologists on how to deal with specific disorders. There is no agreed-on theory from which to deduce unambiguous solutions to problems. As a result, every therapist is now working on his or her own intuition with scant or no help from "science." Is that because there is so little true science? Is it all pretense and illusion? Perhaps we have paid insufficient attention to the real and ultimately moral reasons (as opposed to empirical "stimuli" or conditions) why people feel as they feel, think as they think, and do as they do.

Kant and Hegel must be taken more seriously than they have been historically in our discipline. They surely did not have all the answers, but if we are to recover a more adequate theory in psychology, we cannot afford to continue ignoring them. They offer a challenging and much-needed critical balance to the celebratory frenzy that now tends to characterize psychology's self-understanding.

REFERENCES

Beck, L. W. (1960). *A commentary on Kant's* Critique of practical reason. Chicago: University of Chicago Press.

Cohen, D. (1979). *J. B. Watson: The founder of behaviorism.* London: Routledge & Kegan Paul.

Danziger, K. (1990). *Constructing the subject: Historical origins of psychological research.* Cambridge, England: Cambridge University Press.

Hegel, G. W. G. (1967). *The phenomenology of mind* (J. B. Baillie, Trans., & G. Lichtheim, Ed.). New York: Harper & Row. (Original work published 1807)

Hegel, G. W. F. (1969). *Enzyklopädie der philosophischen Wissenschaften* [Encyclopedia of the philosophical sciences] (F. Nicolin & O. Pöggeler, Eds.). Hamburg, Germany: Felix Meiner Verlag. (Original work published 1830)

James, W. (1890). *The principles of psychology* (Vol. 1). New York: Henry Holt.

Kant, I. (1947). *Kant's Prolegomena to any future metaphysics* (P. Carus, Ed.). LaSalle, IL: Open Court. (Original work published 1783)

Kant, I. (1957). Metaphysische Anfangsgründe der Naturwissenschaft [Metaphysical rudiments of natural science]. In W. Weischedel (Ed.), *Kants Werke, Bd. 5: Kritik der Urteilskraft und Schriften zur Naturphilosophie* [Kant works, Vol. 5: Critique of judgment and writings on natural philosophy] (pp. 11–135). Wiesbaden, Germany: Insel-Verlag. (Original work published 1786)

Kant, I. (1964). *Groundwork of the metaphysic of morals* (H. J. Paton, Trans.). New York: Harper & Row. (Original work published 1785)

Kant, I. (1965). *Critique of pure reason* (N. K. Smith, Trans.). New York: St. Martin's Press. (Original work published 1781)

Kant, I. (1978). *Anthropology from a pragmatic point of view* (rev. ed., V. L. Dowdell, Trans.). Carbondale: Southern Illinois University Press. (Original work published 1798)

Kant, I. (1990). *Kritik der praktischen Vernunft* [Critique of practical reason] (K. Vorländer, Ed.). Hamburg, Germany: Felix Meiner Verlag. (Original work published 1788)

Kitcher, P. (1990). *Kant's transcendental psychology.* Oxford, England: Oxford University Press.

Külpe, O. (1915). *Einleitung in die Philosophie* [Introduction to philosophy] (7th rev. ed.). Leipzig, Germany: Verlag von S. Hirzel. (Original work published 1895)

Pillsbury, W. B. (1929). *The history of psychology.* New York: Norton.

Stace, W. T. (1955). *The philosophy of Hegel.* New York: Dover. (Original work published 1924)

van de Pitte, F. P. (1978). *Introduction to Kant's* Anthropology from a pragmatic point of view (rev. ed.). Carbondale: Southern Illinois University Press.

Watson, J. B. (1961). Autobiography. In C. Murchison (Ed.), *A history of psychology in autobiography* (Vol. 3, pp. 271–281). New York: Russell & Russell. (Original work published 1930)

10

KARL MARX AND WILHELM DILTHEY ON THE SOCIO–HISTORICAL CONCEPTUALIZATION OF THE MIND

THOMAS TEO

Contemporary psychologists study concepts such as memory, perception, consciousness, belief, intention, reasoning, language, and so on to understand the mind. They assume more or less implicitly that these functions or domains belong to an individual, that they change over the life span, and that they indicate certain central tendencies within or between populations that can be assessed in descriptive and inferential ways. Seldom do psychologists realize that they base their theories and research practices regarding the mind on an individualistic as well as on an individual concept of the mind.[1]

The assumption of an individual mind is not surprising and has historical–philosophical roots. When René Descartes (1596–1650; see 1637, 1641/1996) used his widely known *cogito* (I think) argument on which to base knowledge, *cogitamus* (we think) never entered his foundational reflections. On the contrary, he was skeptical of the *cogitamus*, view-

---

[1]The term *individualistic* connotes here a justification for the notion of the individual, while the term *individual* suggests a lack of reflection on the concept in daily research practices.

195

ing it as a source of bias and not seeing the dependence of the *cogito* on the *cogitamus*. Immanuel Kant (1724–1804; see 1781/1982) suggested the *cogito*, the "Ego" as thinking being, to be the subject matter of rational psychology (see Tolman, chap. 9, this volume). Although Kant (1781/1982) used concepts such as community in his epistemological writings, they were not essential in his knowledge–theoretical reflections.

Within the Western philosophical tradition it is not surprising that philosophy and psychology have accumulated a vast literature on the mind–body problem, yet there is only a marginal reflection on the mind–culture or mind–history question. Although philosophers have reflected on external influences on the individual's thinking processes, as suggested, for example, in Francis Bacon's (1561–1626; see 1965) concept of *idola*, this influence was often defined as negative and thus did not result in a cultural–historical or socio–historical conceptualization of the mind. Giambattista Vico (1668–1744) and Johann Gottfried von Herder (1744–1803) formulated ideas that are relevant to a social, historical, and cultural conceptualization of the mind, but the first Western philosopher who systematically elaborated a socio–historical understanding of the mind[2] was Georg Wilhelm Friedrich Hegel (1770–1831).

Hegel (1830/1992) discriminated among the subjective, objective, and absolute mind.[3] The *subjective mind* refers to an individual mind and encompasses sensation, habit, consciousness, perception, reason, desire, memory, imagination, and so on. The *objective mind* is the mind of a social community or era and is expressed in law, morality, and ethics. The *absolute mind*, an infinite entity, is expressed in art, religion, and philosophy (see Tolman, chap. 9, this volume). But Hegel also connected the subjective and objective mind by arguing that no individual "can leap beyond his time" as "the mind of the time is also his mind"[4] (1817/1986b, p. 111).

Critics might argue that Hegel's idealism, according to which the mind was understood as the self-becoming of the Absolute, and his lack of interest in the detailed mechanisms of the relationship between the subjective and objective mind, are not helpful to psychology. However, it must be understood that Hegel's challenge of the empirical individual as the core of a philosophy of the mind has been the stimulus for the socio–historical conceptualization of the mind in 19th-century German philosophical psychology.

Out of the Hegelian challenge have emerged two historically significant, often considered opposing research programs, one founded by Karl

---

[2]The English term *mind* is imprecise as it refers to German *Geist, Seele, Gemüt* as well as to *Bewußtsein* (consciousness). The German term *Geist*, widely used by Hegel, is translated as *spirit* or as *mind*.

[3]Tolman (chap. 9, this volume) translates *Geist* as *spirit*.

[4]Mind of the time (spirit of the times) is a translation of *Geist der Zeit*, which means the same as *Zeitgeist*.

Marx (1818–1883) and the other by Wilhelm Dilthey (1833–1911). Although both rejected the idea of an absolute mind, the concept of an objective mind has played an important role in both of their conceptualizations of the mind. Moreover, both were ambivalent toward Hegel. Marx (1867/1962a) admitted to being a pupil of Hegel, whose dialectics he argued stood on its head, and he considered it his goal to untie Hegel's dialectics "to discover the rational kernel in the mystical shell" (p. 27).[5] Dilthey (1977), who wrote a biography of the young Hegel (see Dilthey, 1959a), used a similar argument in refuting the claim that the Idea provokes historical facts: "This is like assuming that the picture in a mirror is the source of the movement of a person one observes moving in the mirror" (p. 173).[6]

Marx's conceptualization of the mind has indeed influenced psychology in the 20th century. He inspired the Soviet philosophical psychologist Sergej Rubinstein (1889–1960), the cultural–historical school with its mastermind Lev Vygotsky (1896–1934), the French psychologist Georges Politzer (1903–1942), the German psychologist Klaus Holzkamp (1927–1995), and various forms of critical psychology. Followers of the Frankfurt School merged his theories, albeit not his psychological writings, with psychoanalysis and developed a field of research—Freudian–Marxism.[7]

Dilthey's psychological writings have challenged attempts to capture psychological phenomena of the mind through natural–scientific experimentation. Dilthey (1957) called on Wilhelm Wundt (1832–1920) as a witness, who, too, realized that experimental psychology is limited to basic psychological processes and that the study of mental life requires more than causal explanations (see pp. 166–167). He had a significant influence on 20th-century psychology in the form of the *geisteswissenschaftliche Psychologie* of Eduard Spranger (1882–1963) as well as on Karl Jaspers (1883–1969), on Edmund Husserl (1859–1938) and his phenomenological psychology, and on Hans-Georg Gadamer's (born 1900) hermeneutics. In North America his ideas influenced Gordon Allport (1897–1967), and his spirit lives on in various forms of humanistic psychology.[8]

Marx did not discuss Dilthey. However, Dilthey, who was 15 years

---

[5] Translations have been provided by the author of this chapter. In cases of ambiguity the author sought guidance in Kamenka (1983).
[6] Translations have been provided by the author of this chapter.
[7] Marx exercised perhaps his greatest influence in psychology via Vygotsky's developmental concepts (e.g., zone of proximal development). These concepts could be assimilated and accommodated into mainstream research because the cultural–historical school followed a natural scientific methodology in line with Marx's authority.
[8] Despite their real impact on psychology, Marx and Dilthey are hardly mentioned in North American history of psychology textbooks. One of the very few textbooks that recognizes Marx is Robinson (1976). He suggested that Marx failed to influence the course of psychological scholarship because of his Hegelianism and that his nonexperimental and sociological approach to the mind were detrimental to the emerging natural science of psychology. With a focus on intellectual history, however, I do not discuss why Marx and Dilthey were without impact on remodeling the psychology of their time.

younger than Marx, analyzed Marx's economic but not his philosophical or psychological writings.[9] In a review of 1878, Dilthey (1974) argued that Marx's theory of value "stands in unsolvable contradiction to the real facts" (p. 186). According to Marx (1867/1962a, 1898/1962c), value is the crystallization of societal labor, the magnitude of which depends on the amount of labor necessary for the production of the product, while the amount of labor is measured by the time involved. Dilthey criticized Marx—from a psychological point of view—for not taking the needs of individuals into account when determining the value of a commodity. However, he commended Marx's reconstruction of the concentration of capital. This analysis, Dilthey (1974) claimed, was "executed in an extraordinarily brilliant way" (p. 187). Orthodox Marxist scholarship described Dilthey, who was politically a liberal, less favorably and denounced him as a member of late bourgeois philosophy, as irrational, as not understanding the nature of historical laws, and as denying objectivity (Buhr, 1988).

It is the intent of this chapter to demonstrate that both thinkers have more commonalities in their socio–historical understandings of the mind than previously thought. Both were more interested in the historically and socially mediated content of the mind than in its processes, and they both viewed the mind as embedded in human life activity. Notwithstanding these similarities, they differed in their notions of society, history, and action. This chapter outlines Marx's and Dilthey's conceptualization of the nature of the mind and methodologies for studying it—neglected in mainstream psychology but theoretically a historical alternative to German experimental psychology. Too, I hope that it becomes clear that their conceptualization of the mind, although similar in intention, is different from Wundt's and other forms of *Völkerpsychologie*, which Wundt promoted for the nature of higher thought processes, in opposition to experimental psychology that focuses on basic mental processes (see also Danziger, chap. 3, this volume; Teo, 1999).

THE NATURE OF THE HUMAN MIND

Karl Marx

There are difficulties in discussing Marx's ideas on the mind. First, as the object of intense academic research in former socialist countries, a vast literature has been accumulated. However, within Marxism as a state doctrine, socialist countries were seen as the logical and necessary outcome of his thoughts. Second, Marx never wrote a book or an essay on psychology

---

[9]This is understandable, as many of Marx's writings were published long after his death (see below).

in the narrow sense. He did not intend to develop a psychology, as he was primarily interested in philosophy, political economy, and politics. Philosophy's goal is—as Marx expressed in his last thesis on Feuerbach—not to "interpret the world . . . but to change it" (1888/1958, p. 7). He wanted to "overturn all circumstances in which the human is a degraded, a subjugated, a forsaken, a contemptible being" (1844/1956c, p. 385). Third, in his mature writings, Marx no longer participated in discussions on the mind, and psychologists are not mentioned in his writings.[10]

Marx used the term *psychology* in his earlier writings on several occasions. For example, in an article on censorship he suggested that in Prussian criminal suits, judge, prosecutor, and defense counsel are unified in one person. According to Marx (1843/1956a), this unification "contradicts all laws of psychology" (p. 24). Beyond using the word *psychology*, he also laid out a theoretical framework in which the socio–historical quality of the mind was identified as its basic feature. The mind, according to Marx and Engels (1932/1958), "is from the beginning a societal product and remains one" (p. 31). The mind of a single individual is not just the mind of a single person, as the mind is "in connection with the whole of society and part of the whole of society" (p. 167).

The connection of the mind with society finds its equivalent in behavior:

> Even when I am active as a scientist, an activity that I seldom perform in immediate community with others, I am societal, because I am active as a human being. Not only the material of my activity is given to me as a societal product, as is the language in which the intellectual is active, but also my own existence is societal activity. (Marx, 1932/1968, p. 538)

Consequently, Marx urged philosophers to study concrete individuals who live in concrete historical societies and not to reflect on the abstract individual beyond history and society. He criticized Feuerbach for doing exactly that and for not realizing that the "religious mind is a societal product and that the abstract individual he analyzes belongs to a particular form of society" (1888/1958, p. 7).

Marx's socio–historical concept of the mind must be understood within the context of his view on human nature, which again was characterized by its societal dimension: "The essence of specific personalities is not their beards, their blood, their abstract physical features, but their

---

[10]Babbage's works (see Green, chap. 7, this volume) cited by the later Marx were nonpsychological. Althusser (1965/1996, p. 35) classified Marx's writings into the early works (1840–1844), the works of the break (1845), the transitional works (1845–1857), and the mature works (1857–1883). The mature writings are nonanthropological and nonpsychological. The celebrated *Economic-Philosophical Manuscripts of 1844* (Marx, 1932/1968), the *Theses on Feuerbach* of 1845 (Marx, 1888/1958), and *The German Ideology* of 1845–1846 (Marx & Engels, 1932/1958) all belong accordingly to the "pre-mature" works in which Marx's psychological thoughts can be found.

social quality" (Marx, 1844/1956c, p. 222). As Marx (1888/1958) pointed out in the sixth thesis on Feuerbach, "but the human essence is not an abstract idea inherent in each specific individual. In its reality it is the ensemble of societal relations" (p. 6). Although these theses were, according to Engels (1888/1958), "written down in a hurry, absolutely not intended for publication" (p. 547), and thus provide room for speculation and interpretation, this statement did not suggest that humans are solely societal relations.

Marx's term *societal relations* referred to the essence of human beings. Thus, the idea of the relevance of societal relations was not in contradiction to the notion that humans are also natural beings. In contrast to certain readings of Marx, the natural is not in contradiction to the societal in his theory. He repeatedly emphasized the natural dimension of humans in the *Economic-Philosophical Manuscripts* (Marx, 1932/1968). Already in 1860 Marx (1964) stated that Charles Darwin's book on natural selection was "the natural–historical foundation for our view" (p. 131). The difference between Marx and Engels, who highly regarded the evolutionary aspect of Darwin's theory that coheres well with dialectical materialism, and Darwin is that, as Engels (1966) pointed out, "humans produce" (p. 170), whereas animals may collect. Thus, "it is impossible to transfer laws of animal societies at once to human ones" (p. 170).

In the *Economic-Philosophical Manuscripts* (Marx, 1932/1968), which are famous for Marx's discussion of social–psychological topics such as alienation and exploitation, he pointed out that humans are societal and historical beings and thus "history is the true natural history of the human being" (p. 579).[11] He emphasized that "the formation of the five senses is the work of the whole preceding world history" (pp. 541–542). Consequently, the meaning of sensory objects changes according to sociohistorical contexts and according to one's own position in these contexts. Using the example of food, he pointed out that "for starving humans the human form of food does not exist, but only its abstract being as food" (p. 542).

Marx implicitly used the concept of the objective mind when he reflected on the human mind. He moved, however, according to his philosophy with its emphasis on productive activity (labor), from an objective mind understood by Hegel as law, morality, and ethics to viewing the objective mind as industry. Accordingly, one should be able—in the objectified products of human labor—to understand the nature of humans: "One sees how the history of industry and the developing objective existence of industry is the open book of human nature, of . . . human psychology" (1932/1968, p. 542). In the course of this argument, Marx expressed one of the first criticisms of the content of modern psychology: "A psychology, for which this book, the sensuously most tangible and accessible part of

---

[11]Natural history (*Naturgeschichte*) has the meaning of natural science.

history, is closed, cannot become a real science with a genuine content" (p. 543). Not only Marx but also Dilthey desired a psychology with an authentic content.

The socio–historical dimension of the mind (consciousness; Bewußtsein) was discussed extensively in The German Ideology (Marx & Engels, 1932/1958).[12] According to Marx's materialist position, he rejected the idea that the mind was ever pure. On the contrary,

> the mind is a priori afflicted with the curse of being burdened with matter, which makes its appearance in the form of agitated layers of air, sounds, in short of language. Language is as old as consciousness . . . and develops from the need, the necessity of interaction with other humans. (p. 30)

Even more radical than connecting the mind with matter is the idea that the mind changes and develops historically, with production (labor) being the carrier of this development. As suggested within the perspective of a materialist conception of history (see pp. 61–65), Marx (1859/1961) identified a progression of societal formations from an Asiatic, classical, feudal to a modern bourgeois mode of production (p. 9).

Modes of production are power laden as productive humans not only affect nature but also other human beings. They develop relations with other humans and production takes place under these societal relations. Forms of interaction (Vekehrsformen)[13] appear differently at different historical times. However, since primitive communism these relations have appeared in the form of class struggles between exploiters and exploited people. Participants in production relations might be unaware of this structural power and how it is connected with the mind. Marx did not use the term unconsciousness, but the idea is clear: "The ideas of the ruling class are in each epoch the ruling ideas" and "the ruling ideas are nothing but the ideal expression of the ruling material relations" (Marx & Engels, 1932/1958, p. 46). Thus, "morality, religion, metaphysics, all the rest of ideology and their corresponding forms of the mind, thus no longer retain the appearance of independence" (pp. 26–27).[14]

Haug (1984) and other Marxist scholars have emphasized that Marx used the metaphor of a camera obscura to describe ideology or false consciousness.[15] It is not plausible, however, to assume that Marx had a fully

---

[12]The German Ideology was written by Marx and Engels. However, Engels (1888/1962) himself argued that the "largest part of the leading central thoughts . . . belong to Marx" (pp. 291–292). The theory "carries therefore rightly his name" (p. 292). Consequently, I attribute the ideas to Marx.

[13]Marx later used the term production relations (1849/1959, p. 408).

[14]Marx originated the idea that socio–historical formation and class determine thoughts. This idea has been very influential and has been assimilated by contemporary radical theory and includes gender, "race," and sexual preference (see Teo, 1997).

[15]Haug (1984) pointed out that the camera obscura was a common epistemological topic in the 19th century. Dilthey (1977) also compared the working of the eye with a camera obscura (p. 98).

developed concept of false consciousness and used a metaphor for describing it. Applying a critical analysis that begins with real presuppositions, it makes more sense to suggest that Marx knew about optical phenomena such as optical illusions, the invertive function of the eye, and quasi-technological applications such as the *camera obscura* and that he modeled the mind (consciousness) accordingly. These understandings led Marx to the conclusion that the human mind has distorted views of the world (as in optical illusions) and that the mind works upside down (as in the *camera obscura*).[16] This argument is supported by the fact that optical issues formed a reoccurring topic in his writings.

In an article published in 1844 for the *Deutsch-Französische Jahrbücher*, Marx (1844/1956b) criticized Bruno Bauer and radical democrats for the fact that political life appears in their writings as a means, whereas life in bourgeois society is proposed as an end. Marx thought it a puzzle "why in the mind of the political emancipators . . . the end appears as means, and the means as end. This optical illusion of their mind . . . is . . . a psychological, a theoretical puzzle" (p. 367). Marx and Engels (1932/1958) used the image of the *camera obscura* in *The German Ideology* to describe the workings of the mind. Moreover, they identified the causes for the invertive function of the mind:

> If in all ideology humans and their relations appear upside down as in a *camera obscura*, this phenomenon arises just as much from the historical life-process as the inversion of objects on the retina does from the immediate physical process. (p. 26, emphasis added)

A similar image reappeared in the first book of *Capital* (Marx, 1867/1962a) on the fetish-character of the commodity. For example, in religion products of the mind appear as independent objects with life: Angels, products of the mind according to Marx, seem to watch over us. A commodity seems to have a mystical character, too, when societal relations among human beings appear in capitalism as relations between commodities. Marx compared this phenomenon with the sensation of an object on the optical nerve, which is not represented as a "subjective stimulus of the optical nerve itself, but as an objective form of a thing outside of the eye" (p. 86).

As indicated above, it was important to Marx to connect the socio-historical mind with power, and in consequence, with the real-life processes, the material activities, the labor, and practice of humans. Such an idea seems trivial but an examination of the psychology of his time, when cognitive processes were disconnected from real-life activities, demonstrates its significance. Ideas and conceptions of the mind are interwoven with the material activity of human beings: "Imagination, thinking, the mental interaction of humans, appear here as the direct outcome of their

---

[16]The idea of confounding reality and appearance can already be found in Plato's (1997) "allegory of the cave."

202   THOMAS TEO

material behavior. The same applies to mental productions as represented in the language of politics, laws, morality, religion, metaphysics, and so on of a people" (Marx & Engels, 1932/1958, p. 26). It was evident for Marx and Engels (1932/1958) that human beings are the producers of their ideas, "but real active humans, as they are determined by a particular development of their productive forces" (p. 26). Thus, "the mind can never be anything else than conscious existence, and the existence of humans is their real life-process" (p. 26).

This conceptualization of the mind led to the famous statement, "life is not determined by the mind, but the mind by life" (Marx & Engels, 1932/1958, p. 27). This central idea can also be found in the *Manifesto of the Communist Party* of 1848: Ideas of freedom, education, and rights "are results of bourgeois production and property relations" (1848/1959, p. 477), whereas the content of the law can be found in the life conditions of the ruling class; and probably most clearly in 1859,

> the totality of these production relations forms the economic structure of society, the real basis on which is built a legal and political superstructure, and which corresponds with certain societal forms of the mind. . . . It is not the mind of humans that determines their being, but on the contrary it is the societal being of humans that determines their mind. (Marx, 1859/1961, pp. 8–9)

However, out of this expressed determinism arises an explicit problem: If objective relations of a given society determine the mind, then how is it possible to think further ahead? Although Marx had no doubts about the ideological and materialist quality of the mind, he also believed that the mind could be developed further than the *Zeitgeist*. With regard to certain issues "the mind sometimes appears to be further advanced than its concurrent empirical relations, so that in the struggles of a later epoch one can rely on the authority of theoreticians of a previous time" (Marx & Engels, 1932/1958, p. 73).

Wilhelm Dilthey

It may be arduous to discuss Marx, but it is even more challenging to review Dilthey. He provided a wealth of psychological ideas (see Dilthey, 1976; Harrington, 2000; Rickman, 1988) that can hardly be pressed into a single chapter. In addition, in his later writings, after assimilating some of Franz Brentano's thoughts on psychology, the role attributed to psychology as the core science of the *Geisteswissenschaften* (human sciences or mental sciences) changed. Thus, his earlier thoughts should be reinterpreted in the light of his later ones.[17]

---

[17]Given the space constraints, the discussion of Dilthey's thoughts will be more systematic than historical.

Marx understood the mind as societal, as historical, as part of the human life process, and as a topic that must be studied in connection with power, as expressed in production relations, classes, and economic formations. Whereas Dilthey shared with Marx the assumption about the social and historical character of the mind, he did not agree with a materialist view of socio–historical development. Dilthey (1883/1959b) was more than skeptical toward theories of historical progress: "The philosophy of history has never been able to derive directly with sufficient determination a general law of this progress from the historical–social reality" (p. 110). According to Dilthey (1957), we "cannot deduce" historical (or personal) development (see p. 224). Dilthey's (1883/1959b) important distinction between the metaphysical and the modern-scientific mind is not part of a developmental logic. Although he did not share the specifics of Marx's analysis of structural power, he included domination (and dependence) in addition to community as the central external factor that constitutes the external organization of society (1883/1959b, p. 68). However, he suggested a more descriptive understanding of classes, as the "similarity of economic property relations . . . connects individuals to a class that feels united and confronts its interests with those of other classes" (p. 69).

Dilthey (1957) argued that mental life is influenced by the objective mind, an important concept for him: "Language, myth, religious custom, ethos, law, and external organization are products of the whole mind [*Gesamtgeist*] in which human consciousness has become objective, to use a Hegelian term" (p. 180, emphasis added). He conceptualized the term more broadly than Marx's industry and products of labor and maintained that the objective mind can be found in all expressions and effects that humanity has left for the succeeding generations. However, as Marx suggested looking at the products of labor to understand the mind, Dilthey (1957) believed that one must look at the "creations" of humankind, "in order to gain a deeper and more complete understanding" (p. 180). In external objects that represent the uniform character of human creations "psychology has its strong, stable material, which allows a true analysis of human mental life" (p. 226). Whereas Marx provided clear statements on how the objective mind determines the subjective mind, Dilthey (1957) was more cautious in arguing that "the mental constitution of a whole epoch *can* be represented in a single individual" (p. 236, emphasis added). It is a blessing and the basis of hermeneutics, that "historical consciousness allows modern persons to represent in themselves the whole past of humanity" (p. 317).

Dilthey (1958) valued the significance of individual people as much as the objective mind: "The objective mind and the strength of the individual determine together the mental world" (p. 213). Consequently, it is not surprising that Dilthey (1957) included the concept of genius in his reflections: "In the works of geniuses we can study the energetic effects of specific forms of mental activities" (p. 180). It was no contradiction for him to suggest that the individual is central in determining history and that the individual is, at the same time, determined by history. Dilthey (1883/1959b) pointed out that "the human as a history—and society—preceding fact is a fiction" (p. 31), a statement that is reminiscent of Marx's sixth thesis on Feuerbach.

The socio–historical character of the psychological subject matter was expressed several times: "The human being as an object of a sound analytical science is the individual as part of society" (Dilthey, 1883/1959b, pp. 31–32). "The individual is a point of intersection of a multitude of systems that become more finely specialized in the course of the development of culture" (p. 51). Thus, studying historical change is significant for understanding mental life, and "the original tie between psychological forces is dissolved through the work of history" (p. 352). For example, emotions become more complex with the development of art. Increasing differences between individuals are primarily "determined through division of labor and socio–political differentiation" (1957, p. 237).

Dilthey's socio–historical understanding of the mind was not in contradiction to the idea that human beings are natural beings. Like Marx, he emphasized that humans are not only influenced by nature but also influence nature (Dilthey, 1883/1959b, pp. 17–18). However, his focus was not biology but combining the study of psychology with history and the objective with the subjective mind. Dilthey (1957) was well aware of the scope and originality of this attempt. It is a demanding "task to build a bridge between existing psychology and the view of the historical world" (p. 237). Such a goal can only be realized step by step through an inclusion of the "study of historical products" (p. 237) in psychological research. Knowledge of the nature of the human mind is based on the study of the products and lives of the historical mind: "Only this historical self-consciousness of the mind enables us gradually to obtain a scientific and systematic reflection of the human being" (1883/1959a, p. 528).

Marx suggested that history should be the natural science of human beings. Dilthey (1957) echoed that "man cannot learn what he is through meditation about himself, nor through psychological experiments, but only through history" (p. 180). This idea was so crucial that he repeated this argument on several occasions: "What man is, can only be told by his history" (1960, p. 226). "Man recognizes himself only in history, never through introspection" (1958, p. 279). Given the significance of history for understanding humans it is not surprising that Dilthey suggested that "all *Geisteswissenschaften* are based on the study of past history" (p. 278; on the pre-eminence of history in the 19th century, see Shore, chap. 4, and Danziger, chap. 3, this volume).

Dilthey used three labels for psychology: (a) content psychology (*Realpsychologie*), (b) descriptive psychology (or analytical psychology), and

(c) structural psychology. The difference between form and content is a significant philosophical distinction. Dilthey based his argument in his *Habilitationsschrift* of 1864, entitled *Essay on an Analysis of Moral Consciousness* (1962, pp. 1–55), on this distinction. He identified psychology as a formal discipline and suggested that the focus on forms and processes of mental life prevented an examination of the content of the mind: "The psychological laws are pure formal laws; they do not concern the content of the human mind, but its formal conduct and behavior" (p. 43)—a situation that was unsatisfactory to Dilthey. In a manuscript of 1865–1866, Dilthey (1977) argued that "psychological contents are not explained by advancing processes and their laws" (p. 6). As "every experience contains a content" (1958, p. 19), an authentic content psychology includes the totality of mental life. For example, the search for the extension of one's self should be considered a content of emotional life (1957, p. 156). In his *Draft for the Descriptive Psychology* (around 1880), Dilthey (1977) still teaching in Breslau (1871–1882), argued, "however, if man contemplates the meaning of his life, it is the very content through which meaning is formed" (p. 182).

In 1882 Dilthey accepted a professorship at Berlin, a chair held earlier by Hegel (from 1818 to 1831). His famous *Ideas on a Descriptive and Analytical Psychology* (1957, pp. 139–240) were published during this period (in 1894). He promoted the concept of a descriptive psychology as an alternative to the explanatory experimental psychology of his time. Descriptive psychology should focus on the depiction of the parts and connections of mental life as they are experienced in their totality. The idea that the mind is socio–historical was a general framework and important fact for Dilthey, but beyond this general framework Dilthey sought to understand mental life in all its detail and totality. Thus, in contrast to Marx, Dilthey provided an extensive elaboration on the subjective mind.

Dilthey (1957) suggested that *intelligence* is only one part of mental life. The other parts were *instinctual* and *emotional* life, which he considered the center of mental life, and acts of *volition* (p. 180). These three parts —based on a traditional philosophical–psychological distinction—are always interconnected. However, it is possible in a process of scientific abstraction to distinguish them. It was very important to Dilthey to point out that mental life is more than intellectuality: "It is common to oppose thinking, feeling, and desiring as three separate concepts, as if feeling and desiring contain no thinking. That is wrong" (1990, p. 354). Although Dilthey was interested in the structure of the subjective mind, he always emphasized its connection with the objective mind: The subjective and the objective are connected as "the internal psychological connection is determined by the position of a life-unit within a milieu. The life-unit is in interaction with the external world" (1957, p. 212). For example, acts of volition (internal and subjective) and culture (external and objective) are interconnected, and thus psychology should "study the nature, laws, and connection of our acts of volition by looking at the external organization of society, the economic, and legal order" (p. 190).

Dilthey used the term *structural psychology* (*Strukturpsychologie*) explicitly in an unpublished manuscript (1962, p. 317). However, already in his *Ideas on a Descriptive and Analytical Psychology*, Dilthey (1957) emphasized the significance of the concept of structure: "A life-unit is determined by and determines the milieu in which it lives. This leads to an organization of internal states. I label this organization the structure of mental life" (p. 200). According to Dilthey, it would be the task of a descriptive psychology to study this structure and the knots that bind the psychological strings to the totality of life. The concept of structure has theoretical implications: "Mental life does not grow from its parts; it is not built from elements; it is not a composite, not a result of interacting atoms of sensation or emotion: it is originally and at all times an overarching unity" (p. 211). Challenging a psychology that focused on these elements, Dilthey (1957) put forth the notion of the "Gestalt of mental life" (p. 220), a term he already used in the 1860s when referring to the "Gestalt of our mental life as an unexplained synthesis of these mental functions" (1990, p. 27).

The concept of a "mental connective structure," which contains a "stable system of relations of its parts" (Dilthey, 1958, p. 324), represents an alternative to the concepts of natural–scientific psychology. All human experiences are connected and in experiencing the structural connection we accomplish the "totality of life" (1962, p. 317). As the mental structure aims at life's riches, satisfactions, and happiness, the mental structure also has a teleological character (1957, p. 207). The unity and totality of the mind and the person distinguishes mental life from the physical world and explains Dilthey's respect for art. In literature, in the writings of Augustin, Pascal, or Lichtenberg we detect, according to Dilthey, an intuitive understanding of the whole connection. However, a descriptive psychology would have to clarify these ideas in a general way (see p. 153).

Dilthey also linked the concept of structure to the concept of development and emphasized, for example, that each biological age has its own normative right. Developmental research should include the study of bodily development, the influences of the physical environment, and the surrounding mental world. All "these conditions influence the connective structure of mental life" (1957, p. 214). Even further, "development is only possible where a connective structure exists" (p. 218). Each biography is situated in a connective structure which is "organized from the inside and connected to a unity" (1958, p. 325).

Dilthey related mental processes to life activities, not in the sense of labor as a first need (Marx) but in a wider sense. In his inaugural lecture in Basel in 1867, he stated that the "purpose of humans is to act" (1957, p. 27). But Dilthey, who included in his reflections on the mind the whole human being with his or her cognition (intellectuality), emotion, and motivation (volition), saw action as only one expression of life, "only one part of our essence" (1958, p. 206). The problem with action, or behavior for that matter, as a potential core category of psychology is that it does not allow the "complete portrayal of our inner life" (p. 206). This can only be accomplished through the concept of experience (*Erlebnis*) in the sense of a subject's meaningful encounter with the natural, cultural, historical, and human world.

METHODOLOGIES FOR STUDYING THE MIND

It is justifiable to conclude that there are similar threads within the psychological writings of Marx and Dilthey. Both agreed on the socio-historical nature of the mind, but they differed in their understanding of society, history, and action. A similar constellation can be found with regard to methodologies and methods for studying the mind. Both Marx and Dilthey shared a general approach to the problem, which is nonexperimental but rather philosophical and historical, but they differed with regard to the status of the human sciences. Their general methodology may be subsumed under the category of a philosophical–abstractive version of science, which differed from a natural–scientific one—the two basic modes of performing science[18] in 19th-century Germany.

For example, Johann Gottlieb Fichte (1762–1814) and Hegel promoted a philosophical version of science. For Fichte (1794/1972), "a science has a systematic form; all its sentences are connected through a single principle, and unify in this principle to a whole" (p. 31); "a science must be one, a totality" (p. 33); and "a science should be a building; its main purpose is stability" (p. 35). There was no doubt for Fichte that "philosophy is a science" (p. 31) and that "the essence of science is the quality of its content" (p. 32). For Hegel (1807/1986a), "the true form [*Gestalt*], in which truth exists, can only be its scientific system" (p. 14). His dictum that "truth is the whole" (p. 24) contrasts sharply with an experimental version of science that focuses only on parts and moments and not on totality. These philosophical ideas were the core targets of experimental psychologists and recently of postmodernists. However, with the rejection of such a model of science, the possibilities were not explored sufficiently.

Marx and Dilthey endorsed a philosophical–abstractive version of science, different from classical German philosophy but shaped by its spirit. However, Marx (1867/1962a), who maintained a philosophical–abstractive version of science himself, admired the natural sciences and criticized the

---

[18] The term *science* is used in its German meaning *Wissenschaft*, which refers to the study of the natural sciences as well as the study of art, history, or religion.

methods and content of traditional philosophy (p. 27). For example, the first chapter of *Capital* (Marx, 1867/1962a) is a masterpiece in philosophical abstraction; it is not a natural–scientific text. However, a monistic view of science allowed him to interpret processes of capitalist economy and historical development as a "natural–scientific law" (p. 15). Dilthey, in contrast, attempted to establish the foundation for the *Geisteswissenschaften* and a methodology that would do justice to their very subject matters, which meant not to imitate the natural–scientific one. Although he was skeptical of philosophical systems, he demanded from science that research maintain a philosophical intention. In his hermeneutic writings he became skeptical of psychology as the basic science for the *Geisteswissenschaften* and suggested that all *Geisteswissenschaften* are related to understanding and interpretation (see Dilthey, 1958, p. 205).

Karl Marx

Marx (1932/1968) projected a monistic view of science: "The natural science will later subsume the human science as the human science will subsume the natural science: There will be one science" (p. 544). In *The German Ideology*, Marx and Engels (1932/1958) wrote,[19] "we accept only one single science, the science of history. History can be viewed from two sides and divided into the history of nature and the history of humans. Both sides cannot be separated" (p. 18). He also used natural–scientific metaphors for describing his methods. For example, Marx (1859/1961) argued that "the anatomy of bourgeois society must be pursued in political economy" (p. 8).

Marx and Engels (1932/1958) criticized traditional German philosophy for starting with what humans imagine and then arriving at real humans. In contrast he suggested a methodology in which one begins with active humans to understand their ideas and imaginations. To the real presuppositions of human existence and history (pp. 28–30) belongs first the fact that humans must be able to live. They eat, drink, and require clothing and shelter. Another presupposition is that a satisfaction of a need leads to new needs. At a certain point in history humans do not just find their means of living, they produce them. Thus, the history of humankind must be studied in relation to the history of production. Finally, procreation is a necessary presupposition of historical development. In short, he suggested that to study the mind one must study the preconditions that make the mind possible. For scientists of the mind this means that they must reflect on and study the preconditions that make the mind possible before they enter into experimentation.

For the analysis of political economy, Marx (1939/1983) offered a

---

[19] This was crossed out in the original manuscript.

method that can be described as a move from the abstract to the concrete (pp. 34–42). Moreover, he intended this method as a general methodology for the scientific mind. According to this method, the starting point for knowledge is the concrete, which appears in terms of sensible objects. In the process of knowledge acquisition one must identify the essence of these objects, represented in abstract concepts. This is not the end of the scientific process. After the scientific mind has developed abstract concepts, it must move from the abstract to a new form of the concrete. This form of the concrete maintains the abstract concepts but at the same time reproduces mentally the objects in totality. Marx used this method in his analyses of economy, and more recently Holzkamp (1973) successfully applied this method to psychology.

Abstraction and analysis played an important role in Marx's thinking and is an essential part of philosophical–abstractive science. In the preface of the first book of *Capital* (Marx, 1867/1962a) Marx made the comparison: "Neither microscope nor chemical reagents serve for the analysis of economical forms. The power of abstraction must replace both" (p. 12). Dilthey (1883/1959a), too, emphasized abstraction and analysis (analytical psychology) and argued, for example, that psychology depends on "identifying general characteristics developed by psychological individuals . . . through a process of abstraction" (p. 30). Of course, traditional psychology has widely neglected a discussion of the quality of abstraction in the process of discovery and justification.

Marx was open to a variety of methods to access the lives of people. He also used what psychologists might call "concrete empirical methods." He designed a "questionnaire for workers" based on a request from the French journal editor of *La Revue Socialiste,* which contained 100 questions, including "In which trade do you work?" "List the [employees'] sex and age" "Is the work completely or mainly manual or based on machines?" "Report, based on your own experiences, accidents which caused injuries or the death of workers" "How many holidays do you have during the year?" "Report on fluctuations in [your] salary, as far back as you can remember" and "What is the general physical, mental, and moral constitution of workers in your occupation?" (Marx, 1880/1962b).[20]

Wilhelm Dilthey

Dilthey's (1883/1959b) psychological and methodological writings must be understood within the context of his attempt to establish an "epistemological foundation for the *Geisteswissenschaften*" (p. 116). Dilthey sought to develop a critique of historical reason in the same manner as

[20]Marx wrote the original version in English. It has been translated into German for the Marx and Engels edition. This is the author's retranslation into English.

Kant developed a critique of pure reason for the natural sciences (see 1958, p. 278). Epistemological positions as outlined by Auguste Comte (1798–1857) and John Stuart Mill (1806–1873) were unsatisfactory to Dilthey (1883/1959b), as they assimilated history into the concepts and methods of the natural sciences. In contrast, he suggested that the anchor for the *Geisteswissenschaften* is the analysis of human experience, the facts of consciousness, and the mind. The most basic and central human sciences are those that study life-units that "constitute society and history" (i.e., humans; p. 28).

Not surprisingly, psychology is deemed the "first and most elementary among the disciplines of the mind" (Dilthey, 1883/1959b, p. 33). Psychology and anthropology (in the Kantian sense; see Tolman, chap. 9, this volume) study psycho–physical life-units while including the whole of history and all life experiences as their research material. Both disciplines are the "foundation of all knowledge of historical life, as well as of all rules of guidance and development of society" (p. 32). But in contrast to Kant, John Locke (1632–1704), or David Hume (1711–1776), Dilthey—in accordance with his view on human nature—did not limit his reflections to the epistemological subject. Rather, he focused on the total subject, whose psychological essence includes, besides intelligence, emotion and volition.

Dilthey justified philosophically a dualistic view of science encompassing the natural sciences (*Naturwissenschaften*) and human sciences (*Geisteswissenschaften*). The latter include history, political science, law, political economy, theology, literature, and art. More generally, *Geisteswissenschaften* refer to sciences that "have the historical–social reality as their subject matter" (1883/1959b, p. 4). The topic of these *Geisteswissenschaften* is "the historical–social reality as far as this reality has been conserved historically in the consciousness of humankind" (p. 24). Dilthey himself was not completely content with the term *Geisteswissenschaften*, which he borrowed from Schiel, who translated Mill's *On the Logic of the Moral Sciences*. The term *Geisteswissenschaft* "expresses highly imperfectly the subject matter of this study" (p. 5).[21] Dilthey was concerned once more that a focus on the mental (*Geist*) would draw attention away from the emotional and the motivational: "A theory that describes and analyzes social–historical facts, cannot ignore the totality of human nature and limit itself to the mental" (p. 6).

Dilthey (1883/1959b) was cautious about his scientific dualism. On the one hand, he emphasized that natural and mental processes are incomparable (p. 11) and that the "total experience of the mental world" (p. 9) justifies the concept of the *Geisteswissenschaften*, which cannot be executed according to the empirical study of nature. Thus, Hegel, Friedrich Schleiermacher (1768–1834), and Friedrich Schelling (1775–1854) are more rel-

---

[21]Until the middle of the 1870s, Dilthey used the term *moral–political sciences*.

evant for his epistemological reflections than are Comte, Mill, or Herbert Spencer (1820–1903; see Dilthey, 1883/1959b). On the other hand, he emphasized that mental life is only one part of the psycho–physical life-unit and put forth the notion of the "relative independence of the *Geisteswissenschaften*" (p. 17).

Based on the distinction between natural and human sciences and the intention of a psychological foundation for the *Geisteswissenschaften*, Dilthey composed his *Ideas on a Descriptive and Analytical Psychology* (see 1957). He objected that explanatory psychology (Johann Friedrich Herbart, Herbert Spencer, Hippolyte-Adolphe Taine) was not able to study the mind sufficiently, as causal explanations used in the natural sciences cannot be applied to the mental world. Although explanatory (natural–scientific) psychology builds on basic processes such as association or apperception, descriptive psychology separates description and analysis from the explanatory hypothesis. In descriptive psychology "the complete reality of mental life must be used for description and preferably analysis, and this description and analysis must have the highest achievable degree of certainty" (p. 168). To achieve this goal, descriptive psychology must begin with the developed mental life and not with "elementary processes" (p. 169). Hermann Ebbinghaus (1850–1909; see 1896) challenged Dilthey's critique of natural–scientific psychology and suggested that all problems can be handled within explanatory psychology.

Dilthey (1957) considered understanding (*Verstehen*) to be the most appropriate "method"[22] for psychology, simply summarized in the basic dictum: "We explain nature, but we understand mental life" (p. 144). However, he did not exclude other methods of psychology and acknowledged besides understanding a variety of approaches to psychology, including introspection, comparative methods, experimentation, and the study of abnormal psychology (see p. 199). On the basis of his view of the human mind, according to which the objective mind (expressed in the lifestyle, interaction, customs, laws, state, religion, art, and science of a culture) and subjective mind are interconnected, he emphasized the study of the products of mental life as a "very important complement" (p. 199) in the canon of psychological methods.

Even more significantly, Dilthey suggested that understanding is possible only because of the objective mind:

> Each single life-expression [*Lebensäußerung*] represents something common in the realm of this objective mind. Each word, each sentence, each gesture, or each act of politeness, each work of art, and each historical act can only be understood because a commonness [*Gemein-*

---

[22]Rickman (1988) suggested that understanding is not a method. However, Dilthey (1958) himself suggested that "understanding and interpretation is the method which accomplishes the human sciences" (p. 205).

samkeit] connects expression with understanding. (1958, p. 146, emphasis added)

Even the work of "the genius represents common ideas, the mental life [*Gemütsleben*], and the ideal of a time and an environment" (p. 208). From the world of the objective mind, human beings receive nourishment "beginning in early childhood" (p. 208). Consequently, "we can only understand an individual completely, as close as we may be, by getting to know how this individual came to be" (1957, p. 213). The "description of the individual psycho–physical life-unit is realized in biography" (1883/1959b, p. 33).

Dilthey became rather confident about the nature of truth and the outcome of research in the *geisteswissenschaftlichen* context. With regard to metaphysics he suggested that "mental life is in permanent evolution, unpredictable in its further development, at every point historically relative and limited. Thus, it is impossible to connect the latest concepts of these various scientific disciplines in an objective and final way" (1883/1959b, p. 404). However, with regard to psychology, Dilthey believed that an objective knowledge of the processes that constitute the mental life of humankind is possible. It would lead to an "objective science of the mental world" (1990, p. 157).

Thus, Dilthey was not only interested in singularity. On the contrary, he tried to understand the relationship between generality (uniformity) and particularity (singularity), significant for any understanding of mental life. As the mental totality of each human being is particular, it is the "most obvious problem to formulate laws, i.e., uniformities of behavior" (1977, p. 195). He tried to analyze and understand the particular while aiming for general principles. This can be done because "the particular arises on the basis of all these uniformities" (1957, p. 270). He did not envision a purely idiographic description and understanding of the individual but intended an understanding of generalized individuals. His desire for general results can be understood by his emphasis of the notion of an objective mind.

Dilthey's desire for generality can also be seen in his suggestion to develop types. Particular and individual expressions are not random but can be subsumed under a type as "certain basic forms, which we call—for the time being—types, reoccur in the play of variations" (1957, p. 270). Types are not metaphysical constructions as

> humankind contains a system of order just as the objective mind contains an order, which is organized according to types. This system of order leads from the regularity and the structure of the generalized human to types, through which understanding construes individuals. (1958, p. 213)

The focus on types "and what is subsumed under this type" (1962, p. 318) is not arbitrary. It is an essential part of Dilthey's psychology and philosophy. This typological intention can be identified easily in his philosophy of worldviews (Dilthey, 1960) and in the fact that the *geisteswissenschaftliche* psychologist Eduard Spranger (1924, 1914/1928), a follower of Dilthey, developed types of both personality and adolescent experience.

Dilthey is perhaps best known for his elaboration of understanding. This method is important as "the interconnectedness of the psychological cannot be expressed in concepts" (1977, p. 164). Accordingly "totality and its interconnectedness exist only in experience and in immediate consciousness" (p. 165). Humans experience the totality of their essence, and this totality is "reproduced in understanding" (1958, p. 278). Dilthey distinguished between (a) elementary forms of understanding, which are ubiquitous in everyday life in the form of immediate processes (p. 207), and (b) higher forms of understanding should something contradict our everyday experience (p. 210). In higher forms of understanding we start with an examination of the problem, the involved context, and finally reach understanding. An understanding of a person can be modeled on an understanding of poetry, or an interpretation of literature and art. From empathy arises the (c) highest form of understanding, in which the totality of mental life is effective, the re-experiencing (*Nacherleben*) of other people's experiences (see pp. 213–216). It is another feature of a *geisteswissenschaftliche* psychology as "re-experiencing of the psychological world . . . distinguishes all mental operations . . . from the knowledge of nature" (1977, p. 95). The (d) scientific form of understanding and interpretation leads to hermeneutics (1958, p. 217), with the final goal being "to understand the author better than he has understood himself" (1957, p. 331). Besides the category of understanding, Dilthey developed the concepts of experience, expression, and meaning (see 1958).

CONCLUSION

Marx and Dilthey outlined alternative methodologies for the study of the socio–historically embedded mind. These methodologies, unknown to most contemporary psychologists, were not developed with the same institutional support and vigor as experimental psychology. Their conceptualization of the mind did not become part of the mainstream of academic psychology, and their ideas survived only at the fringes of the discipline. The dominance of psychological experimentation at the end of the 19th century, based on a hasty commitment to one methodology, did not solve the problem of the subject matter of psychology or the nature of the mind —it merely excluded methodological ambiguity. Not surprisingly this exclusion led to a reoccurring dissatisfaction with the status of psychology in the history of the discipline as expressed in various crisis-of-psychology discourses. If we take the arguments of Dilthey and Marx seriously, then it seems logical to suggest—in the service of knowledge—that an understanding of the mind is limited as long as the objective dimension of the mind is not recognized. Following such a conceptualization, psychology requires more sophisticated methods for studying the mind. The ideas of Marx and Dilthey, philosopher–psychologists of the 19th century, are not the end but a foundation for this project.

REFERENCES

Althusser, L. (1996). *For Marx* (B. Brewster, Trans.). London: Verso. (Original work published 1965)

Bacon, F. (1965). *A selection of his works* (S. Warhaft, Ed.). Toronto, Ontario, Canada: Macmillan.

Buhr, M. (Ed.). (1988). *Enzyklopädie zur bürgerlichen Philosophie im 19 und 20. Jahrhundert* [Encyclopaedia of bourgeois philosophy in the 19th and 20th century]. Leipzig, Germany: Bibliographisches Institut.

Descartes, R. (1996). *Discourse on the method; and, meditations on first philosophy* (D. Weissmann, Ed.). New Haven, CT: Yale University. (Original works published 1637 and 1641)

Dilthey, W. (1957). *Die geistige Welt: Einleitung in die Philosophie des Lebens* (Gesammelte Schriften V. Band) [The mental world: Introduction to the philosophy of life (Collected writings, Vol. 5)]. Stuttgart, Germany: Teubner.

Dilthey, W. (1958). *Der Aufbau der geschichtlichen Welt in den Geisteswissenschaften* (Gesammelte Schriften VII. Band) [The construction of the historical world in the human sciences (Collected writings, Volume 7)]. Stuttgart, Germany: Teubner.

Dilthey, W. (1959a). *Die Jugendgeschichte Hegels und andere Abhandlungen zur Geschichte des deutschen Idealismus* (Gesammelte Schriften IV. Band) [History of the young Hegel and other essays on the history of German idealism (Collected writings, Volume 4)]. Stuttgart, Germany: Teubner. (Original work published 1883)

Dilthey, W. (1959b). *Einleitung in die Geisteswissenschaften* (Gesammelte Schriften I. Band) [Introduction to the human sciences (Collected writings, Volume 1)]. Stuttgart, Germany: Teubner. (Original work published 1883)

Dilthey, W. (1960). *Weltanschauungslehre* (Gesammelte Schriften VIII. Band) [Philosophy of worldviews (Collected writings, Volume 8)]. Stuttgart, Germany: Teubner.

Dilthey, W. (1962). *Die geistige Welt* (Gesammelte Schriften VI. Band) [The mental world (Collected writings, Volume 6)]. Stuttgart, Germany: Teubner.

Dilthey, W. (1974). *Zur Geistesgeschichte des 19. Jahrhunderts* (Gesammelte Schriften XVII. Band) [On the intellectual history of the 19th century (Collected writings, Volume 17)]. Göttingen, Germany: Vandenhoeck & Ruprecht.

Dilthey, W. (1976). *Selected writings* (H. P. Rickman, Ed. & Trans.). Cambridge, England: Cambridge University Press.

Dilthey, W. (1977). *Die Wissenschaften vom Menschen, der Gesellschaft und der Geschichte* (Gesammelte Schriften XVIII. Band) [Human, social, and historical sciences (Collected writings, Volume 18)]. Göttingen, Germany: Vandenhoeck & Ruprecht.

Dilthey, W. (1990). *Logik und System der philosophischen Wissenschaften* (Gesammelte Schriften XX. Band) [Logic and system of philosophical sciences (Collected writings, Volume 20)]. Göttingen, Germany: Vandenhoeck & Ruprecht.

Ebbinghaus, H. (1896). *Über erklärende und beschreibende Psychologie* [Concerning explanatory and descriptive psychology]. *Zeitschrift für Psychologie und Physiologie der Sinnesorgane, 9,* 161–205.

Engels, F. (1958). Anmerkungen [Comments]. In K. Marx & F. Engels, *Werke Band 3* [Works Volume 3] (pp. 547–567). Berlin, Germany: Dietz. (Original work published 1888)

Engels, F. (1962). Ludwig Feuerbach und der Ausgang der klassischen deutschen Philosophie [Ludwig Feuerbach and the outcome of classical German philosophy]. In K. Marx & F. Engels, *Werke Band 21* [Works Volume 21] (pp. 259–307). Berlin, Germany: Dietz. (Original work published 1888)

Engels, F. (1966). Engels to Lawrow in London: Nov. 1875 [Engels to Lawrow in London: Nov. 1875]. In K. Marx & F. Engels, *Werke Band 34 (Briefe 1875–1880)* [Works Volume 34 (Letters 1875–1880)] (pp. 169–172). Berlin, Germany: Dietz.

Fichte, J. G. (1972). *Über der Begriff der Wissenschaftslehre oder der sogenannten Philosophie* [On the concept of science of knowledge or so-called philosophy]. Stuttgart, Germany: Reclam. (Original work published 1794)

Harrington, A. (2000). In defence of Verstehen and Erklären: Wilhelm Dilthey's ideas concerning a descriptive and analytical psychology. *Theory and Psychology, 10,* 435–451.

Haug, W. F. (1984). Die Camera obscura des Bewußtseins: Zur Kritik der Subjekt/Objekt-Artikulation im Marxismus [The camera obscura of consciousness: On the critique of the subject/Object articulation in Marxism]. In *Projekt Ideologie–Theorie, Die Camera obscura der Ideologie: Philosophie, Ökonomie, Wissenschaft* [Ideology–theory project, the camera obscura of ideology: Philosophy, economy, science] (pp. 9–95). Hamburg, Germany: Argument.

Hegel, G. W. F. (1986a). *Phänomenologie des Geistes* [Phenomenology of the mind]. Frankfurt am Main, Germany: Suhrkamp. (Original work published in 1807)

Hegel, G. W. F. (1986b). *Vorlesungen über die Geschichte der Philosophie II* [Lectures on the history of philosophy II]. Frankfurt am Main, Germany: Suhrkamp. (Lecture given 1817)

Hegel, G. W. F. (1992). *Enzyklopädie der philosophischen Wissenschaften im Grundrisse* [Encyclopaedia of the philosophical science]. Frankfurt am Main, Germany: Suhrkamp. (Original work published in 1830)

Holzkamp, K. (1973). *Sinnliche Erkenntnis: Historischer Ursprung und gesellschaftliche Funktion der Wahrnehmung* [Sensory knowledge: Historical origin and societal function of perception]. Frankfurt am Main, Germany: Athenäum.

Kamenka, E. (Ed. & Trans.). (1983). *The portable Karl Marx*. New York: Penguin.

Kant, I. (1982). *Kritik der reinen Vernunft* [Critique of pure reason] (2 vols., W. Weischedel, Ed.). Frankfurt am Main, Germany: Suhrkamp. (Original work published 1781)

Marx, K. (1956a). Bemerkungen über die neueste preußische Zensurinstruktion [Comments on the newest Prussian guidelines for censorship]. In K. Marx & F. Engels, *Werke Band 1* [Works Volume 1] (pp. 3–27). Berlin, Germany: Dietz. (Original work published 1843)

Marx, K. (1956b). Zur Judenfrage [On the Jewish question]. In K. Marx & F. Engels, *Werke Band 1* [Works Volume 1] (pp. 347–377). Berlin, Germany: Dietz. (Original work published 1844)

Marx, K. (1956c). Zur Kritik der Hegelschen Rechtsphilosophie [Critique of Hegel's philosophy of right]. In K. Marx & F. Engels, *Werke Band 1* [Works Volume 1] (pp. 201–333, 378–391). Berlin, Germany: Dietz. (Original work published 1844)

Marx, K. (1958). Thesen über Feuerbach [Theses on Feuerbach]. In K. Marx & F. Engels, *Werke Band 3* [Works Volume 3] (pp. 5–7). Berlin, Germany: Dietz. (Original work published 1888)

Marx, K. (1959). Lohnarbeit und Kapital [Labor and capital]. In K. Marx & F. Engels, *Werke Band 6* [Works Volume 6] (pp. 397–423). Berlin, Germany: Dietz. (Original work published 1849)

Marx, K. (1961). Zur Kritik der politischen Ökonomie [Critique of political economy]. In K. Marx & F. Engels, *Werke Band 13* [Works Volume 13] (pp. 3–160). Berlin, Germany: Dietz. (Original work published 1859)

Marx, K. (1962a). *Das Kapital: Kritik der politischen Ökonomie (Marx Engels Werke Band 23)* [Capital: Critique of political economy (Marx Engels Works Volume 23)]. Berlin, Germany: Dietz. (Original work published 1867)

Marx, K. (1962b). Fragebogen für Arbeiter [Questionnaire for workers]. In K. Marx & F. Engels, *Werke Band 19* [Works Volume 19] (pp. 230–237). Berlin, Germany: Dietz. (Original work published 1880)

Marx, K. (1962c). Lohn, Preis und Profit [Value, price and profit]. In K. Marx & F. Engels, *Werke 16* [Works 16] (pp. 101–152). Berlin, Germany: Dietz. (Original work published 1898)

Marx, K. (1964). Marx an Engels: 19. Dez. 1860 [Marx to Engels, Dec. 19, 1860]. In K. Marx & F. Engels, *Werke Band 30 (Briefe 1860–1864)* [Works Volume 30 (Letters 1860–1864)] (pp. 130–131). Berlin, Germany: Dietz.

Marx, K. (1968). Ökonomisch–philosophische Manuskripte aus dem Jahre 1844 [Economic–philosophical manuscripts of 1844]. In K. Marx & F. Engels, *Ergänzungsband* [Supplemental volume] (pp. 465–588). Berlin, Germany: Dietz. (Original work published 1932)

Marx, K. (1983). Grundrisse der Kritik der politischen Ökonomie [Outlines of the critique of political economy]. In K. Marx & F. Engels, *Werke Band 42* [Works Volume 42] (pp. 15–768). Berlin, Germany: Dietz. (Original work published 1939)

Marx, K., & Engels, F. (1958). Die deutsche Ideologie [The German ideology]. In K. Marx & F. Engels, *Werke Band 3* [Works Volume 3] (pp. 9–530). Berlin, Germany: Dietz. (Original work published 1932)

Marx, K., & Engels, F. (1959). Manifest der kommunistischen Partei [Manifesto of the Communist Party]. In K. Marx & F. Engels, *Werke Band 4* [Works Volume 4] (pp. 459–493). Berlin, Germany: Dietz. (Original work published 1848)

Plato. (1997). *Complete works* (J. M. Cooper; Ed., & D. S. Hutchinson, Assoc. Ed.). Indianapolis, IN: Hackett.

Rickman, H. P. (1988). *Dilthey today: A critical appraisal of the contemporary relevance of his work.* New York: Greenwood.

Robinson, D. N. (1976). *An intellectual history of psychology.* New York: Macmillan.

Spranger, E. (1924). *Psychologie des Jugendalters* [Psychology of youth]. Leipzig, Germany: Quelle & Meyer.

Spranger, E. (1928). *Types of men: The psychology and ethics of personality.* Halle, Germany: Niemeyer. (Original work published 1914)

Teo, T. (1997). Developmental psychology and the relevance of a critical metatheoretical reflection. *Human Development, 40,* 195–210.

Teo, T. (1999). Functions of knowledge in psychology. *New Ideas in Psychology, 17,* 1–15.

11

EARLY DEVELOPMENT AND PSYCHOLOGY: GENETIC AND EMBRYOLOGICAL INFLUENCES, 1880–1920

FREDRIC WEIZMANN

Maturational models of psychological development have long been criticized (e.g., Hunt, 1961) for their presumed biological predeterminism. In recent years, some developmentalists (e.g., Scarr, 1987, 1993) have argued that these criticisms were misplaced and were based on a faulty model of development that neglected biology. Psychobiologist R. W. Oppenheim (1982) stated that such criticisms embodied serious misinterpretations of both biological concepts and the earlier theorists who relied on them. According to Oppenheim, by around 1900, embryologists had achieved an approach to development that allowed for the operation of environmental influences within the context of an organismic model.

Oppenheim (1982) did admit that the rapid growth of Mendelian genetics after 1900 led to a brief overemphasis on heredity, as well as to some tensions between embryologists and geneticists. He also acknowledged that the eugenics movement did have some influence among scientists prior to 1920 but maintains that its influence among mainstream scientists was limited (but see Kimmelman, 1983; Sapp, 1987). In Oppenheim's view, by 1920 it had become clear that genetic explanations did not rule out an important role for environmental influences.

According to Oppenheim (1982; see also Scarr, 1987, 1993), biological approaches failed to take root in psychology because behaviorists such as John B. Watson and Zir Yang Kuo misinterpreted embryology and genetics. He argued that, although the charge of predeterminism leveled at biological explanations was false, the ensuing debate seriously exaggerated the false and harmful antithesis between environment and heredity and led to the neglect of biological influences by psychologists.

The purpose of this chapter is to examine the issues that Oppenheim raised. Were biological ideas about development in the decades around the turn of the 20th century predeterministic, especially as they applied to humans? Did psychologists simply misconstrue these ideas?

Because biological models of development have been derived largely from the study of early development, one way to approach the topic is to examine historically how embryonic and fetal development have been portrayed. In the remainder of this chapter, I compare ideas about early human development common in biological and medical circles in the 1890s and early 1900s and examine how these ideas had changed by the 1920s, largely because of the influence of the new discipline of genetics. In the process, it will become clear that the history of biological beliefs about the influence of the external environment is more complex and problematic than Oppenheim (1982) suggested. Finally, I examine the impact that this history had on psychological ideas of development.

THE PRENATAL ENVIRONMENT, 1880–1915

One of the central issues for embryology has always been whether intrinsic or extrinsic forces guide development. This issue was marked by the long conflict between *preformationists*, who believed that the organism was in some way prefigured in the ova or sperm, and *epigenicists*, who believed that the organism only gradually developed from an initially homogeneous substance (Gasking, 1964). By the middle of the 19th century, however, most embryologists accepted observational accounts of development that favored epigenesis (e.g., Coleman, 1971/1977).

In the 1880s and 1890s, there was a seeming revival of this debate (Maienschein, 1985). The central protagonists were August Weismann (1834–1914), who emphasized the role of intrinsic factors in determining development, and Oscar Hertwig (1849–1922), who opposed this view. The debate was much less extreme and much more muted than the earlier versions of the conflict, however. Weismann did not believe that the adult form of the organism was literally prefigured in miniature in the embryo but only that the "germ plasm," located in the nucleus of the egg, directed later development. Whereas Hertwig argued that the form of the organism emerged only during development and was influenced by factors external to the nucleus, he did accept the idea that the egg was preorganized to some extent (Maienschein, 1985).

There were also those who believed that neither position could explain all the developmental evidence. In some cases early cellular factors appeared to determine the later development of specific organs or organ systems, whereas in others they did not (Maienschein, 1985). This suggested the existence of intrinsic determinants of development but also cast doubt on the view that development was solely regulated by these determinants. Oppenheim (1982, pp. 38–39) concluded that the conflict between preformation and epigenesis was essentially resolved in favor of this more moderate position by the mid-1890s and that this had become the consensual view by 1900. Certainly several influential American biologists espoused such a middle ground (Maienschein, 1985).

The term *environment* as used by embryologists did not necessarily refer to the external environment but included any factors outside the nucleus of the germ cells, such as the extranuclear cytoplasm of the cell. By the early 1900s, however, experimental embryologists and teratologists had established that various external agents or physical alterations of the embryonic environment, or of the embryo itself, could drastically change the course of ontogenetic development (Gilbert, 1997, p. 509).

Most of this embryological research was carried out in nonmammalian species. However, there was also a significant body of medical and scientific support for the idea that environmental influences operating during the prenatal period could have a powerful effect on mammals, including humans (Stockard, 1921).

It should be emphasized that this view did not simply reflect a belief in the doctrine of "maternal impressions." Historian of medicine Charles Rosenberg (1976) noted that by 1900 many physicians doubted this doctrine, but few would have doubted that prolonged overwork, anxiety, or malnutrition during pregnancy would have had adverse effects on the unborn child.

These beliefs were reflected, for example, in John Ballantyne's (1861–1923; 1902–1904) classic two-volume *Manual of Antenatal Pathology*. Ballantyne was a distinguished Scottish obstetrician. His work, which was still being described as a "must" for teratologists in 1977 (Warkany, 1971), provided a summary and evaluation of teratology and human embryology at the turn of the century. Ballantyne was well aware that many congenital problems were hereditary, but he was also convinced that disease and environmental factors played an important role in prenatal development. Although a strong critic of the belief in maternal impressions, he believed that the general health and well-being of the mother was important for the health of the unborn child.

The work of Franklin Mall (1862–1917) of Johns Hopkins was important in establishing the importance of prenatal conditions for embryonic survival (e.g., Maienschein, 1991, pp. 260–263; Sabin, 1934). Mall had studied embryology in Europe with Wilhelm His, a pioneer in the field of human embryology, and was the first head of the Department of Anatomy at Johns Hopkins University. Mall was also the first director of the Carnegie Institution's Department of Embryology, which was founded largely at his initiative. Mall recognized that several congenital conditions were hereditary; however, he concluded that uterine disease, leading to faulty embryonic implantation and ultimately to inadequate nutrition, was the major cause of prenatal death and defect (Mall, 1908). Although not the first person to propose such a hypothesis, he was, as his student George Corner (1889–1981; 1961) noted, the first to provide it with extensive empirical support.

Mall's work also received important experimental support from the studies of the embryologist C. R. Stockard (1879–1939). Beginning in 1906, Stockard studied the effects of a variety of environmental factors on embryonic development in several species, including mammalian ones. This work led Stockard (1921) to develop the idea of "critical-moments" (later renamed "critical-periods") in development, according to which the effects of an agent on prenatal development depends not on its specific nature but on the stage of prenatal development at which it is active; those organ systems that are developing most rapidly at the time are retarded or arrested. (This idea, of "critical" or "sensitive" periods, of course, later proved itself a powerful and influential one in developmental psychology, e.g., Bornstein, 1989; Oyama, 1979).

The idea that "developmental arrest" can cause developmental deviations dates back at least to Johann Meckel in the 18th century. It was Stockard, building on the experimental work of 19th-century French teratologists (Churchill, 1973), who formalized the idea and provided much of the evidence that led to its general acceptance. Although Stockard (1921) thought that lack of oxygen rather than inadequate nutrition per se was the most likely cause of abnormal development in mammals, his work generally provided powerful support for Mall's views.

In their 1909 text, Bailey and Miller (1909) expressed the balanced view that existed at the time of Mall's and Stockard's work. They noted that, although there were those who emphasized the role of "germinal and hereditary factors" and there were those who upheld the importance of "external factors" in producing malformations, it did "not seem that either can reasonably be considered as the only cause" (pp. 624–625).

THE COMING OF GENETICS

The relatively balanced view of development that existed around the turn of the century was shortly to change, however, with the growing influence of Mendelian genetics after 1900. Some biologists had already begun to differentiate between heredity and development in the 1880s and 1890s (Sapp, 1987, pp. 38–39), but T. H. Morgan (1866–1945) formalized and popularized this separation through his distinction between genotype and phenotype.

In 1903, Wilhelm Johannsen (1857–1927) initially proposed this distinction as a way of statistically differentiating hereditary from nonhereditary variation in populations subjected to selective breeding over several generations (Churchill, 1974). Between 1911 and 1915, Morgan and his group carried out the well-known research that gave rise to modern genetics (Gilbert, 1991). In the course of doing this research, Morgan reinterpreted the genotype–phenotype distinction so that it differentiated heredity from development within the individual (Churchill, 1974). This redefined distinction enabled Morgan to justify his research, which neglected the cell cytoplasm, identified with development, in favor of studying the heredity materials contained in the cell nucleus (Allen, 1979, 1985; Sapp, 1987).

Kurt Danziger (chap. 3, this volume) writes of the importance of constructing boundaries around areas of subject matter as part of the process by which new disciplines are formed and defined. The genotype–phenotype distinction not only served to justify Morgan's research but also allowed Morgan to form a new discipline: genetics. *Genetics*, now defined as the study of heredity, was thus separated from its parent discipline, *embryology*, which was now defined as the study of development (Allen, 1979, 1985; Gilbert, 1991; Sapp, 1987). Many European biologists who studied genes, as well as many other embryologists (Gilbert, 1991; Harwood, 1993), objected to the exclusive focus on the nuclear gene and to the separation of the study of heredity from that of development. However, this separation was widely accepted by geneticists in the United States, the acknowledged leader in genetics at the time (e.g., Sapp, 1987).

On its face, the phenotype–genotype distinction certainly appeared to legitimize the existence of nongenetic influences on development. It seemed to provide a rationale for Oppenheim's (1982) argument that the balanced approach to development first achieved around 1900 continued even after the birth of genetics, and Morgan, himself an erstwhile embryologist, never denied the existence of environmental influences on development.

Once having legitimated the study of the gene, however, many geneticists not only ignored the external environment but also the role of any nongenetic factors in early development. Historian of biology Jan Sapp

(1987, chap. 2) asserted that despite their ignorance about the processes that intervened between genes and the end products of development, American geneticists did not hesitate to claim authority over the entire field (see also Gilbert, 1991). As early as 1917, well-known geneticist L. C. Dunn (1893–1974; 1917) rejected the idea that the cytoplasm regulated development. Instead, he assumed that in time, there would be a physicochemical explanation of "the governance of the chromosomes over development" (p. 299).

For their part, embryologists carried out their research largely independent of genetics (Hamburger, 1980). They approached development from a more holistic and contextual point of view than geneticists. One of their chief concerns, for example, was the phenomenon of embryonic induction, in which development in one region of the organism affects development in other regions. Embryologists believed that genes, which were identical in every cell, could not by themselves explain the developmental processes of differentiation and organization. They viewed attempts to explain development in genetic terms as excursions into their territory. In 1937, distinguished embryologist (and Mall's former student) Ross Harrison (1870–1959; 1937) complained that the "wanderlust" of the geneticists was leading them to trespass on embryological territory (p. 372). He argued that their exclusive focus on the genome was a "hindrance" to understanding development (p. 372).

HUMAN EMBRYOLOGY

The rising influence of genetics was shortly to be reflected in the field of human embryology. By 1920, Mall's views about the environmental vulnerability of the embryo had already been challenged by reports of defective embryos in which the abnormality appeared to occur prior to implantation or in which abnormal embryos were found in apparently healthy uteri. The most important blow to Mall's views, however, came from a former student of his, George Corner.

Corner became one of the founders of the field of reproductive endocrinology (Oppenheimer & Bell, 1982). He was the codiscoverer of the maternal hormone, progesterone, which allowed pregnancy to proceed by suppressing menstruation and ovulation in the mother. Its discovery was a key to the development of the first birth control pill. Corner later became director of the Carnegie's Department of Embryology and, as a recognized authority on human reproduction, was appointed chair of the U.S. National Research Council's Committee on Sex. (He also became a distinguished medical historian as well; see Oppenheimer & Bell, 1982.)

In 1920, Corner (1921) conducted a study in which he examined hundreds of pig uteri obtained from meat packinghouses. Almost 30% of the thousands of embryos they examined manifested a variety of developmental abnormalities. Corner found no evidence of uterine abnormality, endocrine failure, or disease in these cases, however, and most of these uteri contained normal embryos as well.

These findings led Corner to conclude that genetic factors, in the form of lethal genes, were probably responsible for the embryonic failures. He contended (Corner, 1921) that the placental and endometrial damage Mall had observed was due to fetal death and not its cause. In addition, he stated that some of the endometrial inflammation observed by Mall may have been a normal response to gestational hormones, about which little was known when Mall published his monograph.

Corner also attacked the relevance of embryological findings of environmental influences on nonmammalian vertebrates. He believed that the human and mammalian uteri were much better protected from the environment than were nonmammalian ones. As he wrote in a popular book on reproduction 20 years later (Corner, 1941), the human conceptus was not exposed to an attack comparable to the chemicals or to the instruments of the biologist: "It lies out of sight and out of reach, in the uniformly conditioned environment of the uterine cavity" (p. 88).

The genesis of the study was the result of a collaboration between Corner and Charles Benedict Davenport (1866–1944). An early champion of Mendelian genetics in the United States, Davenport was the director of the Carnegie Institution's Station for the Experimental Study of Evolution (SEE) at Cold Spring Harbor in Long Island, a sister organization to Carnegie's Department of Embryology.

He was also the leader of the American eugenics movement (e.g., Allen, 1986; Rosenberg, 1976; for the early history of eugenics, see Fancher, chap. 1, this volume) and directed the Eugenics Record Office (ERO), which was adjacent to the Cold Spring Harbor Laboratory. The Carnegie Institution ran the ERO from 1917 until it was closed in 1939 (Allen, 1986). Davenport also figures in the history of psychology, because he was responsible for involving a number of psychologists, including Robert Yerkes, Edward Thorndike, and Henry Goddard, in the eugenics movement (Chase, 1980; Zenderland, 1998).

As a eugenicist, Davenport was concerned with fertility. He (Davenport, 1920) had proposed that twinning, and large family size generally, was a genetically controlled trait passed on through both male and female lines. This hypothesis was threatened by findings that most human twins were dizygotic, not monozygotic. Dizygotic twins result from the fertilization of two ova, not the splitting of an already fertilized one. Only the mother's genetic lineage would be relevant to any genetic tendency to produce multiple ova.

Davenport's interest in Corner's work came from his attempt to preserve the father's genetic role in the process. He argued (Davenport, 1920) that the tendency to produce multiple ova leading to multiple conception was quite common but that lethal genes, which could be carried by either parent, would lead to embryonic failure.

Davenport had bred a strain of twin-bearing sheep for research purposes but needed an embryologist to determine zygosity, and so he invited Corner to aid him. Following the completion of that task, Corner carried out his study on the pig. The description of how the study was carried out may be found in Corner's published remarks (1921, 1941, 1958).

Corner (1958) consulted with Davenport on the analysis and interpretation of his results, hence it is hardly surprising that Corner's conclusions about lethal genes as the cause of fetal abortion fit so well with Davenport's hypothesis. Corner (1958, p. 41) also credited his stay at Davenport's laboratory with helping him acquire a knowledge of modern genetics. There is no evidence in his writings or personal life that Corner was involved with eugenics. Cold Springs Harbor was a major genetics laboratory, staffed with reputable geneticists. According to Rosenberg (1976) and Cravens (1978), Davenport himself was quite knowledgeable about new developments in genetics.

This episode does, however, reinforce the picture that Diane Paul (1998, especially chaps. 4 & 8) and others (e.g., Kevles, 1985) have painted of the close relationship between genetics, especially human genetics, and eugenics during this period. It also points to the increasing influence of genetics itself. As Corner (1961) put it years later,

> the genetic explanation of congenital malformations developed so rapidly and was so soundly based on experiment that for a time it almost completely displaced the environmental hypothesis, at least in the circle of obstetricians, pathologists and human embryologists with whom I was associated. (p. 11)

In a revealing comment about the changing status of the two disciplines, Corner stated that "just as Mall had turned to experimental embryology for an explanation of his findings so I turned to another new science, genetics, for help" (p. 11).

Corner's study not only reflected but also promoted the genetic viewpoint among embryologists. He later (1961) wrote that his 1920 findings led his colleague, George Streeter (1873–1948), Mall's successor at the Carnegie Institution's Department of Embryology, to give up his attempts to explain intrauterine amputations within Mall's framework and to adopt a genetic explanation instead. Streeter's theorizing, in turn, dominated the field for the next 30 years (Torpin, 1968), and Corner evidently consulted with Streeter in the course of writing his article. In a letter to Davenport, Corner (1923) remarked that Streeter approved of his article "from the embryological side." Streeter later referenced Corner's work prominently (e.g., Streeter, 1926).

Corner (1941) later wrote that for Mall, the development of human embryos was subject to disruption at "critical times" as "surely as the aquatic eggs of the experimenter at Woods Hole" (p. 88). Ironically, the idea of the critical-period became as important to the acceptance of genetic explanations of congenital defects as it had been to Mall's environmental hypothesis.

As Corner (1961) himself indicated years later, if developmental outcomes depend more on the timing than on the nature of developmental influences, then genetic factors could cause defects in humans of the same sort that had been produced in healthy eggs in other species through environmental means. Corner called this an "astonishing fact" (p. 11). Barrow (1971) stated that it was the linkage of genetic theory to the idea of developmental arrest, a linkage that he credits to Streeter, that was the major factor in the victory of the genetic viewpoint over its rivals.

There is, in fact, an ambiguity to the idea that the nature of a developmental influence depends on its timing. If genetic or environmental factors can result in the same kind of abnormality or if the same factor can have different effects at different times, then, as Bailey and Miller (1909) pointed out years earlier, determining whether genes or environmental factors are responsible for particular defects becomes difficult. In the absence of empirical evidence, developmental outcomes, which once might have been interpreted within an environmental framework, could now be interpreted within the newly dominant framework of genetics by default.

Despite Corner's (1961) comments, there was little direct evidence at the time for the genetic regulation of development. Serious work on developmental genetics did not begin until the late 1930s and early 1940s (Gilbert, 1991), and no model of how genes could regulate development existed until 1961, when Jacob and Monod proposed their operon model of gene regulation in bacteria. Although this eventually led to a consensus that cells influenced development through processes of differential gene expression, progress was slow and took several years (Gilbert, 1997).

This emphasis on the role of genetics in prenatal development, to the virtual exclusion of the external environment, lasted for more than 30 years. It was not until the 1950s that the situation began to change and not until 1960–1961, when it was realized that the sedative thalidomide could cause limb malformations in unborn children, that the potential impact of environmental agents on the conceptus was fully realized (Kalter, 1983; Warkany, 1971; Wilson, 1977). Writing about the dominant views that existed prior to these changes, the teratologist J. G. Wilson (1977) wrote that

> it was widely assumed in biology and medicine that the mammalian embryo developed within the virtually impervious shelter of the uterus and the maternal body where it was protected from extrinsic factors.

> This view was consistent with the view that most aspects of normal as well as abnormal development were genetically determined. (p. 47)

According to Wilson (1977), these beliefs about the imperviousness of the unborn to external threats were so strong that neither the discovery of the teratogenic effects of radiation exposure in the 1920s nor the demonstration of the link between environmental factors and congenital malformations aroused much concern. Even the 1941 discovery that mothers could transmit rubella to their unborn child, with rather devastating effects, had only a limited effect in alerting biomedical scientists to the vulnerability of maternal protective mechanisms.

Although embryologists might have been more open than geneticists to the idea of external influences on development, in practice, embryologists were much more concerned with internal (albeit extragenomic) environmental influences on normal development. Once the view that the uterine wall acted to shield the mammalian embryo and fetus from the outside environment became accepted, there was little reason to investigate external influences in mammalian development in any case.

That ideas about the importance of human genetics should have been so influential in the 1930s and 1940s may seem puzzling. The linkage between human genetics and eugenics at the time threw human genetics into disrepute, and so there was actually little research in human genetics during much of this time, especially in the United States (Kevles, 1985; Ludmerer, 1972).

Ludmerer (1972), however, wrote that the lack of research into human genetics did not discourage a belief in the potency of hereditary factors among physicians. If anything, it strengthened it by helping encourage the erroneous belief among physicians that hereditary diseases are untreatable.

Most physicians did not actually receive much education in genetics during this period, but older hereditarian beliefs, often in the form of "like begets like," were widespread (e.g., Rosenberg, 1976). For those not knowledgeable about genetics, the field's successes and prestige may have even been superficially assimilated to and strengthened more traditional hereditarian beliefs. In any case, these attitudes did not appear to be shaken by the vicissitudes of genetic research.

By the 1920s, even some of those who had previously emphasized the importance of environmental factors in development had changed their position. Stockard, for example, had never denied the existence of intrinsic failures in development ("bad eggs"), but in his 1921 article he had clearly emphasized the greater importance of environmental factors in the production of congenital abnormalities (p. 179).

Before this article had even appeared, Stockard had reversed his position, however (see Jones, 1963; Pauly, 1996, for accounts of this reversal). Although he never accepted Corner's view that the fetus was virtually invulnerable to external threats, Stockard, a staunch eugenicist, now argued that the quality of the germ plasm was more important in determining developmental outcomes than deleterious environmental influences; only germ plasm of poor quality would succumb to such influences (Stockard, 1923).

DEVELOPMENT AND HEREDITARIAN THOUGHT

The evidence presented in this chapter indicates that biological views of early development came to emphasize heredity in the years around 1915, an emphasis that did not change markedly until the 1960s. This seems to conflict with the widely accepted view that support for hereditarian views began to decline much earlier. Cravens (1978), for example, suggested that after the nature–nurture disputes of the 1920s, scientific progress undid extreme hereditarian views, and that by the early 1940s, the nature–nurture conflict had been resolved in favor of a more interactional approach (Cravens, 1978, pp. 157–274).

One answer to this seeming conflict may be that these larger changes were more problematic than is usually thought. Cravens, for example, singles out the loss of scientific support for a belief in biological inequality among the races and a similar loss in support for eugenics as two changes that were of special importance in the resolution of the heredity–environment conflict. Recent evidence suggests that, although these changes did occur, they were more equivocal and contentious, as well as less sweeping, than is generally assumed. Moreover, these changes may have had more to do with changes in social attitudes and beliefs among scientists than changes in scientific beliefs per se (e.g., Barkan, 1992; Paul, 1998; Provine, 1986; Weizmann, 1998).

Another possible reason for the contradiction, however, may have been an underlying, if often implicit, belief that birth represents a sharp discontinuity in infant development and that development in the prenatal period differs radically from that in the postnatal period. The idea that the unborn child was perfectly shielded from both the maternal and the external environment reinforced this belief. Because environmentalists generally have emphasized the role of experience in development after birth, they may not have been overly concerned about claims of exclusive genetic control over development before birth.

Insofar as the work on early development during the prenatal period supported a general model of development based on genes and invariant sequences of development, however, it courted potential difficulties. No one doubted that the environment had some effects on development after birth; not only was the extent of those influences unclear and a matter of contention, but it was difficult to know how to incorporate them within a biological model. It is not surprising, therefore, that difficulties would occur when psychologists and child developmentalists attempted to generalize this biological model to childhood.

BIOLOGY AND PSYCHOLOGY

There were several connections between biology and psychology between 1880 and 1920. To begin, the two disciplines grew in parallel ways during this period. Although psychology increasingly identified itself as an experimental natural science separate from philosophy (Cravens, 1991; Shore, chap. 4, this volume; Smith, 1986; Winston, chap. 6, this volume), Garland Allen (1979) suggested that experimental approaches to biology were also growing in importance at the expense of more traditional descriptive ones. (Although several historians interpret this development as a change in emphasis rather than as a radical transformation; see Rainger, Benson, & Maienschein, 1991.)

Moreover, psychology as a discipline was heavily influenced by biology and biologists (Cravens, 1991; Shore, chap. 4, this volume). Jacques Loeb, for example, one of the exemplars of the experimental tradition in biology, played an important role in the development of experimental psychology and behaviorism, through his influence on John B. Watson (1878–1958) and B. F. Skinner (Pauly, 1987; Smith, 1986; Winston, chap. 6, this volume).

Biological approaches to heredity and development certainly influenced the growth of maturational theories of development in psychology (e.g., Cravens, 1991). Watson, despite his later reputation as an arch environmentalist, was one of those who mediated this influence. Cravens (1991) argued that Watson's work in the 1910s helped inspire the subsequent development of a maturational and hereditarian approach to development among psychologists. He ascribed Watson's reputation as a radical environmentalist to his writings after 1920, when Watson left academic life, and also to later interpretations of Watson, which view him through the lens of later developments in behaviorism.

Oppenheim (1982) agreed that early in his career Watson supported the idea of biological influences on development, in the form of instincts governed largely by heredity. Oppenheim (1982, pp. 50–51) argued, however, that Watson's 1914 text on comparative psychology, which Cravens (1991) viewed mainly as an example of Watson's interactional approach to development, embodied a deep misunderstanding of experimental embryology. Watson interpreted embryological research as indicating that the anatomical basis for instincts was already present in fertilized eggs (Oppenheim, 1982). In so doing, Watson wrongly identified embryology with a "crass neopreformationism" (p. 50) long abandoned by biologists.

Oppenheim (1982, p. 51) also supported the contention that Watson mistakenly believed that Johannsen's work on phenotypic and genotypic variation proved that most variation is not inherited. For Oppenheim, it was these misinterpretations of biology that lay at the heart of the nature–nurture conflict and the fight over instincts that emerged in psychology in the 1920s.

Whatever Watson's particular misinterpretations, however, the dominant interpretation that emerged from the biology of development in those years was a hereditarian one. In that sense, whatever the inadequacies of the behaviorist approach to biological aspects of development and behavior, their response to what they viewed as biological predeterminism was not simply based on a misunderstanding.

The maturational viewpoint in psychology, which had developed by the early 1920s (Cravens, 1991), did reflect the hereditarian bias of contemporary biological thought. As I noted earlier, however, the biological model that emerged from the study of early development had difficulty incorporating environmental influences in its purview. This becomes clear when we examine the work of perhaps the most influential and important representative of maturational thought in child development, Arnold Gesell (1880–1961).

Thelen and Adolph (1992) pointed out a central contradiction in his theorizing. Although Gesell viewed development as a universal, genetically driven process, he simultaneously believed strongly in human freedom and the individuality of the child and tacitly recognized the existence of multiple influences on development. Thelen and Adolphe (1992) contended that Gesell was never able to develop an integrated model of development.

Ultimately, he ignored the multiplicity of influences on development because of his emphasis on biological causation. This resulted in "unresolved tensions" in his model, which in turn contributed to his decline as a major theorist (Thelen & Adolph, 1992, p. 370). Although less harsh, Robert Cairns (1983, p. 74) also observed that although Gesell recognized the existence of social and environmental influences in personality development, he never really came to grips with their implications in his theorizing.

The maturational approach to development held sway until the mid-20th century. In view of the earlier discussion of the role of the genotype–phenotype distinction in defining genetics, it is interesting that in an important book advocating the importance of early experience on development published in 1961, Hunt (1961, p. 7) returned to this concept to justify both his stress on the environment and his criticism of maturational theorists such as Gesell.

Hunt's arguments, and his presentation of evidence that cognitive and neural development were partly shaped by the child's early experience were important. Besides encouraging research into early development, especially cognitive development, they also helped influence important social policies, such as the establishment of compensatory education programs, most importantly Head Start (Cravens, 1993). The genotype–phenotype distinction provided a framework that legitimated the importance of early influences on development, just as it had earlier legitimated the study of heredity.

CONCLUSION

As genetics gained influence in the years after 1910, it helped undo the balanced view of biological development that had been reached by embryologists at the turn of the century. In fact, the view that genes played the controlling role in regulating development, normal or abnormal, was accepted long before there was either much direct evidence for such a role or even a model for how genes could regulate development.

When coupled with the prevalent idea that the mammalian fetus was impervious to the effects of the external environment, these beliefs led to a view of human development that had little room to accommodate environmental influences, at least in a coherent way. It was this view, as embodied in maturational theories of behavioral development, against which behaviorists and environmentalists reacted. Behaviorists may have ignored biological influences in the process, but they did not invent the biological determinism associated with this idea of development.

REFERENCES

Allen, G. (1979). Naturalists and experimentalists: The phenotype and the genotype. In W. Coleman & C. Lumbagos (Eds.), *Studies in the history of biology* (Vol. 3, pp. 179–209). Baltimore: Johns Hopkins University Press.

Allen, G. (1985). T. H. Morgan and the split between embryology and genetics. In T. J. Horder, J. Witkowski, & C. C. Wylie (Eds.), *A history of embryology* (pp. 113–146). Cambridge, England: Cambridge University Press.

Allen, G. (1986). The Eugenics Record Office at Cold Spring Harbor, 1910–1940: An essay in institutional history. *Osiris, 2,* 225–264.

Bailey, F. R., & Miller, A. M. (1909). *Textbook of embryology.* New York: Wood.

Ballantyne, J. (1902–1904). *The manual of antenatal pathology and hygiene* (Vols. 1–2). Edinburgh, Scotland: Green.

Barkan, E. (1992). *The retreat of scientific racism: Changing concepts of race in Britain and the United States between the world wars.* Cambridge, UK: Cambridge University Press.

Barrow, M. V. (1971). A brief history of teratology to the early 20th century. *Teratology, 4,* 119–130.

Bornstein, M. H. (1989). Sensitive periods in development: Structural characteristics and causal interpretations. *Psychological Bulletin, 105,* 179–197.

Cairns, R. B. (1983). The emergence of a developmental psychology. In P. H. Mussen (Ed.), *Handbook of child psychology* (4th ed., Vol. 1, pp. 42–101). New York: Wiley.

Chase, A. (1980). *The legacy of Malthus: The social costs of the new scientific racism.* Urbana: University of Illinois Press.

Churchill, F. B. (1973). Chabry, Roux and the experimental method in nineteenth century embryology. In R. N. Giere & R. S. Westfall (Eds.), *Foundations of scientific method: The nineteenth century* (pp. 161–205). Bloomington: Indiana University Press.

Churchill, F. B. (1974). Wilhelm Johannsen and the genotype concept. *Journal of the History of Biology, 7,* 5–30.

Coleman, W. (1977). *Biology in the nineteenth century.* Cambridge, England: Cambridge University Press. (Original work published 1971)

Corner, G. W. (1921). The problem of embryonic pathology in mammals, with observations upon intrauterine mortality in the pig. *American Journal of Anatomy, 31,* 523–545.

Corner, G. W. (1923, January 26). [Letter to C. B. Davenport.] George W. Corner Papers, American Philosophical Society Archives, Philadelphia.

Corner, G. W. (1941). *Ourselves unborn.* Philadelphia: Saunders.

Corner, G. W. (1958). *Anatomist at large.* New York: Basic Books.

Corner, G. W. (1961). Congenital malformations: The problem and the task. In *First International Conference on Congenital Malformations* (pp. 7–17). Philadelphia: Lippincott.

Cravens, H. (1978). *The triumph of evolution.* Philadelphia: University of Pennsylvania Press.

Cravens, H. (1991). Behaviorism revisited. Developmental science, the maturation theory, and the biological basis of the human mind, 1920s–1950s. In K. R. Benson, J. Maienschein, & R. Rainger (Eds.), *The expansion of American biology* (pp. 133–164). New Brunswick, NJ: Rutgers University Press.

Cravens, H. (1993). *Before Head Start.* Chapel Hill: University of North Carolina Press.

Davenport, C. B. (1920). Influence of the male in the production of human twins. *American Naturalist, 54,* 122–129.

Dunn, L. C. (1917). Nucleus and cytoplasm as vehicles of heredity. *American Naturalist, 51,* 286–300.

Gasking, E. B. (1964). *Investigations into generation, 1651–1828.* Baltimore: Johns Hopkins Press.

Gilbert, S. F. (1991). Cellular politics: Ernest Everett Just, Richard B. Goldschmidt, and the attempt to reconcile embryology and genetics. In R. Rainger, K. R. Benson, & J. Maienschein (Eds.), *The American development of biology* (pp. 311–347). New Brunswick, NJ: Rutgers University Press.

Gilbert, S. F. (1997). *Developmental biology* (5th ed.). Sunderland, MA: Sinauer Associates.

Hamburger, V. (1980). Embryology and the modern synthesis in evolutionary theory. In E. Mayr & W. B. Provine (Eds.), *The evolutionary synthesis* (pp. 97–112). Cambridge, MA: Harvard University Press.

Harrison, R. G. (1937). Embryology and its relations. *Science, 85*, 369–374.

Harwood, J. (1993). *Styles of scientific thought: The German genetics community 1900–1933*. Chicago: University of Chicago Press.

Hunt, J. M. (1961). *Intelligence and experience*. New York: Ronald Press.

Jacob, F., & Monod, J. (1961). Genetic regulatory mechanisms in the synthesis of proteins. *Journal of Molecular Biology, 3*, 318–356.

Jones, B. (1963). Prohibition and eugenics, 1920–1933. *Journal of the History of Medicine and Allied Sciences, 18*, 158–172.

Kalter, H. (1983). On the occasion of Josef Warkany's 80th birthday. In H. Kalter (Ed.), *Issues and reviews in teratology* (Vol. 1, pp. vii–viii). New York: Plenum Press.

Kevles, D. (1985). *In the name of eugenics: Genetics and the uses of human heredity*. New York: Knopf.

Kimmelman, B. A. (1983). The American Breeder's Association: Eugenics in an agricultural context. *Social Studies of Science, 11*, 163–204.

Ludmerer, K. M. (1972). *Genetics and American society*. Baltimore: Johns Hopkins University Press.

Maienschein, J. (1985). Preformation or new formation—Or neither or both. In T. J. Horder, J. Witkowski, & C. C. Wylie (Eds.), *A history of embryology* (pp. 73–109). Cambridge, England: Cambridge University Press.

Maienschein, J. (1991). *Transforming traditions in American biology, 1880–1915*. Baltimore: Johns Hopkins University Press.

Mall, F. P. (1908). *A study of the causes underlying the origin of human monsters*. Philadelphia: Wistar Institute Press.

Oppenheim, R. W. (1982). Preformation and epigenesis in the origins of the nervous system and behavior: Issues, concepts, and their history. In P. P. G. Bateson & P. H. Klopfer (Eds.), *Perspectives in ethology* (Vol. 5, pp. 1–100). New York: Plenum Press.

Oppenheimer, J. M., & Bell, W. J. (1982). George Washington Corner (1889–1981). In *Biographical memoirs: Yearbook of the American Philosophical Society* (pp. 460–468). Philadelphia: American Philosophical Society.

Oyama, S. (1979). The concept of the sensitive period in developmental studies. *Merrill-Palmer Quarterly of Behavior and Development, 25*, 83–103.

Paul, D. B. (1998). *The politics of heredity: Essays on eugenics, biomedicine, and the nature–nurture debate*. Albany: State University of New York Press.

Pauly, P. J. (1987). *Controlling life: Jacques Loeb and the engineering ideal in biology*. New York: Oxford University Press.

Pauly, P. J. (1996). How did the effects of alcohol on reproduction become scientifically uninteresting? *Journal of the History of Biology, 29*, 1–28.

Provine, W. B. (1986). Geneticists and race. *American Zoologist, 26*, 857–887.

Rainger, R., Benson, K. R., & Maienschein, J. (1991). Introduction. In R. Rainger, K. R. Benson, & J. Maienschein (Eds.), *The American development of biology* (pp. 3–15). New Brunswick, NJ: Rutgers University Press.

Rosenberg, C. (1976). *No other gods*. Baltimore: Johns Hopkins University Press.

Sabin, F. R. (1934). *Franklin Paine Mall*. Baltimore: Johns Hopkins University Press.

Sapp, J. (1987). *Beyond the gene: Cytoplasmic inheritance and the struggle for authority in genetics*. New York: Oxford University Press.

Scarr, S. (1987). Three cheers for behavior genetics: Winning the war and losing our identity. *Behavior Genetics, 17,* 219–228.

Scarr, S. (1993). Biological and cultural diversity: The legacy of Darwin for development. *Child Development, 63,* 1333–1353.

Smith, L. D. (1986). Psychology and philosophy: Towards a realignment, 1905–1935. *Journal of the History of the Behavioral Sciences, 17,* 28–37.

Stockard, C. R. (1921). Developmental rate and structual expression: An experimental study of twins, "double monsters" and single deformities, and the interaction among embryonic organs during their origin and development. *American Journal of Anatomy, 28,* 115–266.

Stockard, C. R. (1923). Experimental modification of the germ-plasm and its bearing on the inheritance of acquired characteristics. *Proceedings of the American Philosophical Society, 52,* 311–324.

Streeter, G. L. (1926). Single-ovum twins in the pig. *American Journal of Anatomy, 34,* 185–189.

Thelen, E., & Adolph, K. E. (1992). Arnold L. Gesell: The paradox of nature and nurture. *Developmental Psychology, 28,* 368–380.

Torpin, R. (1968). *Fetal malformations caused by amnion rupture during gestation*. Springfield, IL: Charles C Thomas.

Warkany, J. (1971). *Congenital malformations: Notes and comments*. Chicago: Year Book Medical.

Weizmann, F. (1998). Who killed eugenics? Or did they? *History and Philosophy of Psychology Bulletin, 10,* 30–33.

Wilson, J. G. (1977). Current status of teratology—General principles and mechanisms derived from animal studies. In J. G. Wilson & F. C. Fraser (Eds.), *Handbook of teratology* (Vol. 1, pp. 47–75). New York: Plenum Press.

Zenderland, L. (1998). *Measuring minds*. Cambridge, England: Cambridge University Press.

INDEX

Hermann Ebbinghaus's approach to study of, 47–51
in late-19th-century social thought, 68–71
as metaphor, 54–56
organic, 57–58, 70
Wilhelm Wundt's approach to study of, 47–60
Memory (Franz Fauth), 51
Menabrea, Luigi Frederico, 134, 141, 142, 144, 146–147
Mental Philosophy (Joseph Haven), 22
Merryweather, George, 153–155, 162, 166–167
Metaphysical Foundations of Natural Science (Immanuel Kant), xi, 178
Metaphysics, 110, 112–114
Meumann, Ernst, 51, 123
Mill, John Stuart, 6, 10, 108, 112, 117, 138, 211, 212
Mind, 195–215
　Wilhelm Dilthey on, 197–198, 203–208, 211–214
　Georg Wilhelm Friedrich Hegel on, 185–186, 196
　J. F. Herbart's conception of, 55
　as instrument, 155–161
　Karl Marx's conceptualization of, 197–204, 209–210
Mnemonics, 68
Modernism, 69–70, 77–78
Moetley, Randolph, 28–34, 40
Morgan, T. H., 223
Mozart, Wolfgang Amadeus, 88
Müller, Georg Elias, 47
Müller, Johannes, xii, 156
Münsterberg, Hugo, xii, 124

National Education Association (NEA), 68, 80
Nature vs. nurture, 3
Naturwissenschaften, 211
NEA. *See* National Education Association
Neo-Platonism, 92
Neue Lehre von den Proportionen des menschlichen Körpers (Adolph Zeising), 93–94
Newcomb, Simon, 41
Newton, Isaac, 135

On the Economy of Manufacturers and Machinery (Charles Babbage), 137–138
On the Power, Wisdom, and Goodness of God (William Kirby), 163
On the Sensations of Tone as a Physiological Basis for the Theory of Jusic (Hermann Helmholtz), 160

Oppenheim, R. W., 219–221, 223, 230–231
Optical illusions, 77
Organic memory, 57–58, 70
Origin of Civilization and the Primitive Condition of Man, The (John Lubbock), 14–15
Origin of Species (Charles Darwin), 4–6, 158
Outline Study of Man, An (Joseph Haven), 22
Over-soul, 5

Pacioli, Luca, 90–91, 95
Parapsychology, 46
Parsons, William, 142
Patrick, G. T. W., 81–82
Patterson, Donald, 39
Paulsen, Friedrich, 121
Peabody, Selim H., 67
Peacock, George, 135, 144
Pearson, Karl, 3, 114, 117
Peel, Robert, 136
Pfungst, Oskar, 41
Phenomenology of Mind, The (G. W. F. Hegel), 186–190
Philosophy of the Unconditioned (William Hamilton), 7
Phrenology, 21–44
　and character reading, 37–42
　child-rearing advice based on, 35–36
　decline of, 42
　Georg Wilhelm Friedrich Hegel on, 188–190
　and marital counseling, 33–35
　practice of, 25–28
　sample reading, 28–31
　and Scottish commonsense realism, 22–24
　and vocational guidance, 32–33
Physical Dimensions of Consciousness (Edward Titchener), 118

Spottiswoode, William, 15, 16, 18
Spranger, Eduard, 197
Spurzheim, Johann Gaspar, 24
Stewart, Dugald, 22
Stockard, C. R., 222
Strawson, P. F., 180

Taine, Hippolyte-Adolphe, 212
Taylor, Richard, 134
Technique, practice vs., 48
Telegraph, 160–162
Tempest Prognosticator, 153–155, 166–167, 170–171
Testing, psychological, 73–75
Thompson, D'Arcy, 89
Thorndike, Edward, 225
Titchener, Edward Bradford, 79, 108, 117–119
Tolman, E. C., 107
Trace theory, 55
Treatise on Algebra (George Peacock), 144
Turner, Frank, 5
Tyndall, John, 6, 12–15, 17

Upham, Thomas, 22

Vico, Giambattista, 196
Virchow, Rudolf, 145
Vocational guidance, use of phrenology for, 32–33
Vygotsky, Lev, 197

Wallace, Alfred Russel, 16
Ward, William George, 159

Watson, John Broadus, xii, 80, 124–125, 176–177, 182, 220, 230, 231
Wealth of Nations (Adam Smith), 137
Webb, Beatrice Potter, 18
Weber, E. H., xii
Weismann, August, 16, 220–221
Wellington, Duke of, 136
Wells, Samuel R., 38
Wheatstone, Charles, 142, 158, 160, 162
Whewell, William, 108, 135
"White City," 65–67
Wilberforce, Samuel, 7
Wissenschaften, xiii
Wolfe, H. K., 48
Wolff, Christian, 179
Woodworth, R. S., 107
Worcester (MA), 25–28
World's Columbian Exposition (Chicago, 1893), 63–68, 71–76, 78–80, 82–83
World's Congress Auxiliary, 66–67
World War I, xi
Wundt, Wilhelm, 45–60, 108, 198
  and Wilhelm Dilthey, 197
  and Hermann Ebbinghaus, 47–51, 57–60
  and Francis Galton, 18
  and J. F. Herbart, 52–53, 55, 56
  influence of, xii
  voluntarism of, 119

X Club, 15–16, 18

Yerkes, Robert M., xii, 225
Young, Thomas, 136

Zeising, Adolph, 88, 93–96

ABOUT THE EDITORS

Christopher D. Green, PhD, is an associate professor of psychology and philosophy at York University in Toronto, Ontario, Canada, and a Fellow of the History of Psychology Division of the American Psychological Association. He has published research on topics in cognitive science, ancient psychological thought, the golden section, and the history of psychological methods. He is also the founding editor of the Classics in the History of Psychology web site (http://www.psychclassics.yorku.ca/).

Marlene Shore, PhD, is an associate professor and chair of the Department of History, York University, Toronto, Ontario, Canada. She is also a member of York University's graduate programs in history and in social and political thought. She is a specialist in North American cultural and intellectual history; her research focuses on the history of the social and behavioral sciences; and she has written articles and books on the history of sociology, psychology, and historiography. Her major publications include *The Science of Social Redemption: McGill, the Chicago School, and the Origins of Social Research in Canada* (1987) and *The Contested Past: Reading Canada's History. Selections From the* Canadian Historical Review (2001). She is currently working on a book (monograph) on psychology and the culture of modernism from 1890 to 1940.

Thomas Teo, PhD, is an associate professor of psychology and coordinator of the history and theory of psychology program at York University, Toronto, Ontario, Canada. His research areas and publication topics include the epistemological and methodological foundations of critical psychology, psychology as a human science, psychology of liberation, history and theory of the concept of race and racism in psychology, prejudice and multiculturalism, history and theory of developmental psychology, and significance of contexts for development.